Food & Beverage Service

Levels 1&2 S/NVQ

ZOE ADJEY and GARY HUNTER

With contributions from CLARE MANNALL

Food & Beverage Service

Levels 1&2 S/NVQ

DELMAR
CENGAGE Learning™

Australia • Brazil • Japan • Korea • Mexico • Singapore • Spain • United Kingdom • United States

Food & Beverage Service: Levels 1&2 S/NVQ
Zoe Adjey and Gary Hunter with Clare Mannall

Publisher: Melody Dawes

Development Editor: Lucy Mills

Content Project Editor: Jamina Ward

Manufacturing Manager: Helen Mason

Senior Production Controller: Maeve Healy

Marketing Manager: Jason Bennett

Typesetter: Book Now Ltd, London, UK

Cover design: HCT Creative

Text design: Design Deluxe Ltd, Bath, UK

For product information and technology assistance, contact **emea.info@cengage.com**.

For permission to use material from this text or product, and for permission queries, email **clsuk.permissions@cengage.com**.

The Author has asserted the right under the Copyright, Designs and Patents Act 1988 to be identified as Author of this Work.

British Library Cataloguing-in-Publication Data
A catalogue record for this book is available from the British Library.

ISBN: 978-1-4080-0742-6

Cengage Learning EMEA
Cheriton House, North Way, Andover, Hampshire SP10 5BE. United Kingdom

Cengage Learning products are represented in Canada by Nelson Education Ltd.

For your lifelong learning solutions, visit **www.cengage.co.uk**

Purchase your next print book, e-book or e-chapter at **www.ichapters.co.uk**

Printed by Seng Lee Press
1 2 3 4 5 6 7 8 9 10 – 11 10 09

Brief contents

CONTENTS

About the authors

ZOË ADJEY

Originally from Northern Ireland, Zoë attended the College of Business Studies, Belfast, then completed her BA (Hons) Hospitality Management at Thames Valley University, London.

After a period spent travelling and working in Europe, Zoë returned to London and worked in a number of top restaurants. Most recently with Caprice Holdings, originally at J.Sheekey Restaurant before moving to their head office as Group Trainer. She worked on many different training projects within the company both in the UK, Caribbean and the Middle East.

Zoë is a Food and Beverage Lecturer at Westminster Kingsway College. She specialises in teaching restaurant skills to 16–19-year-olds. She is keen to raise the public's recognition of those who have careers in Food and Beverage Service.

GARY HUNTER

Head of Culinary Arts at Westminster Kingsway College, Gary has 14 years' experience of teaching within further, higher and vocational education and has been awarded the City & Guilds Medal for Excellence in recognition of his exceptional work and personal dedication to delivering a continuing high standard of education and training to students and trainees for the catering industry. He has travelled the world as a consultant providing training and seminars on culinary arts. He is also an experienced international culinary competition judge. As the head of the UK's culinary school, he has won numerous awards and competition medals and has worked with and trained many of today's successful chefs. Gary has recently helped to write the diploma in professional cookery qualification at levels 1, 2 and 3.

About the contributor

CLARE MANNALL

Clare is a Curriculum Team Leader for Hospitality Higher Education at Westminster Kingsway College. Clare has a Masters in Hospitality Management and had previously trained in the industry, opting to specialize in Finance. Since joining the college in 2000 Clare has become an advocate for employer engagement in the classroom and in assessment. She also maintains the belief that to meet the needs of modern day students, 'anywhere, anytime learning' is now part of their culture and that colleges need to be innovative in the way they present their resources. She is a keen developer of the online resources, piloting online assessment and marking for students in the college and sharing good practice in the wider field of Hospitality.

Foreword

The hospitality industry has emerged in recent times as one of the cornerstones of our economy. It employs over two million people and contributes to the economic wellbeing of the nation. It provides an insight into what Britain stands for as a Tourist destination, as well as linking together aspects of modern business life and social interaction. Hospitality tempts us with its vast array of destinations, environments, activities, entertainments, products and services. We have come to regard these elements as an essential part of our daily lives, central to the way in which we define our lifestyles and indeed, ourselves. Much has been written about the significance of the modern kitchen, its use of ingredients, the value of culinary techniques, organisation and expertise. This book highlights the vital role service plays in providing great hospitality. It investigates the various aspects of what defines excellent service, exploring the key elements involved in delivering superb service. It demonstrates how service plays a vital part of what contributes to the customer experience and enjoyment. It illustrates clearly how to become proficient in each of the key areas of professional food service – and then how to build on these essential skills.

Without great service, there would not be hospitality. Without great hospitality, Britain's identity and reputation as a major business and tourist destination would not exist.

Take time to learn the key aspects of exceptional service and to understand the key contribution it makes to the success of this great industry. Take a moment to reflect on the vast array of potential career opportunities it offers, as you discover the world of hospitality. By exploring this book, you have already begun to take the first steps towards developing your understanding of this key area of hospitality.

Enjoy the journey.

Geoff Booth
CEO for the Professional Association For Catering Education

Acknowledgements

The authors and publishers would like to thank the following:

Personal acknowledgements
Zoe Adjey:
Simon Clayton and Finn Clayton

Gary Hunter:

Sarah Jane Hunter	Charlotte Hunter	Estelle Hunter

Veronique Bonnefoy-Croft and Johanna Wimmer for their professional inspiration and support
All at the Restaurant Association and especially the superb Young Chef Young Waiter Competition
Iron Maiden and Metallica for maintaining my sanity!

Clare Mannall:

Ann Mannall	Michael Mannall	Mungo Mannall	Rachel Sansom
Bev Boughen	Clare Rowland		

Reviewers
Briege McRory, South West College
Margaret Calver, Yorkshire Coast College
Edward Trimingham, Boston College
James McDonagh, Southgate College

Industry profile contributors

Alain Kerloc'h	Brian Silva	Karen Mcconnell	Marc Stroobandt
Matthew Hobbs	Matthew Mawtus	Richard Harden	Robin Rowland
Stephane Palluault	Vincent McGrath	Anna Hansen	

For providing pictures for the book
William 'Bill' Hull, Professional Photography www.billhullphotography.com

Aerobie Inc	Crane Merchandising Systems	Diageo PLC	42 Technology
Drinkstuff.com	Eureka	www.hotfoodvending.com	IMC Ltd, www.imco.co.uk
The Publican	The British Hospitality Association	i-stock photography	Riedel Glassware

Every effort has been made to trace the copyright holders, but if any have been inadvertently overlooked the publisher will be pleased to make the necessary arrangements at the first opportunity. Please contact the publisher directly.

Introduction

The purpose of this book is to guide you through the skills and foundation knowledge required to become a professional waiter, bartender or other food service staff in the Hospitality and Catering industry.

Through the cooking, serving and eating of food, communication – both professional and sociable – has improved across the world. Food is served as a gift, as a medicine, to create friendship, to nourish, to celebrate, to generate business and to stimulate happiness and conversation. The late gastronome Anthelme Brillat-Savarin reminds us that eating out in restaurants is now firmly established as one of the top leisure pursuits for the public, saying 'tell me what you eat, and I will tell you what you are'. People are now becoming much more conscious of the standards of food and drink service than ever before and therefore have greater expectations in their requirements of good service.

The basic principles of being a worthy professional food service staff member are to combine informative service with good techniques and skills, a firm knowledge of food and drink with attention to detail, and a positive and friendly personality. Only then will you have the foundations to show your food and drink service skills and creative talents.

This book will also illustrate some of the top food service personnel in this country whose talent, dedication and energy have helped them achieve heights of excellence in the Hospitality industry today. They share their thoughts and experience for you to learn from. Finally, it will provide you with an important reference point to develop the professional skills and knowledge for today's demanding customer requirements.

Enjoy learning.

Zoe Adjey & Gary Hunter

A quick reference guide to the qualification

NVQs (National Vocational Qualifications) are nationally recognized and follow a common structure and design across all vocational subjects. To be awarded an NVQ/SVQ demonstrates that you have the competence (having sufficient skill and knowledge) to perform a job at a certain level. *Assessment* will take place once you and your assessor consider you to be competent.

Each NVQ/SVQ is divided into *units*. The unit relates to a specific task or skill area of work. The *element/s* that makes up a unit describes in detail the *skill and knowledge* components of the unit. To pass a particular unit you will need to accomplish various tasks.

- What you must do – gives information on the actions to be undertaken to pass each element within a unit.
- What you must cover – gives a range of situations, recipes, commodities and tasks for you to cover.
- What you must know – this is the underpinning knowledge or theory section that proves you understand the subject covered in the chapter.
- Evidence requirement – this addresses how much you need to cover by assessment using observation and alternative methods of assessment.

To achieve an NVQ/SVQ there will be a set of specific tasks and processes to go through.

1. At the commencement of any programme of study you should receive an *induction*. This should give you a detailed explanation of the qualification and the support that is available for you to use.

2. An *initial assessment* should be undertaken to assess your current degree of understanding and skills level for the qualification and to set out an action plan of the particular units you will undertake to complete the NVQ/SVQ. This assessment system will also identify specific areas of training and teaching that you will require.

3. Your competence and ability to carry out a task will be *assessed* by your assessor when you both consider that you are ready. Your assessor will regularly observe the tasks that you are carrying out, of which the outcomes will be recorded into your *portfolio of evidence*.

4 Your understanding and the background knowledge of the unit subject is also measured through questions asked by your assessor. The questions are usually required to be answered in a written format or verbally and then recorded in your portfolio of evidence. This is known as *underpinning knowledge*. The activities and theory covered in this book will provide you with plenty of examples, knowledge and practice to help with these.

5 The portfolio of evidence will be eventually completed by you and your assessor. It is designed to help you demonstrate your competence at a particular level. At this stage and usually during the process of training and assessment an *internal verifier* will check the consistency of the assessor's work.

6 Finally the *awarding body* (the body responsible for checking the qualification and awarding you the certificate) will appoint an *external moderator* to carry out final checks before certification.

This book will cover the breadth of knowledge and skills necessary to meet the qualification requirements at NVQ/SVQ Levels 1 and 2. Moreover it will give you the opportunity to enhance your knowledge of the industry with modern up-to-date service techniques alongside classical skills that are the fundamentals of good waiting staff.

The performance criteria

What you must do

The performance criteria of an NVQ/SVQ will list the required actions that you must achieve to complete the task in a competent manner. This means demonstrating the practical skill in an acceptable, professional and safe way to your assessor. In all NVQ/SVQ portfolios this is now stated in the form of 'what you must do'.

As an example, the what you must do criteria for element 1GEN1.2 Help to maintain a hygienic, safe and secure workplace states that to achieve the national standard the candidate must:

1 Keep a look out for hazards in your workplace

2 Identify any hazards or potential hazards and deal with these correctly

3 Report any accidents or near accidents quickly and accurately to the proper person

4 Follow health, hygiene and safety procedures in all your work

5 Practise emergency procedures correctly

6 Follow your organization's security procedures

All of these criteria must be adequately assessed against the next stage called 'what you must cover'.

What you must cover

This next section clearly states exactly what skills should be covered on a range of different types of hazards and ways of dealing with hazards which also include emergency procedures. The 1GEN1.2 element covers the following as an example:

1 **Hazards**
   a) relating to equipment
   b) relating to areas where you work
   c) relating to personal clothing

2 Ways of dealing with hazards

a) putting them right yourself
b) reporting them to appropriate colleagues
c) warning other people

3 Emergency procedures

a) fire
b) threat
c) security

It is important to understand that all of the three aspects in bold above have to be assessed in order to pass the element. The NVQ/SVQ portfolio will normally state the minimum requirements that are needed to pass the element through observation of the physical task and how the rest of the assessments can be covered, usually by professional witness statements or questioning.

What you must know

Further assessment of a candidate's knowledge and understanding of the skills relating to the element may be assessed through theoretical tasks such as questions or assignments. This stage is known as the 'what you must know' section. Any questioning should be performed under certain test conditions that have been set by the Sector Skills Council (People 1st):

■ In an environment that the candidate feels comfortable to take the assessment
■ That is supervised to ensure the assessment is authentic
■ That it is conducted in line with the appropriate Awarding Body guidelines

Assignments can also be used under the assessment strategy. The strategy allows centres to use materials that have been developed, and the use of assignments is an option within this.

A centre wishing to use an assignment will need to get the Awarding Body's prior approval before using the assignment. Assignments will also need to be administered within controlled conditions by the centre or college.

Witness testimony

Testimonies are used as a type of supplementary evidence whereby they can confirm performance evidence in two ways:

■ *Witness testimony*, for example from a customer, supplier or colleague that provides evidence towards a candidate's assessment; or
■ *Expert witness testimony* that provides authoritative evidence of competence, which may be sufficient for an assessor to consider that competence has been proved.

Expert witnesses may be other approved assessors who are recognized to assess the relevant occupational area and level, or line managers, that may not be approved assessors but whom the awarding body agrees has sufficient occupational qualifications or experience to make a judgement on the competence of a candidate. Expert witness testimony must be used in line with all Awarding Body requirements.

About the book

Mapped to the qualification
Each chapter addresses a specific unit of the Levels 1 or 2 Food and Beverage Service S/NVQ qualification.

3
Give customers a positive impression of yourself

Unit 503 Maintain customer care
1GEN3.1 Deal with customers.
1GEN3.2 Deal with customers' problems.

Unit 601 Give customers a positive impression of yourself
2GEN1.1 Establish effective relationships with customers.
2GEN1.2 Respond appropriately to customers.
2GEN1.3 Communicate information to customers.

What do I need to do?
■ You need to meet and greet customers.
■ You need to communicate information to customers.
■ You need to be able to locate information for customers.
■ You need to deal with customer complaints.

What do I need to know?
■ You need to know and understand the different aspects of legislation relating to your customer's information.
■ How to communicate positively, professionally and confidently.
■ How to recognize when a customer is angry and how to resolve their problems.

35

Learning objectives at the start of each chapter explain the skills and knowledge you need to be proficient in and understand by the end of the chapter.

STEP-BY-STEP: MAKING A MACCHIATO

1 Make a double espresso (see 'making an espresso' on page 348)

2 Spoon some of the froth only on to the espresso

3 When placing the cup and saucer in front of the customer, place the hand of the cup facing to the right- hand side and the teaspoon from top to right

! REMEMBER

Macchiato can be served as both a double and a single drink.

STEP-BY-STEP: MAKING A HOT CHOCOLATE

1 Place two dessert spoons of chocolate chips into a glass

2 Pour a small amount of hot milk into the glass and stir until the chocolate has completely melted

3 Top up the glass with hot milk

Step-by-step sequences
illustrate each process and provide an easy-to-follow guide.

Assessment of knowledge and understanding

You have now learned about the responsibilities you have to work effectively in a carvery operation. This will enable you to ensure your own positive actions contribute effectively towards the whole team.

To test your level of knowledge and understanding, answer the following short questions. These will help to prepare you for your summative (final) assessment.

Preparing for assessment checklist
■ Ensure that you know how to prepare all the areas of the buffet/carvery.
■ Write a checklist of your duties during buffet/carvery service

Project 1
1 Write a list of items needed to prepare a carvery serving roast beef and roast chicken.

2 What duties are performed by the waiter behind a buffet?

3 What are the portion sizes for each dish on the buffet?

4 What is the procedure if a customer asks for another portion of an item from the buffet?

Project 2
1 What is the correct procedure if a buffet runs out of an item?

2 How should spillages be dealt with?

3 Why is it important that each different item on a buffet has its own serving cutlery?

4 If two platters of sandwiches are half-finished on a buffet and there are more customers to come, what should the waiter's actions be? What must be checked?

Assessment of knowledge and understanding
at the end of each chapter contains questions, so you can test your learning.

Key words to define the key terms relating to the unit.

INDUSTRY PROFILE

Name: VINCENT MICHAEL McGRATH
Position: DIRECTOR OF FOOD AND BEVERAGE (F&B)
Establishment: THE SAVOY HOTEL – FAIRMONT HOTELS AND RESORTS

Current job role and main responsibilities:
Director of food and beverage for the Savoy Hotel, Fairmont. Annual turnover of £24 million. Responsible for the entire day-to-day operations of the division and long term strategy planning. The hotel is closed at present for a £100 million renovation project, due to reopen in summer 2009. Working on all new F&B concepts, menu design, FF&E and recruitment for the entire F&B Team. Responsible for a team of over 240 employees working between two bars, restaurant, in-room dining, banqueting, lounge, kitchen and stewarding.

What is the most exciting thing about working at the Savoy?
The history of such an iconic hotel and the attention to detail we strive to achieve.

When did you realize that you wanted to pursue a career in the food service industry?
From an early age at school, I always had an interest in cooking and experimenting and it was the only thing I wanted to do.

Training:
Cauldon College – Staffordshire three years; City and Guilds, HCIMA, Wine and Spirits; three-month practical experience in Aviemore Scotland; casual work at the North Stafford Hotel whilst studying; first job full-time: Four Seasons Hotel, London, as a commis waiter.

Experience:
Four Seasons Hotel, Park Lane, London, 5 Star Deluxe: commis waiter, server, headwaiter, supervisor, kitchen commis, room service night manager. *Hyatt Regency Hotel*, Birmingham, Pre-opening team, 5 Star: assistant restaurant manager, assistant catering ops manager, director of catering. *Dorchester Hotel*, Park Lane, London 5 Star Deluxe: deputy food and beverage manager. *Conrad International Hotel*, Dublin, Ireland 5 Star: director of food and beverage. *Four Seasons Hotel*, Park Lane, London, 5 Star Deluxe: director of food and beverage. *Four Seasons Hotel*, Hampshire: Pre-opening team, 5 Star Deluxe: director of food and beverage.

What do you find rewarding about your job?
The guest experience: meeting and exceeding expectations turning moments into memories. Working with the most talented and passionate team members.

What do you find the most challenging about the job?
Every day is different: you need to be prepared for the unexpected – today will be unlike any other day in the world of hospitality. A challenge but also an achievement.

What advice would you give to students just beginning their career?
Training – learn as much of the technical aspects of the job and treat one another with respect and dignity. Teamwork – work together to achieve your goals, and enjoy – it's a great industry to be part of.

Who is your mentor or main inspiration?
There have been two great mentors throughout my career: Mr Gemelli the restaurant manager at the Four Seasons, Park Lane, when I started my career as a commis waiter. I learnt so much from his experience, determination and the important fundamental parts of service and guest experience. John Stauss, regional VP and GM Four Seasons, London, always pushing you to exceed and achieve, inspiring and motivational hotelier

What traits do you consider essential for anyone entering a career in the food and drink sector?
Energy and determination and willing to achieve and stand on your own two feet.

A brief personal profile
My biggest achievement has to be where I am today within the industry. My love for the industry lies in F&B, every day is a different day. I am a member of the Champagne Academy and Alsace wine association. Travelling is also a great interest of mine.

Can you give one essential management tip or piece of industry advice?
Determination! Never give up, as long as you have the right attitude, personality, passion and drive you will be successful.

KEY WORDS

Colleagues
People who work at the same level as yourself in your own organization or other organizations, and staff whose work you are responsible for.

Hazards
A hazard is something with the potential to cause harm.

Risk
A risk is the likelihood of the hazard's potential being realized.

Workplace
The place where an employee will work.

Customers
These include individual clients, plus other departments within your organization and external organizations to whom you may provide a service (internal and external users of your service).

Legislation
Legislation is a law which has been circulated by the government. The term may refer to a single law, or the collective body of enacted law, while 'statute' is also used to refer to a single law. Before an item of legislation becomes law it may be known as a bill, which is typically also known as 'legislation' while it remains under active consideration.

Health
Achieving health and remaining healthy is an active process. Maintaining effective strategies for staying healthy and improving one's health is of utmost importance.

Hygiene
Hygiene is the practice of keeping the body clean to prevent infection and illness, and the avoidance of contact with infectious agents.

Security
Being protected against danger or loss. Security is a concept similar to safety. Individuals or actions that infringe upon the condition of protection are responsible for the breach of security.

Industry Profiles provide advice from leading industry figures and an insight into what motivated them during their training.

 REMEMBER

Continuing Professional Development (CPD) is the term used by professionals to describe constantly updating their skills. Every opportunity to continue to update and learn new skills, techniques and knowledge should be explored.

Remember boxes draw your attention to important and relevant information.

 ACTIVITY

Stand in front of a mirror wearing your uniform.

■ Is your uniform clean, neat and tidy?

■ Fold your arms. How do you look to a customer?

■ Stand upright with your hands by your sides and your weight evenly distributed on each foot.

This is how you should be standing in your workplace.

Activity boxes help you explore and research the industry and put your knowledge into practice.

✓ **TIP**

All employees within food service spend long periods standing. Make sure you have good flat footwear that is comfortable. It will make a big difference to your working day!

Tip boxes share the authors' experiences of the industry, with helpful suggestions for how you can improve your skills.

1

Maintain a safe, hygienic and secure working environment

Unit 1GEN1.1 Maintain personal health and hygiene

Unit 1GEN1.2 Help to maintain a hygienic, safe and secure workplace

What do I need to do?

■ Identify the correct attire for the waiter or waitress in the workplace.

■ Indicate potential hazards in the workplace and how to effectively deal with them.

■ Identify the legislation and action enabling the reduction of hazards and risks at work.

What do I need to know?

■ Understand the implications and responsibility in the workplace for personal health and hygiene.

■ Be able to report illnesses and minor accidents.

■ Recognize the importance of security in the workplace and how to enforce emergency procedures.

Information covered in this chapter

This unit is about enabling the candidate to develop proficiency and put into practice knowledge of the health, safety and hygienic practices within the workplace. It discusses the health and safety requirements and policies that you will need to know about if you are to work safely and responsibly in the restaurant environment. This will also include information on the resources at the disposal of the hospitality worker to help implement any government and sector guidelines and legislation.

KEY WORDS

Colleagues
People who work at the same level as yourself in your own organization or other organizations, and staff whose work you are responsible for.

Hazards
A hazard is something with the potential to cause harm.

Risk
A risk is the likelihood of the hazard's potential being realized.

Workplace
The place where an employee will work.

Customers
These include individual clients, plus other departments within your organization and external organizations to whom you may provide a service (internal and external users of your service).

Legislation
Legislation is a law which has been circulated by the government. The term may refer to a single law, or the collective body of enacted law, while 'statute' is also used to refer to a single law. Before an item of legislation becomes law it may be known as a bill, which is typically also known as 'legislation' while it remains under active consideration.

Health
Achieving health and remaining healthy is an active process. Maintaining effective strategies for staying healthy and improving one's health is of utmost importance.

Hygiene
Hygiene is the practice of keeping the body clean to prevent infection and illness, and the avoidance of contact with infectious agents.

Security
Being protected against danger or loss. Security is a concept similar to safety. Individuals or actions that infringe upon the condition of protection are responsible for the breach of security.

INTRODUCTION

Whatever function you have in the hospitality industry, everyone is required to behave safely and professionally. Reasonable care must be taken for the health and safety of yourself and others who may be affected by what you do. You must always be responsible for your own behaviour and ensure that your actions do not cause a health and safety risk to yourself, others that you work with or customers. This includes co-operation with your employer, owner or manager to ensure that health and safety procedures are followed.

PERSONAL HEALTH, HYGIENE AND APPEARANCE

The safeguarding of personal health is important to prevent the introduction of germs and bacteria into food preparation areas. It is essential to maintain physical fitness through sufficient rest, good exercise and a nutritious diet.

The appearance of a waiter or food server should promote a high standard of cleanliness and professionalism. Employees in the workplace should always reflect the desired image of the profession that they work in.

A waiter's uniform is both smart and functional. From a smart viewpoint, it is a compelling symbol of all that the particular workplace stands for. Many workplaces now supply uniforms to help ensure that a standard dress code is maintained in the front-of-house area at all times.

As with all types of work dress, it should always fit correctly and be of a design that allows freedom of movement. Footwear is often overlooked, but because front-of-house staff are likely to spend most of their time on their feet, shoes of a sturdy, comfortable and safe design should be worn.

Uniforms must be changed on a shift-by-shift basis. It is good practice to change uniforms when a spillage takes place, although this cannot always be achieved. The clothing should be of an easily washable material.

The wearing of jewellery can be a debatable issue. There should be no jewellery worn whilst undertaking any type of food preparation with the exception of plain wedding bands

A waiter in uniform

(even this can lead to danger when operating machinery or can harbour germs and bacteria). All outward and visible jewellery must be removed during these types of tasks.

Many restaurants will not allow the use of jewellery because it could fall off into the food being served, unknown to the wearer. Cosmetics, such as make-up if used, should be used in moderation and a light deodorant or perfume can be used but should not be overpowering.

Waiters wearing the same uniform in a restaurant

Maintaining personal hygiene

It is vital that the waiter maintains a high standard of personal hygiene. Bodily cleanliness is achieved through daily showering or bathing. Anti-perspirant or deodorant may be applied to the underarm area to reduce perspiration and thus the smell of sweat. Clean underwear should be worn each day.

Hands

Hands and everything that has been touched are covered with bacteria, and although most of these are harmless, some can cause ill health. Hands must be washed regularly and frequently, particularly after visiting a toilet, before commencing the service of food and drink and during the handling of food. They should be washed using hot water with the aid of a nail brush and an antibacterial gel or liquid. The frequent use of sanitizing wipes to disinfect hands is convenient for killing a wide range of bacteria and can be used on a day-to-day basis.

To ensure good health and safety practice some employers insist on the use of plastic disposable or cotton gloves when serving food items. It must be remembered that when wearing these the gloves should be changed regularly if your hands come into contact with food, to prevent cross-contamination. Gloves may be worn in the contract catering sector during counter service of food and also some high-class restaurants and hotels will ask their waiters to wear white cotton gloves to prevent fingerprints marking elaborate silver serving cutlery or plates.

Fingernails should always be kept clean and short. Nails should be cleaned with a nailbrush and nail varnish should not be worn. Dirt can easily accumulate under the nails and then be introduced into food.

Hair

Hair should be clean, washed regularly and tidy. It should be cut and maintained on a frequent basis. If hair is worn long it should be tied back. The hair should never be touched whilst preparing or serving food as bacteria can be transferred to the fingers and potentially the food or drink that is being served.

A waitress with her hair tied back

Feet

Feet should be kept fresh and healthy by washing them daily and drying thoroughly. Deodorizing foot powder can be applied and toe nails should be short and clean.

Mouth and teeth

There are many germs within and around the area of the mouth. Therefore it is essential that the mouth does not come into contact with utensils or hands that will come into contact with food. Coughing over foods and working areas is to be avoided at all costs for the prevention of spreading bacteria from illness.

The avoidance of bad breath by brushing teeth at least twice daily is essential to good health and standards. Visit the dentist regularly to maintain healthy teeth and gums.

Smoking

Smoking must never take place near food preparation areas. This is because when a cigarette is taken from the mouth using the fingers, bacteria from the mouth can be transferred onto the fingers and therefore onto food. Any ash found on food is unacceptable and it is an offence to smoke whilst preparation of food is ongoing. It is now illegal for anyone to smoke in the workplace and this includes restaurants, pubs, bars and all areas where food and drink is now served.

Smoking prohibited sign

FIRST AID

Employers must have appropriate and adequate first aid arrangements in the event of an accident or illness occurring. All employees should be informed of the first aid procedures including:

■ Where to locate the first aid box.

■ Who is responsible for the maintenance of the first aid box.

■ Which member of staff should be informed in the event of an accident, illness or emergency occurring.

The Health and Safety (First Aid) Regulations 1981 state that workplaces must have first aid provision. An adequately stocked first aid box should be available. The Health and Safety Executive (HSE) has recommended a minimum standard for first aid kits used in food production areas. These should contain a minimum level of first aid equipment, although this is by no means restricted.

CONTENTS OF A FIRST AID BOX FOR A KITCHEN

NUMBER OF EMPLOYEES	1–10	11–50
First aid guidance notes	1	1
Triangular bandage	4	8
Sterile eye pad	2	6
Sterile dressings – large	3	5
Sterile dressings – medium	5	11
Blue detectable plasters	20	60
Blue fingerstalls	2	12
Blue detectable tape	1	1
Blue disposable polythene gloves	1 pair	3 pairs
Moist wipes	6	20
Safety pins	6	12
Burn gel sachets	3	3

> **! REMEMBER**
>
> - First aid should only be administered by a qualified first-aider.
> - A first aid certificate is only valid for three years. After this period it must be renewed with additional first aid training.
> - Know what action you can take within your responsibility in the event of an accident occurring.

Cuts

All cuts should be covered with a waterproof dressing after the cut has been cleaned and dried. The dressing used should be coloured blue to help identify this quickly if it falls into food. When there is substantial bleeding it should be slowed as much as possible before transferring the person to professional medical care. The bleeding may be reduced by applying direct pressure or by the use of a firm bandage being attached to the wound.

Burns and scalds

Types of burns:

- Dry – caused by flames, hot metal and friction.
- Scalds – caused by steam, hot water and hot fat.
- Electrical – caused by domestic current, high voltage and lightning.
- Cold – caused by freezing metal or liquid nitrogen.
- Chemical – caused by industrial and domestic chemicals.
- Radiation – caused by exposure to the sun or extreme heat in an oven.

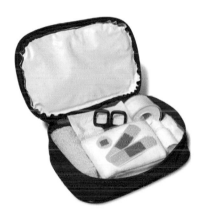

Example of a first aid box

As soon as possible place the injury under slowly running cold water or place an ice pack on top for a minimum of ten minutes. Whilst cooling check the patient's breathing and pulse. If the burn or scald is serious the wound should be dressed with a sterile dressing and professional medical help sought immediately. It is important that adhesive dressing, lotions or kitchen cloths do not come into contact with the injury.

Sometimes, due to the significance of the burn or scald, the person may go into a state of shock. The signs are clammy skin with a pale face, faintness, lethargic characteristics and sometimes sickness. The person in shock should be treated by keeping him/her comfortable at all times, laying down in the recovery position and keeping warm with a light blanket.

With an electric shock, switch off the current immediately if possible. Any burns should be dealt with as above and professional medical advice should be sought once the person is comfortable.

Reporting of Injuries, Diseases and Dangerous Occurrences Regulations (RIDDOR) (1995)

All injuries must be reported to the member of staff responsible for health and safety. This includes injuries involving guests, visitors and staff. The kitchen accident book must be completed with basic personal details of the person or persons involved, together with a detailed description of the incident. Each accident report book should comply with the recent Data Protection Act 2003. There may be legal consequences because of the injury and all witnesses must provide a clear and accurate statement of events.

The Act's key message is, you must report:

- Any fatal accidents.
- Work related diseases.
- Major injuries sustained whilst at work.
- Any potentially dangerous event that takes place at work.
- Accidents causing more than three days' absence from work.

LEGAL RESPONSIBILITIES

If you cause harm to a customer, or place them at risk, you will be personally held responsible and could be liable to criminal prosecution. There are many legislative directives relating to health and safety and the details are widely available. It is your duty to become aware of your own accountability and responsibilities towards this.

The Health and Safety at Work Act (1974)

The Health and Safety at Work Act (1974) covers employees, employers, self-employed, customers and visitors. It describes the minimum standards of health, safety and welfare required in each area of the workplace. It is the employers' legal responsibility to implement the Act and to ensure that so far as is reasonably practicable, they manage health and safety at work for the people they are responsible for. The Act's key message is that when working in a kitchen you must maintain a safe and healthy working environment at all times.

Health and Safety (Information for Employees) Regulations (1989)

The regulations require the employer to provide employees with health and safety information in the form of posters, notices and leaflets. The Health and Safety Executive provides relevant publications.

Each employer of more than five employees must formulate a written health and safety policy for that establishment. The policy must be issued to each employee and should outline their safety responsibilities.

Regular health and safety checks should be made to ensure that safe practices are being used. Employees must co-operate with their employer to provide a safe and healthy workplace. As soon as any hazard is observed, it must be reported to the designated authority or line manager so that the problem can be rectified. Hazards can include:

- Obstructions to corridors, stairways and fire exits.
- Spillages and breakages.
- Faulty electrical machinery.

> **! REMEMBER**
>
> Always ensure that the accident report book is in an accessible place for everyone to use and that everybody is trained in the documentation of accidents. It is important that the report book is checked to monitor for regular occurrences.

Health and Safety Law poster

The Workplace (Health, Safety and Welfare) Regulations (1992)

This Act covers a set of benchmarks to cover the legal requirements necessary in a working environment such as ventilation, indoor temperature, lighting and staff facilities. The Act's key message is that when working in the hospitality industry you must maintain a safe and healthy working environment. Another issue that is covered is the maintenance of the workplace and equipment, cleanliness and the handling of waste materials.

> **! REMEMBER**
>
> When unpacking a delivery always ensure the product packaging is undamaged to help avoid possible personal injury from broken goods.

The Manual Handling Operations Regulations (1992)

These regulations apply where manual lifting occurs. The employer is required to carry out a risk assessment of all activities undertaken which involve manual lifting.

The Act provides guidelines on how to protect oneself when lifting heavy objects.

Stand with your feet apart

Your weight should be evenly spread over both feet

Bend your knees slowly keeping your back straight

Stand with your feet apart

Tuck your chin in towards your chest

Get a good grip on the base of the box

Bring the box to your waist height keeping the lift as smooth as possible

Keep the box close to your body

Proceed carefully making
sure that you can see
where you are going

Lower the box, reversing
the lifting procedure

Sequence showing how to lift heavy objects

The Control of Substances Hazardous to Health (COSHH) Regulations (1999)

COSHH is a workplace policy that is relevant to everyday working practices. Chemicals that are toxic such as detergents are hazardous and present a high risk. They must be stored, handled, used and disposed of correctly in accordance with COSHH regulations.

Hazardous substances are usually identified through the use of symbols, examples of which are shown below:

COSHH: A brief guide to the Regulations
What you need to know about the Control of Substances Hazardous to Health Regulations 2002 (COSHH)

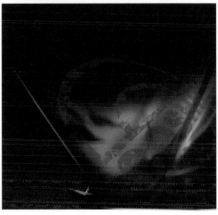

Hazard warning signs

Any substance in the workplace that is hazardous to health must be identified on the packaging and stored and handled correctly.

Hazardous substances can enter the body via:

- The skin.
- The eyes.
- The mouth (ingestion).
- The nose (inhalation).

The COSHH regulations were recently consolidated in 2002 and employers are stated as being held responsible for assessing the risks from hazardous substances and for controlling the exposure to them to prevent ill health. Any hazardous substances identified should be formally recorded in writing and given a risk rating. Safety precaution procedures should then be implemented and training given to employees to ensure that the procedures are understood and will be followed correctly.

Electricity at Work Regulations (1989)

With the often heavy use of electrical equipment in the hospitality industry this Act is particularly important. These regulations require that every item of electrical equipment in the workplace is tested every twelve months by a qualified electrician.

In addition to this annual testing, a trained member of staff or qualified electrician should regularly check all electrical equipment for safety. This is recommended every three months but generally most employers undertake this annually. A quick visual inspection before using an electrical item on a daily basis is a good method of reducing potential accidents or breakdowns. Records must be kept of the check and will include:

- Electrician's name/contact details.
- Itemized list of electrical equipment complete with serial number for identification purposes.
- Date of purchase or disposal.
- Date of last inspection.

General checks should be undertaken and reported for potential hazards, such as: exposed wires in flexes; cracked plugs or broken sockets; worn cables; and overloaded sockets. Although it is the responsibility of the employer to ensure all equipment is safe to use, it is also the responsibility of the employee to always check that the equipment is safe to use and to never use it if it is faulty.

Any electrical equipment that appears faulty must be immediately checked and repaired before use. It should also be labelled or have the plug removed to ensure that it is not used by accident before being repaired.

HAZARDS AND RISKS

The Health and Safety Act covers all full-time and part-time employees and unpaid workers (such as students on work placements). Everyone needs to be aware of their legal duties for health and safety in the workplace as required by the Health and Safety at Work Act 1974.

The Health and Safety Executive (HSE) is the body appointed to support and enforce health and safety in the workplace. They have defined the two concepts for hazards and risk:

1 A hazard is something with the potential to cause harm.
2 A risk is the likelihood of the hazard's potential being realized.

A hazard has the potential to cause harm and everyone must identify working practices within the work environment which could harm people. All staff are required to make sure that all equipment and the workplace in general is well-maintained and safe to use.

Two examples of this are as follows:

1 A light bulb that requires replacing is a hazard. If it is one out of several it presents a very small risk. But if it is the only light within a 'walk-in' storage cupboard, it poses a high risk.
2 A pan of hot fat on a guéridon trolley is a potential hazard that can fall off, causing spillage onto clothes, causing burns and creating a slippery floor surface unless cleared away immediately. Therefore it is high in risk.

Warning signs in the workplace

Safety signs are used in the workplace to help identify hazards, obligatory actions and prohibited actions for all staff, customers and visitors. Usually these signs are predominantly displayed and should be made in laminated plastic. All signage should comply with the relevant health and safety regulations and different colours signify different actions:

▪ – Warning signs to alert people to various dangers such as slippery floors and hot water.

■ – Mandatory signs to inform everyone what they must do in order to progress safely through a certain area. Usually this would indicate the need to wear protective clothing.

■ – Prohibition signs are designed to stop persons from certain tasks in a hazardous area, such as no smoking or no access.

■ – Escape route signs, designed to show fire and emergency exits to staff, visitors and customers.

Warning signs in the workplace

The Local Authority Environmental Health Department enforces the Health and Safety at Work Act, and an environmental health officer visits and inspects local business premises on a regular basis.

The inspector identifies any area of danger and it is the responsibility of the employee to remove this danger within a designated period of time. The inspector will issue an improvement notice. Failure to comply with the notice will lead to prosecution. The inspector also has the authority to close a business until he/she is satisfied that all danger to employees and public has been removed.

FIRE

The Fire Precautions Act 1971 declares that all staff must be aware of and trained in fire and emergency evacuation procedures for their workplace. The emergency exit route will be the easiest route by which all staff, customers and visitors can leave the building safely. Fire action plans should be prominently displayed to show the emergency exit route. A fire certificate is a compulsory requirement of the Act if there are more than 20 employees, or if more than 10 employees are on different floors at any one time.

The Fire Precautions (Workplace) Regulations 1997

This requires that every employer must carry out a risk assessment for the premises, under the Management of Health and Safety Regulations 1999:

■ Any obstacles that may hinder fire evacuation should be identified as a hazard and be dealt with.

■ Suitable fire detection equipment should be in place.

■ All escape routes should be clearly marked and free from obstacles.

■ Fire alarm systems should be tested on a weekly basis to ensure they are in full operational condition.

Fire fighting equipment should be easily accessed in a specified area of every kitchen. This should only be used when the cause of the fire has been identified because the use of a wrong fire extinguisher can make the fire worse. Only use fire fighting equipment when correctly trained to do so.

Fire extinguishers are available to tackle different types of fire. It is important that these are checked and maintained as required.

CAUSE OF FIRE AND CHOICE OF EXTINGUISHER

CAUSE	EXTINGUISHER	LABEL COLOUR
Electrical fire	Carbon dioxide (CO_2)	Black
Flammable liquids	Foam	Cream/yellow
Solid material fire	Water	Red
Vaporizing liquids	BCF (or) Dry powder	Green Blue

Fire blankets are used to smother a small, localized fire such as a hot fat fire or burning caramel.

A range of different fire extinguishers

Fire can only occur when three factors are present:

1 Fuel.

2 Air (oxygen).

3 Heat.

Should any one of these factors be removed, ignition cannot take place. Therefore it is essential that flammable materials should be stored safely and securely in a locked fireproof cupboard. Gas canisters are kept stored away from direct sunlight and any other direct heat source.

It is important that everyone should be completely aware of their surrounding work environment and the potential risk of fire.

In the event of a fire it is essential that no one is placed at risk and that the emergency alarm is operated as soon as possible to alert others. The emergency services should also be contacted as fast as possible. Fires can spread quickly and easily – so it is important to leave the building at once, closing doors to prevent the spread of fire and report at the identified fire assembly point.

ACTIVITY

Think of several potential causes of fire in the front-of-house area. How could each of these be prevented?

Fire blanket

SECURITY AND OTHER EMERGENCIES

The security of the workplace is associated with the following areas:

- Protection of personal and customer property.
- Correct locked storage of flammable materials.
- Workplace security procedures.

The workplace should have a clearly defined set of security procedures for every employee, visitor and customer to follow. It is essential that employees are fully aware of these measures to help identify potential breaches of security.

Usually there is a set of useful telephone numbers in the office such as local plumbers, gas engineers, electricians, emergency services and local maintenance persons.

In the event of possible threats to security, such as a bomb alert, all employees must be trained in the appropriate emergency procedures. This will involve the recognition of a suspect package, how to deal with a bomb threat, evacuation of staff and customers and contacting the emergency services. Your local Crime Prevention Officer can advise on bomb security and the security of the premises in general.

Security concerns should be taken into consideration to prevent loss of stock through theft:

1 The restaurant/service/public area should be designed to be in full view of employees and with a security camera placed for additional security if needed.

2 Stock should be kept in a secure area, accessed only by those with authority to do so.

If there is suspicion that a customer has stolen from the premises, and that there is sufficient evidence, the employer has the right to make a citizen's arrest under the Police and Criminal Evidence Act 1984. It is critical that the employer's policy on theft is totally understood.

Assessment of knowledge and understanding

You have now learned about the health and safety responsibilities for everyone in the workplace. This will enable you to ensure your own actions reduce risks to health and safety.

To test your level of knowledge and understanding, answer the following short questions. These will help to prepare you for your summative (final) assessment.

Health and safety risks

1 State the main responsibilities under the Health and Safety at Work Act 1974.

2 State the frequency that electrical equipment should be safety tested.

3 Identify the person responsible for reporting health and safety matters in the workplace.

4 State the procedure for lifting a large box from floor level to be placed onto a work surface.

5 Explain the reason for regular health and safety checks to be carried out in the workplace.

Hazards and risks in the workplace

1 Explain the word risk.

2 Explain the word hazard.

3 State the reason for immediately removing obstructions that prevent access.

4 Identify the effects that unprofessional behaviour will have on your colleagues and clients.

5 Identify the term RIDDOR and its meaning.

6 How would you deal with the following:

a Wet, slippery floor.

b Broken glass.

Taking the correct action

1 State the procedure for dealing with an accident in the workplace.

_____

2 Explain the reasons for a fire drill. State the frequency that a fire evacuation procedure in the workplace should be tested.

_____

3 In a staff room, you discover a smoking bin, in which the fire has been caused by an un-extinguished cigarette. State how this fire should be extinguished.

_____

4 Explain the action to take in the event of a bomb alert.

_____

5 Hazardous substances can enter the body via:

  a The skin.

  b The eyes.

  c The mouth (ingestion).

  d The nose (inhalation).

Describe **one** instance for each method that could happen in a restaurant environment.

_____

_____

_____

_____

Research task

Evidence is important when creating your portfolio within your own work role. Provide some detailed examples on how you have taken steps to reduce those health and safety risks which you may come into contact within the front-of-house area.

2

Contribute to effective teamwork

Unit 1GEN4 Contribute to effective teamwork

What do I need to do?

- Follow instructions.
- Keep your work organized and organize your workspace as efficiently and cleanly as possible.
- Maintain good working relationships.
- Deliver clear and effective communication within the team.
- Deal with feedback in a positive manner.

What do I need to know?

- Continue to learn and develop yourself.
- Create an efficient learning plan.
- Understand the importance of providing work on time to the exact specifications.
- Identify your responsibility as a team member.

Information covered in this chapter

This unit is about developing and putting into practice the effective organization of your own work and the contribution that can be made to produce an efficient team. It discusses the importance of communication, working relationships and behaviour issues. This will also include information on how to improve yourself and your own skills and knowledge.

KEY WORDS

Colleagues
People who work at the same level as yourself in your own organization or other organizations, and staff whose work you are responsible for.

Communication
Giving and receiving information, listening and understanding.

Confidential information
Information that you should only share with certain people, for example, your manager or personnel officer.

Customers
These include individual clients, plus other departments within your organization and external organizations to whom you may provide a service (internal and external users of your service).

Limits of your job role
What you are and are not allowed to do in the workplace.

Feedback
Giving colleagues and team members your assessment of the positive and negative aspects of the way they work and potential outcomes from set objectives.

In writing
For example, short memorandums and messages.

Prioritizing
Placing your aspects of your work in order of the most important.

INTRODUCTION

Working within a team environment involves many process skills, interpersonal skills and personal qualities. These skills are important to the effectiveness of the team when undertaking various projects (e.g. preparing for a large function). It includes co-operation with your employer, owner or manager to ensure that health and safety procedures are always followed.

WORKING AS A MEMBER OF A TEAM

One of the most vital skills any employer will seek is the ability to become a valued member of a team. Therefore the skills shown below are essential in the contribution to the effectiveness of a team and its overall performance.

Process skills

- Target setting.
- Planning.
- Clarifying roles and responsibilities.
- Organizing.
- Obtaining resources.
- Reviewing the work.

Interpersonal skills

- Teamwork and supporting co-workers.
- Communicating ideas and needs.
- Listening to others.
- Showing assertiveness.
- Negotiating support.
- Asking for help and feedback.
- Handling disagreement and conflict.

Teamwork

Personal qualities

- Reliable.
- Confident.
- Empathetic.
- Self-aware.
- Open to feedback.
- Willing to learn from experience.
- Persistent.

Effective teamwork is an essential ingredient in all successful organizations. The traditional restaurant team has always been a strong team that is usually made up from smaller groups with specific tasks and roles. Nowadays these traditional hierarchies have given way to flatter structures and waiters and

Setting a table for a function

WORKING AS A MEMBER OF A TEAM

> **! REMEMBER**
>
> When working in a restaurant, regardless of whether it is a large company chain or a small independent restaurant, you are an important member of the team. You will be working with other people that you do not know, and yet will have to develop an instant working relationship with them. As an integral part of the team you will need to quickly establish who the other members of the team are, who is responsible for different things and who you need to go to for any help and guidance.

waitresses have become more multi-skilled. Some teams can be relatively permanent, and repetitive tasks and familiar work mean that each team member has a fixed role. Experience shows that team working increases creativity, makes the most of a range of skills and knowledge, improves understanding, communication and a sense of shared purpose and overall it will improve efficiency.

ORGANIZING YOUR OWN WORK

Planning is a crucial part of work in a front-of-house operation and in the workplace generally. In order to complete a task effectively and on time planning is always involved. Larger tasks will need to be broken down into smaller sized, more manageable tasks, with 'milestones' along the way. Planning needs to be undertaken to:

- Identify what needs to be done, when and by whom.
- Help to foresee any potential problems so plans can be developed on how to tackle them.
- Provide a method for monitoring and controlling work, helping to ensure that things are done to the correct standard and on time.

Action plans will vary in detail depending on the level of task that needs to be completed. At every level, the first stage is to identify the steps that need to be taken to get the task done. It is often helpful to begin by brainstorming a list of tasks and then sketching a rough diagram, using boxes and arrows, rather than by trying to list the steps in order from the start. Sometimes this is referred to as a 'work-flow diagram'.

It can be difficult to estimate how much time is required to carry out a task. Other activities will also need to be thought about, such as cleaning cutlery, polishing glasses and organizing the tables for service. These activities are essential to the successful completion of a specific task and are collectively referred to as 'mise-en-place'. This is a French term that means 'getting everything ready and in its place'.

In order for your restaurant to be successful you will need to plan carefully for the service or function that you will be involved with.

All service functions have common characteristics and you will have come across many of these already:

- Individuals must have clear objectives and outcomes so that all members of the team are clear about the goals of the service of food and drink.
- Preparation ('mise-en-place') must have a start time and a realistic end time to ensure that they do not overrun.
- Tasks can be broken down into a sequence of smaller tasks so that they can be tackled by the team more effectively.

Being involved in a café, function room or restaurant will often involve working co-operatively as part of a team to reach common business goals. As a team you will first need to decide what needs to be done and then decide who will do what within the team.

Reading the menu carefully

Reading the menu carefully is important so that everyone in the front-of-house understands implicitly all of the dishes on the menu. The menu is the primary sales tool for any restaurant operation and it follows that product or menu knowledge is important. Aside from issues concerning allergies, special diets or preferred tastes, astute customers will expect the waiting staff to have a thorough understanding of all dishes both in terms of ingredients, preparation and cooking. Good menu knowledge is an essential aid to the sales process which provides an opportunity to up sell more profitable dishes or match a wine to any particular dish.

A strong knowledge of the menu will help guests to make informed choices and enhance their enjoyment of the meal

Identifying the tools and equipment required

As a menu is studied before service, the waiter should be making a note of which cutlery, crockery, glassware and service equipment will be required for each dish. If a specific piece of service equipment is not available, can another one be substituted without jeopardizing the service of a particular dish?

Gathering the necessary accompaniments

Once the dishes on the menu have clearly been established and the tools and equipment are readied to professionally serve each dish, other potential accompaniments to each dish should be prepared for service. For example, any classical accompaniments should be gathered beforehand to prevent any unnecessary running around during service looking for specific ingredients.

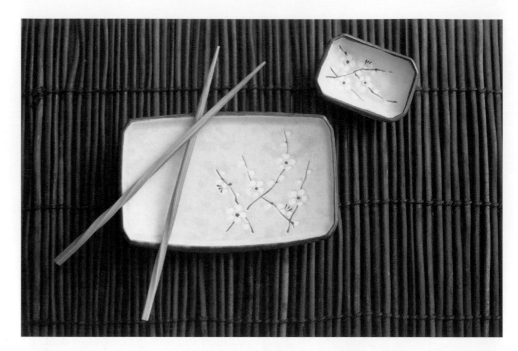

Table set for service in a Japanese restaurant

Bartender

Working to deadlines

Working to realistic deadlines is an important factor for a waiter or waitress, especially during a busy luncheon or dinner service. Doing this effectively depends on the prior skills of estimating how long a certain task will take and being able to prioritize individual jobs. Once that is achieved, it may be helpful to set intermediate deadlines related to relatively short and defined drink or food service-based tasks.

Restaurant staff working at the kitchen passe

Time management is an important skill for front-of-house staff working in the hospitality industry. In order to manage your time more effectively you must have a realistic assessment of all the tasks required and then plan the workload accordingly.

The ability to set shared targets and make plans is essential to successful teamwork. If staff do not know what they are aiming to achieve, they cannot determine what has been achieved. Summarily, if there is no real planning, progression cannot be properly monitored to review how well things are going and to be able to learn from the experience. It is during these stages that team members can support each other and provide help where necessary to achieve the end result.

Support the work of your team

Working collaboratively as a team will require you to develop your interpersonal and communications skills. When working in a team it is important to:

- Listen to the opinions of others.
- Respond in an appropriate manner to the feelings of other people if there are disagreements.
- Offer support and encouragement to team members in times of difficulty.
- Each member of the team works to his or her own strengths.
- The workload is evenly distributed amongst the team.
- Decide who is accountable for which tasks.
- Have a fully negotiated agreement among the team.

 REMEMBER

Find out which tasks take priority. Some jobs are more important or urgent than others and will need to be done first. Remember: if you have to leave a task halfway through, make sure that you get back to complete it at the earliest convenient moment.

REMEMBER

It is important to be aware of cultural and gender variations in the meaning of some gestures, posture and facial expressions.

Teams often have to agree targets and plans when preparing a luncheon, special function or dinner. The most effective plans have SMART targets that clearly set out what needs to be done to achieve the targets. The acronym SMART is often used to describe an effective target.

SMART TARGETS	
Specific	Outlining exactly what the group aims to do, rather than expressing vague general aims.
Measurable	Outlining how the group will know it has met the targets and what evidence will show this.
Achievable	Challenging for the group, but not too difficult.
Realistic	The opportunities and resources should be available.
Time-bound	There should be both interim and final deadlines.
Targets can be even SMARTER. They can be:	
Enjoyable	
Rewarding	

It is important that during this early stage job roles are clearly defined and set to specific employees. Each job role should be considered to strategically meet the requirements of the organization and to successfully contribute to the effectiveness of the team.

Communication skills

To become effective in communication such as speaking and listening, you should have an understanding of non-verbal communication (NVC), or body language.

NVC can take many forms:

1 Touch: greetings, agreements, apologies, goodbyes.
2 Posture: sitting or standing straight, leaning forward or back.
3 Proximity: distance between people, personal territory.
4 Dress: clothes, hair, appearance.
5 Eye contact: indicates interest and attention or the opposite.
6 Hand gestures: agreement, disagreement, impatience, welcome.
7 Facial expression: shows emotions and provides feedback.

Asking questions or making a point during discussions is an essential element to effective communication. Many people will want to ask questions but some will not do so because they lack the confidence to put their thoughts across at the right moment. It is a key sign of support if you can ask questions in a positive manner.

Good communication is an essential tool for a thriving restaurant business

- Briefly express your appreciation of the speaker, e.g. 'That was a really interesting point'.
- Briefly summarize the point made by the speaker, e.g. 'I was particularly interested in what you said about . . .'
- Ask your question: If you need to, write it down and read it out and try to make it clear, concise, relevant, informed and non-aggressive.

Listening skills are essential for effective communication and teamwork. They ensure that we obtain the right information from the right people, help us understand what information or support other people need and help us to work more effectively as a group.

Always remember that a good listener aims to get a thorough understanding of what the other person is saying before starting to form an opinion about it.

Other forms of communication are the telephone and via a written format (e.g. email, memorandum, fax or letter). The telephone is a fast and effective way of communicating specific requirements or orders to a supplier or to communicate events from another location that may affect the overall outcome of a specific task. It should be noted that when using the telephone, your face cannot be seen and it is important to consider your tone of voice and to speak clearly.

With the advent of information technology and the email system it is now easier than ever to record conversations and attach relevant documents. Suppliers can now usually accept orders electronically by email which makes it easier to see potential mistakes in the order and gives a greater sense of clarity to the order. Staff training in areas of communication and especially IT awareness is imperative if the organization is to develop and succeed.

Respect is the key foundation for a strong working relationship, and being able to have self-respect will encourage your views on your colleagues and the organization. It is much easier to see positive aspects in colleagues and treat them with due respect.

Another means to forming effective relationships is to confront differences directly. Differences between colleagues create a diverse environment. In a meeting where each person pays full attention to the other colleagues, they may discover a new fact that integrates two opposing perspectives. This is more rewarding than the alternatives – for example, withdrawing, becoming rebellious, or complaining to someone else. Learning to understand differences takes time and can be uncomfortable, but confronting and attempting to understand them is a good, learning exercise.

CONTRIBUTE TO YOUR OWN LEARNING AND DEVELOPMENT

Appraisal or progress reviews are an important method of communication, where one member of staff looks at the way another employee/member of staff is performing in their job role. It is usual for an employee to receive an appraisal from their line manager.

Appraisals provide an opportunity to review individuals' performance against targets set. Each team member will have their own strengths and weaknesses and it is important to utilize those strengths and action a plan to build upon and improve the weaknesses with appropriate personal goals.

Performance appraisal will identify:

- Results achieved against pre-set targets.
- Any additional accomplishments and contributions.

This may seem overwhelming, but it is an important and useful process. It can also be used to one's own advantage:

- Identify with your line manager the tasks that need to be accomplished, and how these will be met.
- Identify training needs. This will provide you with a greater range of skills and expertise and ultimately will improve your opportunities for promotion, giving you increased responsibilities.
- Identify obstructions which are affecting your progress.
- Identify and amend any changes to your current job role.

> **! REMEMBER**
>
> Continuing Professional Development (CPD) is the term used by professionals to describe constantly updating their skills. Every opportunity to continue to update and learn new skills, techniques and knowledge should be explored.

- Identify what additional responsibilities you would like.
- Identify and focus on your achievements to date against the targets set.
- Update your action plan, which will help you achieve your targets.

If personal targets are not being met it is important to identify the problem. Following this, new performance targets should be put in place to resolve any difficulties. At the next appraisal the agreed objectives and targets set for the previous period will be reviewed.

In order to develop personally and to improve your skills professionally, it is important to have personal targets against which you can measure your achievement. If these are confidential, the workplace policy on confidentiality should be observed. As mentioned earlier all targets set should be SMART (see p. 28).

IMAGE COURTESY OF THE BRITISH HOSPITALITY ASSOCIATION

To an employer it is important that you are consistent. You must always perform your skills to the highest standard and present and promote a positive image of the industry and the business you represent.

You can develop your skills by entering culinary competitions where you will have the chance to meet and compete against other food and drink service peers and this will give you the opportunity to see new techniques and exchange ideas. This is an enormous personal learning strategy and will also give a positive reputation to both yourself and your place of work. There are many different competitions both on a local and national basis with categories for juniors and seniors, such as the Young Chef Young Waiter competition run by the British Hospitality Association (www.bha.org.uk).

Waiters and restaurant managers can also learn and develop through the membership of professional associations. Developing a network of associates, friends and peers is very important for business and learning. Waiters, sommeliers, employers, suppliers, training providers and managers are able to exchange ideas and discuss ways to help meet industry targets such as training, profitability and links to other industries across the world. Examples of various associations that can be of great influence in a career are the National Restaurant Association and the British Hospitality Association.

The continuation of learning is essential to succeed in this industry and the prospect of continuing to acquire knowledge and to further develop skills to advance one's career is a very real incentive. Colleges have diverse study courses to help match your development plan and they assess the future skills that the industry requires in order for your job to be carried out effectively and for you to progress in your profession.

Your individual learning plan can be based on the chart below. It is imperative that you revisit the chart on a regular basis to review your progress and match your aims and objectives against this.

A typical individual learning plan

Winners from the Young Chef Young Waiter Competition 2008

Assessment of knowledge and understanding

You have now learned about the responsibilities you have to work effectively as a team member and the importance of communication and improving yourself. This will enable you to ensure your own positive actions contribute effectively towards the whole team.

To test your level of knowledge and understanding, answer the following short questions. These will help to prepare you for your summative (final) assessment.

Organizing your own work

1 State two important aspects of effective team work.

i) _____

ii) _____

2 Identify three ways of maintaining good working relationships with other team members.

i) _____ ii) _____

iii) _____

3 Explain the French term 'mise-en-place'.

_____

4 Name four steps you can take to make your work organized.

i) _____ ii) _____

iii) _____ iv) _____

5 Explain the importance of providing any requested work on time and within the required standards.

_____

6 Name four interpersonal skills.

i) _____ ii) _____

iii) _____ iv) _____

7 Identify what the term SMART represents.

_____

Supporting the work of your team

1 State the reason effective teamwork is important and the contribution it has to the team's overall success.

_____

2 Explain the value of helping team members in their work.

_____

3 Identify the significance of being able to communicate effectively.

_____

4 List three examples of effective teamwork.

i) _____ ii) _____

iii) _____

5 Explain the term NVC.

_____

6 Feedback on your job role performance may not always be positive and may identify areas for improvement:

a State the importance in responding positively to such feedback.

_____

b Explain how this information can improve your performance in the future.

_____

Contribute to your own learning and development

1 State the purpose of an appraisal or performance review.

_____

2 Explain the importance of improving your own knowledge and skills to help the work of your own team.

_____

3 Describe the types of activity that can help you learn.

_____

4 Give an explanation of an individual learning plan.

_____

5 State the importance in reviewing your learning plan on a regular basis.

_____

Research task

Evidence is important when creating your portfolio within your own work role. State five learning aims that you would like to achieve in the next six months and make them into SMART targets.

i) _____ ii) _____

iii) _____ iv) _____

v) _____

3

Give customers a positive impression of yourself

Unit 503 Maintain customer care

1GEN3.1 Deal with customers.

1GEN3.2 Deal with customers' problems.

Unit 601 Give customers a positive impression of yourself

2GEN1.1 Establish effective relationships with customers.

2GEN1.2 Respond appropriately to customers.

2GEN1.3 Communicate information to customers.

What do I need to do?

- You need to meet and greet customers.
- You need to communicate information to customers.
- You need to be able to locate information for customers.
- You need to deal with customer complaints.

What do I need to know?

- You need to know and understand the different aspects of legislation relating to your customer's information.
- How to communicate positively, professionally and confidently.
- How to recognize when a customer is angry and how to resolve their problems.

Information covered in this chapter

- Body language.
- Dealing with customers.
- Legislation.
- Dealing with customers' problems.
- Dealing with angry customers.

KEY WORDS

Body language
How a person's physical appearance and actions can indicate what they are thinking and feeling.

Legislation
Laws that apply to a specific area.

Equal opportunities
The term applied to the laws that prevent discrimination.

Discrimination
The unfair treatment of a person or group of people.

INTRODUCTION

How customers are spoken to and communicated with will impact greatly on their experience in a food service outlet. Customers are not attracted to restaurants and bars solely because of the food served or the ambience, the warmth, efficiency and professionalism of the service will impact greatly too.

Body language and how a member of staff acts impacts greatly on how customers perceive the individual and the establishment. How questions are answered can ensure that a customer is treated with the utmost professionalism at all times. There are important laws that need to be adhered to when giving out information to customers and about customers.

If there is a problem and a customer becomes upset or angry this can affect the entire establishment and the service within it. Preventing a problem from arising is better than trying to appease an angry customer. However, dealing with an angry customer is a skill that needs to be learned. A customer who has a bad experience and is helped will return to a establishment; one who is ignored will not.

BODY LANGUAGE

There are times when our actions can speak louder than our words. The ability to project positive body language to your customers will help make a positive impression. Although body language is not an exact science there are rules that apply.

Make eye contact: When dealing with customers, be sure to make eye contact with them, but do not stare. This will make them feel that attention is being paid to them and also will make sure they hear what has been said. It is difficult to hear someone if they are not looking at you when being spoken to.

Appear friendly: Everyone has bad days, there is no need to take it out on the customers. Smile and try to help in a friendly way. Be careful not to appear over friendly as this can be off-putting to a customer as well.

Pay attention to the customer: Be sure to give customers your full attention when assisting them. If you are busy with a customer when another is trying to attract your attention, make eye contact and let the customer know that you will be with them.

Your facial expressions will let everyone know what type of mood you are in. Be courteous. Smile, even if it hurts. Always be polite and courteous to your customers.

To let a customer know that you are listening and concerned with what they are saying, perhaps nod to allow the customer to know you are listening. Also, face the customers with your entire body to show them they have your undivided attention.

TIP

All employees within food service spend long periods standing. Make sure you have good flat footwear that is comfortable. It will make a big difference to your working day!

Receptionist

A further part of body language is neatness and personal hygiene. How we look has a big impact on how people perceive us.

How you look

The first impression that you give to customers will set the standard for the rest of their time within your establishment.

Most establishments will require some form of uniform to be worn. Some will provide them, in others you will be expected to provide them yourself. But there will be an expectation of how you wear your uniform. It is important to

TIP

Always make sure that you have a freshly laundered uniform ready before you commence work each day.

remember that uniforms have two purposes, one is so that customers can readily identify you as an employee of the establishment, and the other is to protect food that is being served from contamination.

CHECKLIST FOR UNIFORMS

- ✓ Ensure that all parts of the uniform fit correctly.
- ✓ Launder and iron each item daily.
- ✓ Always wear correct footwear.
- ✓ Keep make-up natural and light.
- ✓ Do not wear overpowering perfumes when serving customers.
- ✓ Keep hairstyles classical.
- ✓ If you are missing a button or have a tear, repair it immediately.

Smart uniform

Your surroundings

The area that you work within is another good indication to a customer of the establishment's standards. It is important both from hygiene and professional perspectives that all work areas are kept clean and tidy at all times.

 ACTIVITY

Stand in front of a mirror wearing your uniform.

- Is your uniform clean, neat and tidy?
- Fold your arms. How do you look to a customer?
- Stand upright with your hands by your sides and your weight evenly distributed on each foot.

This is how you should be standing in your workplace.

DEALING WITH CUSTOMERS

Customers are the lifeblood of any food service establishment. They pay the money for the products that are served, which then in turn pays for the staff. Good manners and politeness are essential at all times.

CHECKLIST

✓ Always address the customers as sir, madam or Mr ___ or Mrs ___ unless invited by them to call them something else.

✓ Always refer to a customer as a lady or a gentleman, never as he or she.

✓ When answering a question give a complete answer, never just one word.

✓ Try not to use jargon or specific words that the customers may not be familiar with.

✓ If you do not know the answer to a question, politely tell the customer, 'I am sorry I don't know the answer but I will go and find out'.

✓ Speak clearly, do not mumble or mutter.

Each restaurant or establishment will have their own customer service practices and rules. Some are general across the entire industry and others are individual to each establishment.

There is basic information that all members of staff should know and be able to answer when asked. This information includes the address and telephone number of the premises, opening hours of the establishment, the names of the general manager and the head chef, and a description of the menu. Other information that staff may know includes transport directions to and from the establishment and other local amenities or who designed the restaurant.

LEGISLATION

When dealing with customers there are some important pieces of legislation that need to be understood. Their purpose is to both protect the customer and help the establishment.

Data Protection Act 1998

The Date Protection Act 1998 is a law that is in place to protect information about people that has been entered onto or stored in a computer. It is there to protect information and to stop people using information for criminal purposes.

It is important that a customer's names, addresses and personal details are not given out to any other person. Within a restaurant or food service

Legislation

establishment details may be held about individual customers within booking or reservations systems. These details may include names, addresses and credit card details.

It is important that only authorized members of staff have access to customers' details on a computer database. There must be a method with which these details may be changed if necessary. No members of the public may see these records and it is an offence to let them do so.

However, it is essential that if a customer asks a question or seeks information about another customer that the question is dealt with correctly.

EXAMPLE

A customer, Mr Smith, asks for the telephone number of another customer, Mr Jones. Mr Smith has lost his mobile phone which contains Mr Jones' number. As they are both regular customers you know that they both know each other very well. Unfortunately you are not allowed to give the number out as it contravenes the Data Protection Act 1998. As a member of staff you want to be able to help your customers as much as possible. Therefore you must NOT say 'Sorry, I can't help you, it's against the rules'. The way in which to negate this is to say 'I am sorry we cannot pass on a customer's details but if you give me your telephone number I could ring him and ask him to contact you'. By doing this you are giving the customer an alternative solution without passing out details.

Equal Opportunities and Disability Discrimination

Over the last thirty years much legislation has been introduced to ensure that all sections of society have the same opportunities both in their work and leisure time. It is illegal to discriminate against people because of their sex, religion, sexual orientation, disability, colour, or ethnic origin.

This means that a public restaurant must be prepared to allow everyone who approaches it as a customer to enter and must offer the same service and items to everyone. The rules only change slightly in the case of clubs who by their definition will set out criteria for joining.

Equal opportunities

EXAMPLE

A golf club may only permit male members to join, this will be written in its rules of eligibility. The golf club will have to allow all males who fulfil the eligibility criteria to enter.

When serving guests who have disabilities it may not always be practical or economical to have all the equipment necessary in a small establishment. Not many restaurants have menus in Braille or large print, but staff are encouraged to spend extra time with these customers describing the dishes on offer and helping them make their selection.

It is a requirement in all premises constructed or renovated since 2005 that toilets are available for those with limited mobility. It is important that all members of staff are aware of these facilities or the arrangements for these customers.

ACTIVITY

Find out what the arrangements are within your premises for physically handicapped customers.

DEALING WITH CUSTOMERS' PROBLEMS

When customers have a problem it is best to deal with it as quickly as possible. If it is not dealt with promptly the customers can become more frustrated and angry and this will have an impact on their experience.

TIP

Do not ignore a customer's problem, this will only cause it to escalate. Be proactive and offer help as soon as possible.

Male receptionist on telephone

If guests appear to be unhappy or angry the waiter should approach them. Using positive language the waiter should say 'May I help you?' rather than 'What's wrong?'. This will start the interaction on a positive note. Listen carefully to what the customers say. Apologize, make sure that you do so sincerely and make eye contact. Deal with the problem, apologize again and ensure that your supervisor knows about the situation.

Once the situation has been dealt with take extra time and energy to ensure that the customers have no further problems.

DEALING WITH ANGRY CUSTOMERS

There is no excuse for anger or bad behaviour within any workplace but it is a fact of life that people can be angry in public places. It can be very stressful dealing with angry customers and it is very easy to take an angry customer's comments personally.

Customers can become angry for many different reasons, none of them are acceptable but it is important that you find the underlying reason for their anger.

WHY CUSTOMERS CAN BECOME ANGRY
✓ They may not have received the items or service that they require.
✓ They may have become drunk.
✓ They may have had a bad experience before entering the premises.
✓ They may just be having a bad day.
✓ They may be frightened about a situation that they have no control over.

How to recognize that someone is angry

■ They may have raised voices.

■ They may be agitated.

■ They may be rude.

■ Their facial expression will not be positive.

Don't respond with anger

✓ TIP

Looking after an angry customer correctly can turn him/her into a loyal customer in the future.

It would be easy to feel that an angry customer should be responded to in a similar way. It may be justified, but it definitely will not help with the situation. Responding with anger can make the situation worse because:

■ The customer will get even more angry and unreasonable.

■ The employee will become stressed and unhappy.

■ Staying calm is the best way to resolve the situation.

The nature of anger is that the customer will try very hard to make the employee feel guilty. As a waiter there are many things within an establishment that are out of your control but the customers do not want to know that, they want the situation to be rectified as quickly as possible. If a waiter feels guilty they will carry this feeling on to their next tables and this will affect the rest of the customers.

If a customer's order is incorrect and they receive the wrong item, the waiter may well be to blame but that will not help the waiter improve the situation. Apologize and rectify the order, take the customer seriously and ensure that the supervisor knows what has happened.

When people get angry they lose a sense of perspective and it becomes difficult to reason with them. It is good to deal with the situation in a way that pacifies them without going into too much detail. People who get angry don't want to lose face, so it is important to give them a way out.

- Do not panic. They may feel it is the most important thing in the world, but sometimes a moment's silence can calm the situation.
- Acknowledge the issue.
- Apologize for their inconvenience. If you think their complaint is unjustified, you can apologize in a very unspecific way. This gives an apology without having to admit that they are right.
- Say you will inform the supervisor.

RESPONDING TO CUSTOMERS' PROBLEMS

GOOD THINGS TO DO WHEN RESPONDING TO ANGER	THINGS NOT TO DO WHEN RESPONDING TO ANGER
Be calm, polite and dignified. This is the best way to get a customer to behave reasonably.	Be sarcastic. Sarcasm is the lowest form of wit, angry people have lost their sense of humour so will not appreciate it.
Apologize for their inconvenience.	Get angry yourself.
Smile and maintain eye contact.	Feel guilty.
Be sympathetic and empathetic.	Worry about it after the event.
Thank them for bringing the issue to your attention.	Chat about what happened to other members of staff.
Offer steps that could be taken to rectify the situation. Please ensure the offer that you make is within your area of responsibility.	Roll your eyes or make facial expressions that are negative.
Refer them to someone else. If you feel out of your depth it is a good idea to refer to a supervisor. Make sure that the supervisor has all the details of the situation.	Tell your supervisor half the story or omit important details.
Don't directly say they are wrong; if you do not agree, maintain a dignified silence.	Argue with the customers.

Keep calm when talking to customers

IMAGE COURTESY OF JAMES STEIDL

Assessment of knowledge and understanding

You have now learned about the responsibilities you have to work effectively as a team member and the importance of giving customers a positive impression. This will enable you to ensure your own positive actions contribute effectively towards the whole team.

To test your level of knowledge and understanding, answer the following short questions. These will help to prepare you for your summative (final) assessment.

Preparing for assessment checklist

■ Draw a diagram of the uniform that you are required to wear. List how it should be maintained.

■ Write out a list of common customer questions about your establishment, ensure your answers are as comprehensive as possible.

■ What is the procedure for dealing with customer's complaints in your establishment?

Project 1

1 A dish that a guest has ordered was cold when it was served to him. What is the procedure for dealing with this situation?

2 Write a description of how to find your establishment by public transport. Where is the nearest car park and how much does it cost to park?

_____

_____

3 A customer has had to wait for half an hour for his table to be ready. When you are serving him what steps would you take to ensure that the rest of his meal is successful?

_____

_____

Project 2

1 Write a log describing when you have dealt with a customer who has had a problem. How did you deal with it? Who did you get to help you?

_____

_____

2 Write a log describing the information that you are normally asked for by customers in your establishment.

_____

_____

INDUSTRY PROFILE

Name: **KAREN McCONNELL**
Position: RESTAURANT MANAGER
Establishment: PLAS BODEGROES RESTAURANT WITH ROOMS

Current job role and main responsibilities:
I am the restaurant manager but as we only have 11 rooms I'm very much involved with the hotel too. My main responsibilities are guest relations, the set up of the restaurant for evening service and organizing bookings for rooms and restaurant.

In your opinion, what is it that sets your service apart from the average and makes it worthy of a Michelin star?
Our service is incredibly attentive from the moment the guests arrive when we take their coats to the very last minute when they leave and we bid them goodnight. Although we are a MIchelin starred restaurant the service is unstuffy and welcoming but we do pride ourselves on efficiency from the ordering of cocktails to delivery of food to clearing tables – it's done under the eye of the customer but they don't notice what is going on.

When did you realize that you wanted to pursue a career in the food service industry?
I fell into the hospitality industry when I moved to East Africa and I haven't looked back since. Although the hours are strange it's great fun and rewarding most of the time.

Training:
I have no formal training but have learnt from three dynamic owner/occupiers who have each passed down tips and know-hows to me. Listen to these people and remember if it ain't broke don't fix it. You don't have to make your mark by changing procedures especially if they work really well.

Experience:
All my previous experience has been in Kenya and Tanzania.
Wasini Island Restaurant: assistant manager. This was a restaurant on an island off Kenya where we dealt in large numbers of clients so authority was a much needed personality trait.
Gibb's Farm Hotel, Tanzania: assistant manager. I was responsible for the wellbeing of all the hotel clients. We also had a large restaurant where we served lunch to passing guests again in very large numbers so good organization is a must.
Kusini Camp, Tanzania: joint camp manager. I was responsible for the preparation of the menus, food ordering and the guests. It was a small operation but was completely guest focused where we actually hosted each dinner so good conversational skills were much needed.

What do you find rewarding about your job?
I find the feedback rewarding, when guests have really enjoyed their stay and I have been a part of that. I really enjoy meeting people from all walks of life so this is the perfect job.

What do you find the most challenging about the job?
Sometimes the pronunciation of food names!!! Other than that it is unreasonable people but luckily they are few and far between.

What advice would you give to students just beginning their career?
Think long and hard if this is what you want to do. You will work anti-social hours and this will be tested by family opinion, boyfriends/girlfriends, not being able to go out on a Saturday night. You will have to be dedicated, if you are ill your colleagues will have to cover for you and it's not a popular move. The pay is not always good to start with but once you have proved your dedication you will be in demand.

Who is your mentor or main inspiration?
My three previous and current employers. They have all worked so long and hard for this end product.

What traits do you consider essential for anyone entering a career in the food and drink sector?
A happy disposition, dedication, diplomacy, efficiency.

A brief personal profile
My interests are travelling, food and wine, theatre and cinema. I am proud of how I have moved up in the hospitality industry which ended up in me owning my own business but I also happily sold it. I would rather someone else does the paperwork!

Can you give one essential management tip or piece of industry advice?
Treat your colleagues equally as you need to be a strong team behind the scenes and do your swan impression – gliding effortlessly whilst underneath you are paddling like hell.

4

Maintain food safety when storing, holding and serving food

Unit 2GEN4 Maintain food safety when storing, holding and serving food

2GEN4.1 Keep yourself clean and hygienic

2GEN4.2 Keep your working area clean and hygienic

2GEN4.3 Store food safely

2GEN4.4 Hold and serve food safely

What do I need to do?

■ Identify the correct attire for the waiter in the workplace.

■ Maintain clean and hygienic work areas and equipment.

■ Check food into the premises and identify specific labels.

■ Identify food bacteria and other organisms and food hazards in the workplace.

What do I need to know?

■ Be aware of your responsibility for personal cleanliness during food service and storage in the workplace and unsafe behaviour.

■ Understand the correct use of storage control, the stock rotation system and keeping records.

■ Know how to safely defrost food and thoroughly wash food.

■ Know the regulations for the safe holding and the safe service of food.

Information covered in this chapter

This unit is about the current food safety guidance in the UK and integrates the key topics of cleaning and preventing cross-contamination. It provides the learner with the knowledge and skills of reviewing hazards and using hazard-based procedures as a part of a team maintaining food safety. It discusses the health and hygiene requirements and policies that you will need to know about if you are to work safely and hygienically in the front-of-house area. This will also include information on the resources at the disposal of the waiter or waitress to implement regulations to store, hold and serve food safely.

KEY WORDS

Personal hygiene
Hygiene refers to practices associated with ensuring good health and cleanliness.

Food bacteria
Bacteria were first observed by Antoine van Leeuwenhoek in 1676, using a single-lens microscope of his own design. Food bacteria are a group of single cell micro-organisms, and although the vast majority of bacteria are harmless or beneficial, a few bacteria are pathogenic and these are food bacteria that will cause illness.

Stock rotation system
This is the practice used in restaurants and food production areas, of moving products with an earlier sell-by date to the front of a shelf, so they get picked up and sold first, and of moving products with a later sell-by date to the back.

Food hazards
Is a term used by food safety organizations to classify foods that require time and temperature control to keep them safe for human consumption. Foods that contain moisture, protein and are neutral to slightly acidic are typically labelled as a potential food hazard and strict storage conditions are imposed.

Staphylococci
Staphylococcus can cause a wide variety of diseases in humans and other animals through either toxin production or invasion. Staphylococcal toxins are a common cause of food poisoning, as they can grow in improperly stored food.

Cross-contamination
If a chopping board is not cleaned properly before another food is cut on the same board a transference of contamination can happen.

INTRODUCTION

The waiter or waitress must be particularly conscious of the need for hygiene; many commodities have to be handled, stored and served to the customer without any type of heat treatment. High standards of hygiene are essential to prevent food poisoning, food spoilage, loss of productivity, pest infestation and potential criminal prosecution for malpractice.

Food hygiene implies more than just the sanitation of work areas; it includes all practices, precautions and legal responsibilities involved in the following:

1 Protecting food from risk of contamination.
2 Prevention of organisms from multiplying to an extent which would pose a health risk to customers and employees.
3 Destroying any harmful bacteria in food by thorough heat treatment or other techniques.

PERSONAL HYGIENE

Good hygiene systems are required to be followed by all food handlers and servers. Chapter 1 (Maintain a safe, hygienic and secure working environment) covers the features of personal hygiene in some depth but some aspects need to be highlighted in this chapter in relation to the subject matter.

Regular hand washing is a requirement of all front-of-house personnel. The following procedures should apply:

1 An approved hand washing detergent should be provided by the employer, preferably in liquid form and from a dispenser.
2 Hot water and an approved drying system should be in place.
3 The application of an alcohol based hand disinfectant allows for maximum disinfection.

Hand washing must be undertaken:

- Before commencing work (to wash away general bacteria).
- After using the toilet.
- After breaks.
- Between touching raw food and cooked food.
- Before handling raw food.
- After disposing of waste.
- After cleaning the workspace.
- After any first aid or dressing changes.
- After touching face, nose, mouth or blowing your nose.
- Hand washing and sanitation should take place at every possible opportunity.

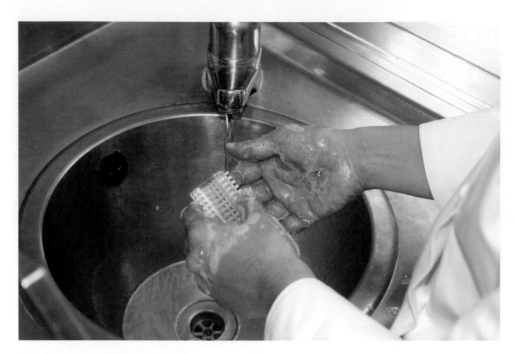

Hands must be washed regularly

Tasting food whilst cooking during guéridon service

Sometimes the waiter or waitress at some high-class establishments will be required to prepare or cook certain dishes in front of the customer. This can be referred to as guéridon service. Whilst it is good practice for a waiter to taste the food during cooking to ensure that the dish is seasoned correctly, a spoon that is washed between tasting must always be used. The practice of tasting food from the fingers should always be prohibited. The mouth is likely to harbour *staphylococci* and food servers should never chew gum, eat sweets while working, spit or constantly touch their mouth or nose.

Hair

This should be washed regularly and kept in good condition. It should be tied up if shoulder length to keep it away from the face. Certain restaurants will have in-house rules about hair styles and sometimes this will be as much about the image of the restaurant as it is about hygiene. To maintain food hygiene standards there are now many types of hat available from suppliers for food servers working behind a counter, many of which are disposable. They also present a professional image in serving areas that are visible to the public and customers.

Cuts, boils and septic wounds

Food handlers and servers should always cover cuts, grazes, boils and septic wounds with the appropriate dressing or with brightly coloured (blue)

waterproof plasters. Cuts on fingers may need extra protection with waterproof fingerstalls or in certain cases latex disposable gloves.

Smoking

This is prohibited where food is being served due to the following issues:

- The danger of contaminating food by *staphylococci* from the fingers which may touch the lips and from saliva from the cigarette end.
- It encourages coughing.
- It is now illegal to smoke in places that serve food and drink.

Jewellery and cosmetics

Food handlers and front-of-house staff should be discouraged from wearing earrings, watches, rings or piercings because they can harbour dirt and bacteria. Plain wedding bands are permitted, but these can still harbour significant levels of bacteria. Strong smelling perfume may cause food to be tainted or be too overpowering for customers to enjoy their food and make-up should be used minimally.

Appropriate clothing

Every person handling food must wear protective clothing. It should be lightweight, washable and strong. White clothing has the advantage of showing up dirt more easily. However, it is important that food handlers or staff that serve food from behind a counter wear the following protective garments in a food service environment:

1 A hat to cover the hair.

2 A clean, light shirt that is comfortable.

3 Apron – long and made from heavy cotton.

4 Non-slip, safe shoes.

Protective clothing is worn to protect the food from risk of contamination and to help protect the food server from spillages of any kind. Protective clothing should not be worn outside food premises and not for travelling to and from work.

A well-dressed team

Waiters and waitresses in restaurants, hotels, corporate catering and outside catering will usually be asked to meet the requirements of the employer with regards to standardized clothing. Every employee should fully understand the standards and requests for clothing or how a uniform should be worn.

Often a customer's first contact will be with a restaurant receptionist, *Maitre d'* or waiter. It is this first impression that will help to distinguish the type of outlet that the customer may want to dine in. Some restaurants such as TGI Fridays have a uniform that depicts a bright, fun and slightly laid-back atmosphere. In contrast, a five star hotel restaurant will expect their waiting staff to be correctly turned out in an elegant and sometimes stylish full waiter's uniform. Once again this uniform will represent the grandeur of the restaurant experience.

Reporting of illness or infection

RIDDOR regulations (reporting injuries, diseases and dangerous occurrences) were introduced in 1995. This Act requires all work-related accidents, diseases and dangerous occurrences to be reported by employees to employers and by employers to the National Incident Contact Centre. Each accident report book should comply with the recent data protection act.

It is important that if you are feeling unwell you should report this to your line manager or employer as soon as possible. The risk of passing on illness or infection to other members of the team may be too hazardous depending on your condition.

A CLEAN AND HYGIENIC AREA

The use of premises which are clean and can be correctly maintained is essential for the preparation, cooking and service of food. Cross-contamination risks should be minimized by the provision of separate preparation areas for the various raw and cooked foods and separate storage areas too.

Work surfaces and equipment for the storage and service of food should be impervious and easy to clean. Equipment should be constructed from materials which are non-toxic, corrosion resistant, smooth and free from cracks. Apparatus such as a bain-marie should be able to store hot food for up to two hours at an ambient temperature of 63°C and regular temperature checks should be taken. The surfaces should be easy to clean even when hot and should allow the food to be served in an attractive manner.

Worktops and chopping boards

It is very important to keep all worktops and chopping boards clean because they touch the food your customers are going to eat. Even chopping boards that are used to slice lemons for cocktails are subject to bacterial infection. If they are not properly clean, bacteria will spread to food and potentially make your customers ill. The following steps are easy actions to take to help ensure the hygienic use of all worktops and chopping boards:

- Always wash worktops before you start preparing food with hot water with a light detergent added.
- Wipe up any spilt food immediately.
- Always wash worktops thoroughly after they have been touched by raw ingredients.
- Never put ready-to-eat food, such as tomatoes or fruit, on a worktop or chopping board that has been touched by raw meat, unless you have washed the worktop or chopping board thoroughly first.

If you have a dishwasher, this is a very effective way to clean plastic chopping boards. Dishwashers can wash at a very high temperature, which kills bacteria. Otherwise, wash chopping boards thoroughly with hot water and detergent.

It is standard practice to have separate chopping boards for different food preparation tasks. A standardized system of coloured boards and knife handles to help minimize cross contamination are widely available. The coloured code for chopping boards should be as follows:

- Red Raw meat and poultry
- Yellow Cooked meat and poultry
- Blue Raw fish (in this book, white and wooden backgrounds may be used for photographic purposes)
- Brown Vegetables
- Green Fruit and salads
- White Dairy and pastry items

These boards must be cleaned between each use, ideally with a specialist sanitizer and clean cotton cloth. On a regular basis they should be soaked overnight in a sterilizing solution. If boards become damaged they should be discarded because bacteria can multiply in cracks and blemishes, and be the cause of contamination.

Colour-coded cutting boards

Waiters' cloths and tea towels

Dirty and damp cloths are the perfect breeding ground for bacteria. So it is very important to wash waiters' cloths and other cleaning cloths, sponges and abrasive materials regularly and leave them to dry before using them again.

Ideally, try to keep different cloths for different jobs. For example, use one cloth to wipe worktops and another to wash dishes. This helps to stop bacteria spreading.

The safest option is the use of disposable towels to wipe worktops. This is because you throw the towel away after using it once, so it is less likely to spread bacteria than cloths which you use again.

Tea towels can also spread bacteria, so it's important to wash them regularly and be careful how you use them. Remember, if you wipe your hands on a tea towel, this could spread bacteria to the towel. If you then use the tea towel to dry a plate, the bacteria will spread to the plate.

Glassware

The use of the bartenders' method for speedy wine glass washing is the best way of cleaning wine glasses. Holding the base, pump the glass vigorously in hot soapy water, and quickly pump it in hot clear water (cooler water may shatter the glass). Dry it upside down on a cotton towel. Alternatively, glasses

Polishing wine glasses

can be dried by rotating them in a dry tea towel (preferably linen or plain cotton). A damp cloth drags a cold surface and could pull out a piece of the rim. Hold stemmed glasses firmly by the bowl as the stem is easily broken. For extra shiny streak-free glasses, add a little vinegar or borax to the final rinse water.

Never use hot water, harsh soaps, ammonia or washing soda on silver or gold rimmed glasses. The action of a dishwasher and detergent will etch and dull the surface of lead cut crystal. Ideally they should be hand washed singly in a warm solution of washing-up liquid, rinsed in a bowl of water and dried whilst warm. However, there can be potential problems or hazards with certain glass products, such as:

Chipped glass rims: Provided the chip is shallow and the glass is valuable, have the rim ground down but it will be shorter than the rest. Alternatively, the glass should be disposed of immediately.

If two glasses are stuck together: Fill the inner glass with iced water and repeatedly dip the outer glass in a bowl of warm water. Gradually increase the temperature of the warm water until the outer glass has expanded sufficiently for the two glasses to be separated. Always increase the temperature gradually otherwise the glass may break.

Decanter stopper stuck: Wrap the neck of the decanter in a fairly hot, damp towel and use the handle of a wooden spoon to gently tap opposite sides of the stopper. Or pour two or three drips of cooking oil around the decanter's rim and leave in a warm place.

Stained decanters: To remove stains in the base of a decanter half fill with warm, soapy water and add two tablespoons of uncooked rice. Swirl the mixture round several times over 30 minutes and then pour it out. Rinse thoroughly and stand upside down to drain dry.

To remove the remains of sticky labels: This does depend on the type of adhesive used on the label as some are impervious to water. Rub with a cloth dipped in methylated spirits or sprinkle on a little talcum powder and rub with your finger.

Cutlery and utensils

Cutlery in a washer tray

It is important to keep all cutlery and utensils clean to help stop bacteria spreading to food. It is especially important to wash them thoroughly after using them with raw ingredients, because otherwise they could spread bacteria to other food. Once again, a dishwasher is a very effective way to clean knives, forks, spoons and other utensils because dishwashers can wash at a very high temperature, which kills bacteria. Otherwise, wash them thoroughly with hot water and a detergent before drying and polishing with a clean cotton cloth.

> ! **REMEMBER**
>
> As a result of changes in European food hygiene regulations in January 2006, the Food Standards Agency has issued new guidance on temperature control in England, Wales and Northern Ireland. The guidance contains advice on the types of foods that are required to be held under temperature control and on the circumstances in which some flexibility from the temperature control requirements is allowed. The guidance is intended to complement best practices in the food industry, which might involve, for example, keeping foods at chill temperatures below the legal maximum and thereby providing additional assurances of food safety.

HAZARD ANALYSIS CRITICAL CONTROL POINTS (HACCP)

Hazard Analysis Critical Control Points are an internationally-recognized and recommended system of food safety management. They focus on identifying the critical points in a process where food safety problems (or hazards) could arise and putting steps in place to prevent things going wrong. This is sometimes referred to as controlling hazards. Keeping records is also an important part of HACCP systems.

HACCP involves the following seven steps:

- Identify what could go wrong (the hazards).
- Identify the most important points where things can go wrong (the critical control points – CCPs).
- Set critical limits at each CCP (e.g. food holding temperature/time).
- Set up checks at CCPs to prevent problems occurring (monitoring).
- Decide what to do if something goes wrong (corrective action).
- Prove that your HACCP plan is working (verification).
- Keep records of all of the above (documentation).

Your HACCP plan must be kept up-to-date. You will need to review it from time to time, especially whenever something in your food operation changes. You may also wish to ask your local Environmental Health Officer for advice. Remember that, even with a HACCP plan in place, you must comply with all requirements of current food safety legislation.

The Food Hygiene (England) Regulations 2006 provide the framework for the EU legislation to be enforced in England. There are similar regulations in Wales, Scotland and Northern Ireland. The Food Safety (General Food Hygiene) Regulations 1995 and the Food Safety (Temperature Control) Regulations 1995 do not apply any more. Many of the requirements of these regulations are included in the new EU legislation, so this means that what businesses need to do from day-to-day has not changed very much. The main new requirement is to have 'food safety management procedures' and keep up-to-date records of these.

Disposal of waste is another HACCP matter, as bacteria and pathogens can multiply at an alarming rate in waste disposal areas. In ideal circumstances the areas for cleaning crockery and pots should be separate from each other and from the food preparation area.

 REMEMBER

Food handlers and servers must receive appropriate supervision, and be instructed and/or trained in food hygiene, to enable them to handle food safely.

A dirty kitchen

The reporting of maintenance issues

Food and drink must be served using surfaces that are hygienic and suitable for use. Work surfaces, walls and floors can become damaged, and they too can be a source of contamination and a danger to customers and staff alike. Signs of damage should be reported to your line manager. A maintenance reporting system can easily be designed to suit each establishment. Good practice is to have a weekly maintenance check and a set procedure for repairing or replacing equipment. If this is done it can lead to a more economical maintenance programme as it much cheaper to repair little and often than to wait until equipment is dangerous and perhaps risk injury or litigation. Areas for attention are:

- Cracks in walls.
- Damage to tables and work benches.
- Equipment such as plates, glassware, cutlery and utensils.
- Windows, sanitary systems and lights.
- Flooring and any other structural issues.
- Electrical equipment relating to that particular operation.

SAFE FOOD STORAGE

A HACCP food management system will also examine the point of food storage. It should cover the receiving of goods where the core temperatures and condition of the delivery is thoroughly checked. Fresh meat that has been delivered should have a core temperature of a maximum of 8°C. All fresh produce should be delivered in unbroken, clean packaging and in clean delivery vehicles that are refrigerated. If you suspect a delivery has not met the requirements of your HACCP it should not be accepted and returned immediately to the supplier. A goods inwards sheet showing the company, invoice number, core temperature, any problems and how they were dealt with, allows received goods to be monitored.

After the commodity has been received it needs to be correctly stored. Raw meat and fish should be stored, covered, in separate refrigerators at 4°C. However if there is not enough capacity for two separate refrigeration systems, *cooked products must be stored above fresh meat*. Fish should be stored as low in the refrigerator as possible. This is the coldest part of the refrigerator and a layer of crushed ice will help to keep the temperature down. This method eliminates cross-contamination from storage and optimizes quality. All foods should be labelled with the date of delivery/ production, a description of the contents and the recommended use-by date.

Types of bacteria that cause food poisoning

Salmonella

There are approximately 2000 types of salmonella, the most common varieties are *salmonella enteriditis* and *salmonella typhimurium*. These organisms survive in the intestine and can cause food poisoning by releasing a toxin on the death of the cell. The primary source of salmonella is the intestinal tract of animals and poultry and will therefore be found in:

- Human and animal excreta.
- Excreta from rats, mice, flies and cockroaches.

- Raw meat and poultry.
- Some animal feed.

Staphylococcus aureus

About 40–50 per cent of adults carry the organism in their nose, mouth, throat, ears and hands. If present in food, *staphylococcus aureus* will produce a toxin which may survive boiling for 30 minutes or more. The majority of outbreaks are caused by poor hygiene practices which result in direct contamination of the food from sneezing or uncovered septic cuts and abrasions. Frequently, the cooked food has been handled whilst still slightly warm and these storage conditions have encouraged the organism to produce its toxin.

Clostridium perfringens

This is commonly found in human and animal faeces and is present in raw meat and poultry. This organism forms spores which may survive boiling temperatures for several hours. Outbreaks can involve stews and large joints of meat which have been allowed to cool down slowly in a warm kitchen and either eaten cold or inadequately reheated the following day.

Bacillus cereus

This is a spore-forming organism. The spores survive normal cooking and rapid growth will occur if the food has not been cooled quickly and refrigerated. This bacterium will induce nausea and vomiting within five hours of ingestion.

A well-laid-out storeroom

FOOD STORAGE AND TEMPERATURES

- **Raw meat, poultry and game and charcouterie**
  4°C or below — *Store away from cooked meat and cooked meat products to avoid any risk of cross-contamination.*

- **Cooked meat**
  4°C or below — *Keep away from raw meat and meat products.*

- **Uncooked fish**
  4°C or below — *Keep in separate compartments or in plastic fish trays with lids if possible and away from other foods which may become tainted.*

- **Frozen food**
  −18°C or below — *Thaw only immediately prior to using the commodity.*

- **Fish (smoked or cured)**
  8°C — *Keep in chilled storage away from other foods, which may become tainted.*

- **Fruit (fresh and dried)** — *Store in cool, dry, well-ventilated area. Away from other food, at least 15 cm from the ground. Discard at the first sign of mould growth. Do not overstock.*

- **Pasta, rice and cereals** — *Store in self-closing tightly lidded containers in dry cool storeroom or cupboard.*

- **Eggs**
  Refrigerate at 8°C or below — *Use strictly in rotation and ensure the shells are clean.*

- **Fats, butter, dairy and non-dairy spreads**
  8°C or below — *Keep covered and away from highly flavoured food, which may taint.*

- **Milk and cream**
  8°C or below — *In a separate dairy refrigerator that is used for no other purpose and in strict rotation.*

- **Prepared desserts**
  4°C or below — *Should be prepared only on day of use.*

- **Sauces and soups**
  8°C or below — *Should be prepared only on day of use and stored in plastic containers with a tight fitting lid.*

- **Salads and fresh herbs**
  8°C or below — *Always wash before use.*

- **Canned and bottled goods** — *Cool, dry, well-ventilated storage area. Blown, rusty or split tins must not be used.*

- **Root vegetables** — *Store in sacks or nets as delivered in cool, well-ventilated area.*

- **Leaf and green vegetables**
  8°C — *Use on day of delivery.*

Freezers, whether upright or chest freezers, should be maintained at a maximum temperature of −18°C. All food should be covered to prevent freezer burn and labelled with the date of production and a use-by date.

Ambient stores should be clean and well-ventilated, with mesh over windows and doors to help with pest control. All foodstuffs must be stored away from the floor and be rotated on a first in and first out basis.

Chilling food not for immediate use should ideally be achieved in blast chillers where the core temperature is brought down from 70°C to 4°C in 90 minutes or less. With these temperature ranges both pathogenic and bacterial growth is inhibited although not completely stopped.

If food that has been cooked is not for immediate consumption, or is to be frozen, it should be well covered with cling film or ideally vacuum-packed to create an airtight barrier and prevent freezer burn. Storage should be within manufacturer's guidelines and the foods must be clearly labelled as previously mentioned.

HAZARD ANALYSIS

Critical points to note in the preparation and cooking of food come in the following forms:

- *Bacterial* and other organisms.
- *Chemicals* (such as degreasers, polishes, detergents and sanitizers), must be stored in a designated area away from food production.
- *Allergenic*: An allergy to food is the hypersensitivity of constituents in food. Examples are:
  - *Lactose intolerance*: A condition in which lactase is not present and the body cannot process lactose. Lactose is present in milk and dairy products.
  - *Coeliac disease*: Intolerance to gluten. Proteins present in wheat, rye, barley and oat products.
  - *Peanuts and tree nuts*: Nuts, especially peanuts can cause extreme reactions and even death. It is impossible for the chef to guarantee a nut-free diet to the guest.
  - *Eggs*: Intolerance to the proteins in egg whites or yolks or sometimes both.
  - *Fish*: Fish allergies are more common in children than adults; even the smell can bring on asthma in a sensitive person. Common fish known to cause symptoms are cod, salmon, trout, herring, bass, sword fish, halibut and tuna.
  - *Shellfish*: Reactions to the ingestion of shellfish can be severe even to the level of inhalation of cooking vapours. Great care should be taken to avoid cross-contamination between shellfish products and all other foodstuffs that might be in contact with the diner. The shellfish

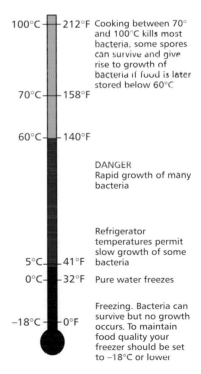

Food temperature safety guide for temperature controls when cooking and storing food

commonly known to cause allergic reactions include shrimp, crab, crayfish, lobster, oysters, clams, scallops, mussels, squid, and snails. People allergic to shrimp often suffer from respiratory allergy. Crab is also a potent allergen. Shrimp, lobster, and crayfish contain common major allergens, making cross reactivity between shrimp and crab, and lobster and crayfish possible.

AREAS WHERE HAZARDS MIGHT OCCUR IN THE SERVICE AND STORAGE OF FOOD

STEP	HAZARD	CONTROL
Purchasing	■ Contaminated high risk foods ■ Damaged goods ■ Growth of pathogens during delivery	■ There must be sufficient storage facilities for purchases ■ Purchase only from approved suppliers ■ Deliveries to be delivered under suitable conditions Chilled food at 8°C or below Frozen food at −18°C or below
Receipt of goods	■ Contaminated high risk foods ■ Damaged or decomposed goods ■ Incorrect specifications ■ Growth of pathogens between the time of receipt and storage	■ All deliveries inspected and checked by a staff member ■ Appropriate labelling ■ Prompt and correct storage
Storage	■ Contamination of high risk foods ■ Contamination through poor handling ■ Contamination by pests ■ Spoilage of food by decomposition	■ Correct usage of refrigeration regimes ■ Foods must be suitably stored in the correct packaging or receptacles ■ Materials that are in direct contact with food must be of food-grade quality ■ A contract for a pest control service must be in place ■ Correct stock rotation ■ Out-of-date and unfit food stuffs must be segregated from other foods and removed from the premises
Hot hold	■ Growth of pathogens and toxin production ■ Contamination by staff and customers especially in self-service operations	■ Maintain food at 63°C and discard after two hours ■ Keep containers covered when not in service ■ Use sneeze screens ■ Supervise self-service
Cold hold	■ Growth of pathogens and toxin production ■ Contamination by staff and customers especially in self-service operations	■ Keep food at 8°C and discard after four hours ■ Keep containers covered when not in service ■ Use sneeze screens ■ Supervise self-service
Cold takeaway	■ If the food is kept at ambient temperature there can be increased growth of pathogens and toxin production whilst in the possession of the customer	■ Keep food refrigerated at 8°C until being sold ■ Meals to be given out no longer than four hours prior to the time of consumption ■ Use insulated containers and freezer pack
Hot serve	■ Growth of pathogens, spores = toxin production ■ Contamination	■ Serve immediately on removal from holding equipment ■ Keep food covered when service is not in progress

General points to consider concerning hazard controls

■ Regular servicing of equipment.

■ Use a temperature probe to check on food storage.

■ Use a temperature probe to check on food storage equipment.

■ Investigate all complaints of suspected food-borne illnesses.

■ Regular inspections by a health and safety officer.

■ Frequent self inspections.

■ Comprehensive cleaning programmes in place.

■ Adequate staff training in food handling and hygiene practises.

In every professional restaurant or food service area a working system of the purchase and use of all ingredients needs to be maintained. It should detail the work-flow to prevent hazards from occurring during the storage, preparation, cooking and service of food.

A set table featuring pristine cutlery and glassware

Assessment of knowledge and understanding

You have now learned about the responsibilities you have to work effectively to maintain food safety at all times. This will enable you to ensure your own positive actions contribute effectively towards the whole team.

To test your level of knowledge and understanding, answer the following short questions. These will help to prepare you for your summative (final) assessment.

Maintaining a hygienic condition

1 State the food **safety hazards** that wearing jewellery can cause.

_____

2 State **five** basic principles on washing hands.
i) _____ ii) _____
iii)_____ iv)_____
v) _____

3 Identify who health hazards are **reported** to.

_____

4 Identify the importance of **reporting illnesses** quickly and the significance of stomach illnesses.

_____

5 Explain the **importance** of the avoidance of touching the nose, mouth or blowing the nose during food preparation.

Keeping the working area clean

1 State **three** reasons that work surfaces and chopping boards should be clean and hygienic.
i) _____ ii) _____
iii)_____

2 Describe the importance in using clean and suitable cloths when cleaning between tasks.

_____

3 Explain the importance of clearing and **disposing of waste** promptly.

_____

4 State the significance of damage to walls and floors as a potential **hazard** to food safety.

_____

5 Explain the reason for regular maintenance checks.

_____

6 State the cleaning procedure for the following:
a Wine glasses _____
b Cutlery _____
c Work surfaces _____

Taking the correct action

1 Explain the importance of storing food at the correct temperature.

_____

2 State the importance of ensuring that food deliveries are undamaged.

_____

3 Define the difference between these two terms:
   a Raw food.
   b Ready-to-eat food.

4 Describe the term **stock rotation**.

_____

5 State the reason for labelling food to store in a freezer.

_____

Research task

Explain the process of cross-contamination.

_____

Provide three examples of how this might occur.

i) _____ ii) _____

iii)_____

INDUSTRY PROFILE

Name: **MATTHEW HOBBS**
Position: OPERATIONS MANAGER
Establishment: CAPRICE HOLDINGS LTD

Current job role and main responsibilities:
Liaise with the board of directors, especially the CEO, and communicate their decisions around the group.
I provide operational support on all issues and respond to requests from the General Managers.
I link in with the marketing department and develop the websites.
I am currently the coordinator for all new projects ensuring the construction meets the standard of Caprice Holdings.

How do you keep yourself and your staff up-to-date with any changes to your wine lists?
Our wine supplier informs each bar manager directly on a weekly basis. We have wine tasting sessions on a weekly basis.

When did you realize that you wanted to pursue a career in the food service industry?
When I was at school I worked part time in an Italian restaurant and realized I loved the business, particularly food and wine.

Training:
I completed a year of a 2 year course (HND) in a further education college in Scotland where I was living at the time.

Experience:
The Ivy restaurant: Commis, chef de rang, Headwaiter, assistant restaurant manager
Sohohouse New York: Restaurant MGR, F&B Director
Caprice Holdings: General Manager of Scott's
Caprice Holdings: Director of operations, Birley group
Caprice Holdings: Director of operations and new projects

What do you find rewarding about your job?
Being involved at all levels of the business and working closely with the decision makers means I am at the sharp end of the business.
I particularly enjoy working in a quality driven company where we give people using the establishments a really great experience.

What do you find the most challenging about the job?
Being fully involved in all the restaurants at all times. Not enough hours in the day.

What advice would you give to students just beginning their career?
Have an open mind, work hard and enjoy yourself.

Who is your mentor or main inspiration?
I have been very lucky with my bosses over the years. However, two stand out.
Mitchell Everard, General Manager of The Ivy really developed my career and Nick Jones of Sohohouse was the most creative boss and showed me a different part of the industry.

What traits do you consider essential for anyone entering a career in the food and drink sector?
Passion for food and beverage are fundamentally important, as is a desire to learn. I learn every day in my job and the people I respect most are inquisitive and prepared to educate themselves continually.

A brief personal profile
Having started at the most junior position at The Ivy and leaving after 7 years as the assistant restaurant manager I feel that I can relate to (and manage) everyone involved in the front-of-house team.
Being offered the opportunity to work in New York was a once in a lifetime chance and taught me a huge amount.
Opening Scott's Restaurant was another opportunity that taught me how to build a restaurant as well as running one.
I really enjoy the creative part of an opening, and there's a fantastic sense of team work in everything involved.

Can you give one essential management tip or piece of industry advice?

Management tip: Invest in your team, they are the people working most closely with the guests.

Industry advice: Put yourself in the guest's position as much as you can.

5

Prepare, serve and clear areas for table/tray service

Unit 507 Advise and consult with clients

1FS1.1 Prepare and clear areas and equipment for table/tray service

1FS1.2 Prepare customer dining areas for table tray service

1FS1.3 Clear dining and service areas after service

Unit 508 Provide a table/tray service

1FS2.1 Greet customers and take orders

1FS2.2 Serve customer orders

What do I need to do?

■ Know how to set up a canteen area for service.

■ Understand and participate in a canteen-style service.

■ Know how to break down and clean a canteen area after service.

What do I need to know?

■ Why preparing an establishment correctly is important.

■ How to work in a safe and effective manner during service.

■ Why cleaning up after a service is important.

Information covered in this chapter

■ What a canteen is.

■ How it should be set up.

■ How service is undertaken.

■ How a canteen is broken down.

KEY WORDS

Canteen

A type of foodservice outlet in which customers can help themselves, assisted in their choice by the employees.

Condiment

Salt and/or pepper.

INTRODUCTION

Canteens or self-service restaurants are a form of food service outlet. Their function is to serve large volumes of customers a variety of meals, beverages and snacks with a low amount of service staff.

There are defined areas within the canteen and the amount of customers that need to be served at any one time will dictate the layout and flow of the operation.

Examples of tray service canteens can be seen in many workplaces, hospitals, airports and shopping centres. Canteens can provide many different types of meal at any one time. Some customers may want a quick snack or cup of coffee, some may require a three-course meal. Canteens are required to provide all these services.

Customers are expected to go to a counter to choose their own food and beverages, collect any cutlery or condiments and take them to a table of their choice.

SETTING UP A CANTEEN FOR SERVICE

As with every food service outlet, to run effectively a canteen needs to be set up properly before each service. To ensure that the necessary amount of people are served it is essential that all members of staff carry out their duties when service is occurring. After service the area needs to be cleaned, restocked and prepared for the next service.

THE ADVANTAGES AND DISADVANTAGES OF A CANTEEN-STYLE SERVICE

THE ADVANTAGES OF A CANTEEN SERVICE	THE DISADVANTAGES OF A CANTEEN SERVICE
High volume of people can be served.	Queues can form at peak meal times.
Few staff needed.	Tables and chairs may not always be cleaned in time for customers.
Can offer a wider range and variety of food and beverage than a traditional restaurant.	Customer may be held up waiting for an item to be prepared or restocked.
Customers can see and choose for themselves.	Customers with disabilities or mobility problems or small children will need extra assistance.
Can be opened for longer hours than a traditional outlet.	Dishes may not be presented as well as in a more formal kitchen.

Suggested different areas in a canteen

The layout of a canteen will differ depending on the style of service necessary and the differing meals and snacks that are to be served.

DIFFERENT AREAS IN A CANTEEN
✓ Tray pick up
✓ Cold drinks refrigerators
✓ Cold drinks/fruit juice dispensers
✓ Hot drinks dispensers
✓ Sweeteners, sugars and stirrers
✓ Salad bar/cold starters
✓ Sandwich bar/sandwich counter
✓ Hot food area
✓ Dessert area/fresh fruit
✓ Bread, pastry area with toaster, butter and preserves
✓ Cutlery, condiments, seasonings and sauces, napkins
✓ Payment point
✓ Tray return and dirty crockery and cutlery area

The flow of canteen service

The canteen may use the island system or may have one long counter as its service area.

If a canteen serves a variety of different meal types during the day (breakfast, mid-morning snack, lunch, afternoon tea, dinner), different parts of the canteen need to be prepared and used at different times.

The first item to be picked up will be a tray, following that any of the different areas could appear. At the front of the area there will be a rack for the customers' trays to be held while the customers make their choice.

The island system breaks up the various food and beverage areas into different counters and the customers may flow among them, picking up what they require.

Some of the areas may have staff to help serve the dishes, especially the hot dish selection. At others the customers will be expected to do it themselves, e.g. the sandwich area or salad bar.

Once the customers have made their selection they need to pick up their cutlery, napkins, sauces and seasonings. At this point they may also choose a beverage. Once customers have made their selection they will take their tray to the payment area.

After the customers have paid they are then free to choose their tables.

Once finished the customers may be encouraged to take their dirty dishes, cutlery and trays to a wash up area.

Soup in a canteen

 ACTIVITY

Go in to a local shopping centre or department store and observe their canteen.

■ What type of meals or snacks are the customers buying?

■ Are there any queues and if so at which area?

■ Are there plenty of clean tables for the customers to sit at?

Preparing the canteen area

Preparation in all food and beverage outlets is vitally important. If an establishment has not been set up correctly it can impact on the customer's experience.

AREAS TO BE CHECKED BEFORE THE CANTEEN IS OPENED

AREA	SET UP
Counters	Should be wiped and checked for cleanliness.
	Hot lamps and bain-maries must be switched on in good time in preparation for service.
	Any service cutlery, tongs, spoons and ladles should be set out.
Refrigerators	All refrigerators should have their temperatures checked and recorded.
	Drinks and sandwiches should have their 'use-by' dates checked. Any items which have passed their 'use-by' date must be discarded. The most recent date must be at the front of the shelf.
Menus	The menus should be checked to ensure that they are up-to-date.
	Menu boards or specials boards should be written up and priced correctly.
Crockery and cutlery	Trays should be checked for cleanliness and placed at the beginning of the counter.
	Plates, bowls, cups and glasses should be checked and adequate stocks placed in the areas where they will be required.
	Cutlery should be polished, sorted and put in place near the payment counter with napkins.
Retail items	Chocolates, biscuits, crisps and soft drinks should have their 'use-by' dates checked. Any items which have passed their 'use-by' date must be discarded.
	These items should be restocked.
Condiment and cutlery pick up	Sugar dispensers, cups and stirrers should be refilled.
	Salt and pepper should be refilled.
	Sauces, dressings and accompaniments should be replenished and checked to ensure they match with the menu items.
	Cutlery trays should be replenished.
Tables and seating area	Tables and chairs should be sanitized and put into position. Tables should have cruets and any promotional items placed on them.
	The floors should be checked for any debris and tripping hazards.
	Waste bins should be empty with fresh bin liners.
Tray drop off	The area the customers use to return dirty trays and waste items must be checked for cleanliness.
	Trolleys to take dirty trays should be empty and in place.
	Cleaning products should be checked and put in place in preparation for service.

CANTEEN SERVICE ROLES

A canteen self-service counter

For employees there are several different roles that need to be filled within a canteen setting.

- *Serving behind the counter*: Helping customers choose from hot options available.
- *Replenishing the counters*: Ensuring that all the cold options, retail items and drinks are fully stocked.
- *Working at the payment point*: Take payment for the items that the customers choose.
- *Preparing hot beverages*: Preparing customers' hot drink orders.
- *Keeping the tables and chairs clear*: Ensuring that the customers have somewhere clean and clear to sit.

Members of staff can rotate all these roles over the course of the working week. The size and amount of customers that an establishment has will change and vary these roles.

 TIP

All the roles in a canteen are visible to customers, it is important to maintain personal hygiene standards at all times.

Order of service for a canteen

As customers arrive in the establishment they may need to be guided to the different areas or counters.

Customers at a canteen self-service

As the customers make their food and beverage selections, any dietary requirements need to be indicated to them. This can be done either verbally by a member of staff or with the use of signs. A member of staff should be on hand at all times to help customers make their selections and to restock food items and remove any empty dishes.

During this period the cold food selections, retail items and cold drinks need to be refilled. The crockery, cutlery, glasses and cups need to be checked and replenished when necessary. The customers can then help themselves to cutlery, glasses, cups, sauces and napkins.

Once the customers have made their selections they then must pay for their items. This can be done at a payment counter or till area. The customers will then choose their seats and enjoy their meal or snack.

As customers finish with their dishes these can be removed by employees, depending on the amount of staff working. Once the customers have finished, they should be encouraged to take their trays and dirty cutlery and crockery to the specified area.

When the customers have left, the table should be cleaned and the chairs straightened in preparation for the next customers.

A salad bar

HEALTH & SAFETY

One of the many hazards within a canteen is the possibility of customers slipping or tripping on the floor. The most hazardous areas are:

■ In front of the food counters.

■ Near drinks dispensers.

■ Around vacated tables.

Special attention must be paid to these areas at all times. A clean mop with a fresh bucket of hot water and a dustpan and brush must always be available so that spillages can be cleaned up quickly.

CLOSING PROCEDURES FOR A CANTEEN

In order for the quality of customer service to be maintained and the establishment to be kept to a hygienic standard it is important that the breaking down or closing procedures are followed completely.

A typical school luncheon tray

CANTEEN AREAS THAT SHOULD BE BROKEN DOWN AFTER SERVICE

AREA	SET UP
Counters	■ Should be washed and sanitized. ■ Hot lamps and bain-maries should be turned off. ■ Any service cutlery, tongs, spoons and ladles should be removed and washed.
Refrigerators	■ All refrigerators should have their temperatures checked and recorded. ■ Drinks and sandwiches should have their 'use-by' dates checked. Any items which have passed their 'use-by' date must be discarded. ■ All handles and doors on refrigerators should be washed and polished.
Menus	■ Menu boards or specials boards should be cleaned.
Crockery and cutlery	■ Trays should be washed. ■ All dirty and used plates, bowls, cups and glasses should be washed.
Retail items	■ Chocolates, biscuits, crisps and soft drinks should have their 'use-by' dates checked. Any items which have passed their 'use-by' date must be discarded. ■ These items should be restocked.
Condiment and cutlery pick up	■ Sugar dispensers, cups and stirrers should be refilled. ■ Salt and pepper should be refilled. ■ Sauces, dressings and accompaniments emptied and stored in appropriate containers.
Tables and seating area	■ Tables and chairs should be sanitized and put into position. ■ Tables should have cruets and any promotional items removed. ■ The floors should be brushed and mopped.
Tray drop off	■ Waste bins should be emptied and washed out. ■ All shelves and surfaces should be washed down.

Assessment of knowledge and understanding

You have now learned about the responsibilities you have to work using a table/tray service system. This will enable you to ensure your own positive actions contribute effectively towards the whole team.

To test your level of knowledge and understanding, answer the following short questions. These will help to prepare you for your summative (final) assessment.

Preparing for assessment checklist

■ Check the preparation for the canteen in your establishment.

■ Whilst working within your establishment make notes about the menu, what is being served and when.

Project 1

1 Set up your canteen; write a checklist of the areas that you have prepared.

2 When service has finished which areas need to be washed down?

3 Where are the sauces and condiments stored?

4 What are the temperatures of the refrigerators?

Project 2

1 During service who is responsible for the following:

a Clearing and cleaning trays? _____

b Restocking plates? _____

c Replenishing beverage stirrers? _____

d Cleaning the tables? _____

2 How are customer complaints dealt with?

3 What options are on the menu for vegetarians?

4 What time is your outlet open from and does it serve different products at different times of the day?

6

Provide a trolley service

Unit 511 Provide a trolley service

1FS5.1 Prepare a catering trolley for service

1FS5.2 Serve products from a catering trolley

What do I need to do?

- Check and set up a trolley for service.
- Serve food and beverages from a trolley.

What do I need to know?

- Why the set up procedures must be correct.
- How to maintain the trolley during service.

Information covered in this chapter

- Preparing trolleys for service.
- Airline trolley service.
- Trolley service.
- Cleaning and clearing trolleys.

KEY WORDS

Refrigerated trolleys
Trolleys with a chiller unit to keep food items at a safe temperature.

Eye contact
Look directly at the face of a person.

Waste items
Rubbish to be thrown away or recycled.

Tetrapaks
The generic term for cartons that contain liquid.

INTRODUCTION

Trolleys are used to bring a food and beverage service to customers who cannot move to a counter. Trolleys are used on aeroplanes, ferries and trains, in hospitals and sometimes in the workplace.

Trolleys can serve complex hot meals or simple snacks depending on the type and style necessary. In the upper class cabin of a long-haul airline, trolleys will be used to serve up to three meals, several snacks and drinks, all of which will be included in the cost of the ticket. On a budget airline or train, sandwiches, snacks and hot and cold drinks will be served to the passengers who will pay as they order.

ITEMS THAT MAY BE SERVED FROM A TROLLEY

✓ Hot and cold beverages and soups.

✓ Sandwiches, snacks, crisps and savoury items.

✓ Cakes, pastries, biscuits, chocolates and sweets.

✓ Pre-packed hot meals.

✓ Non-food items, magazines, newspapers.

PREPARING THE TROLLEY

 TIP

Check that the trolley itself is in good working order prior to setting it up.

Everything that is to be sold needs to be on the trolley before it begins its journey. No-one can predict what customers are going to select from the trolley, therefore a selection of each item should be included.

There may be menus or booklets provided for the customers to select which items they wish to have prior to the server and the trolley arriving. It is from this menu that the set up must be done.

To ensure that the stock items are paid for and not lost or mislaid from the trolley a count of the items must be taken prior to the trolley leaving. This list will be the responsibility of the employee and when the trolley finishes its circuit the money taken must match the items sold.

When setting up the trolley it is important to remember that the customers will look at it to help them choose the items that they require. It is important to display items clearly and keep the trolley tidy.

If the trolley is damaged in any way please report it immediately to your supervisor. If the trolley does not move smoothly or the brakes do not work correctly when applied, then it could roll away and cause injury to a customer or member of staff. Any doors on the trolley need to close properly to avoid swinging open and catching.

PREPARING A TROLLEY

ITEM	PREPARATION
Wines, beer and spirits	Served from small individual bottles, accompanied by plastic or glass cup, ice should be offered with spirits, a small napkin is often offered to act as a coaster.
Soft drinks, fruit juices and water	Served in small cans, tetrapaks or bottles. Accompanied by cup or glass, ice should be offered, a small napkin is often offered to act as a coaster.
Sandwiches, crisps and cold snacks	Served pre-packed perhaps with a small plate and napkin. These should have their 'use-by' dates checked. Items that need refrigeration need to be kept chilled while the trolley is moving.
Hot items	These can either be heated prior to the trolley starting or can be heated to order and delivered to the customer. Often hot drinks are served with lids to prevent spills.
Service items	Cups, plates and napkins should be checked and restocked.
Payment	A float needs to be organized; credit/debit card machines need to checked to ensure that they function.
Waste bins	Rubbish bins or bags need to be prepared and placed on the trolley ready for use.

AIRLINE TROLLEY SERVICE

Some airlines still offer hot meals during the flight. On flights within Europe hot meals are generally only offered in the first or business-class cabins. This type of service is also offered in the first-class carriage of long distance trains.

 TIP

Care must be taken when serving hot drinks and items, especially on moving vehicles, as they can spill quite easily.

A flight attendant serving drinks

These meals are served from a trolley to the passengers at specific times during the journey.

Prior to the meal being served the drinks trolley passes through the cabin or carriage, offering the passengers pre-dinner drinks. Then the food trolley will serve the main meal. Depending on the time of the flight this could consist of a salad as a starter, a hot main course and a cold dessert or cheese.

The trays will be stacked within the trolley and may already contain the cold items. These trolleys may be kept in refrigerators to ensure that the cold items stay within their correct temperature. The hot items will be kept in refrigerators until they need to be reheated.

On long-haul airlines there are set times for meals through the flight. Prior to these times the hot element of these meals needs to be reheated. This is done in ovens within the galley.

The trolley then needs to be loaded. In order to speed up service there may be two or three trolleys each starting at different parts of the aeroplane, one at the back, one in the centre and one from the front.

As each customer is served in turn the flight attendants 'build' their trolleys to suit their needs. The different options may include, vegetarian, vegan, non-fish and there also may be a choice of wines. Care must be taken to ensure that the passengers don't get burned or scalded.

After-dinner drinks, teas and coffees may be offered after the main meal, these may be offered from a different trolley. Once all meal items are finished a further trolley can pass through the cabin collecting the waste items and used trays and removing all debris.

 TIP

When customers place their order, remember to repeat it back to them to ensure that it is correct.

A flight attendant with trolley

Trolley service

The employee must make sure that the trolley is loaded with adequate stock. Prior to moving, the trolley must be checked to ensure that the stock is safely loaded and does not pose a safety risk to either the employee or customers.

As the trolley approaches each customer, care must be taken to apply the brake once it has stopped. The employee should greet the customer clearly making eye contact. As customers select their items from the trolley, the employee will give each item and cups and napkins can be offered. Once the customers have completed their order, payment will be taken.

As the trolley passes on its circuit stock items may become low. Depending on the location, the trolley may need to be restocked during its circuit or customers told that the item is out of stock.

Customers may be encouraged to put their waste items into nearby bins. Alternatively the trolley may pass through the area again to collect waste items.

 ACTIVITY

When moving with a trolley list what safety precautions should be taken.

What is the procedure for moving the trolley between floors of a building or moving it upstairs?

How can you ensure that the trolley passes easily through a narrow space?

Cleaning and clearing the trolley

Once the trolley has finished its circuit its stock should be counted. The takings should then be counted. These should match and any disparity should be recorded.

A trolley of pastries

All items should be removed from the trolley and the trolley cleaned. The trolley's wheels and brakes should be checked and any maintenance issue reported to the line manager. Any items that need to be stored in a refrigerator should be removed.

Waste bags and bins should be emptied. The trolley should be restocked in preparation for its next trip. The trolley should be secured when not in use to ensure that none of its stock is removed or goes missing.

Trolley service can be a fast and effective way of serving items to customers who have limited mobility. It needs to be prepared with all necessary items and presented in a way that will appeal to customers. The stock on a trolley needs to be accounted for and the employee will be asked to keep a record of the items sold and tally that against the takings. Trolley service can also be used to serve up-market meals in the first-class compartments of trains and aeroplanes. This service may not require payment but the employee will need a more in-depth knowledge of the products being served.

Assessment of knowledge and understanding

You have now learned about the responsibilities you have to provide an effective trolley service. This will enable you to ensure your own positive actions contribute effectively towards the whole team.

To test your level of knowledge and understanding, answer the following short questions. These will help to prepare you for your summative (final) assessment.

Preparing for assessment checklist

- Check the preparation procedures for your trolley.
- Write a list of the items that are served.

Project

1 Draw a diagram of the trolley and how it should be set up.

2 What service items are needed?

3 What is the procedure if a stock item runs out?

4 How are the sales recorded?

5 How are cold drinks served?

6 If the trolley is damaged what is the procedure to arrange its repairs?

7

Assemble meals for distribution via conveyor belt

Unit 1SF6 Assemble meals for distribution via conveyor belt

1SF6.1 Prepare conveyor belt ready for run

1SF6.2 Assemble tray sets on the conveyor belt

What do I need to do?

■ Know how to check trays.

■ Know how to restock as required.

■ Know how to store unused items.

■ Know how to place equipment, cutlery and condiments on the tray.

■ Know how to present food items correctly on plates or food containers.

What do I need to know?

■ How to check the conveyor belt and service area are clean, undamaged and ready for use.

■ How to prepare sufficient stocks for the belt run and store them correctly.

■ How to select menu items.

Information covered in this chapter

This unit is about preparing the conveyor belt and service equipment and assembling both food and drink items. It also covers presenting the food on trays, and maintaining levels of stock during the process.

KEY WORDS

Conveyor belt

This consists of two or more pulleys, with a continuous belt that rotates around them. One or both of the pulleys are powered, moving the belt and the material on the belt forward. The powered pulley is called the drive pulley while the unpowered pulley is called the idler.

Stock level

Stock level is a term used to describe an amount of stock that is maintained below the cycle stock to buffer against running out of any particular ingredient. Safety stock levels exist to counter uncertainties in supply and demand. For example, if a restaurant were to continually run out of ingredients, they would need to keep some extra stock of ingredients on hand so they could attempt to meet demand.

Cutlery

This refers to any hand implement used in preparing, serving and eating food. It is more usually known as silverware, whereas cutlery can have the more specific meaning of knives and other cutting instruments.

Crockery

Crockery is the general term for the dishes used in serving and eating food, including the plates and bowls.

Napkins

A napkin or serviette is a rectangle of cloth or paper used at the table for wiping the mouth while eating. It is usually small and folded.

Accompaniments

Items of food that are served to complement the main dish such as a sauce, relish or seasoning.

INTRODUCTION

Conveyor belts are used in many industries to transport goods and materials between stages of a process. Using conveyor systems is a good way to reduce the risks of injury in tasks or processes that involve manual handling, as they reduce the need for repetitive lifting and carrying. This system of food production also ensures a high volume of food can be manufactured quickly and consistently.

Traditionally, airline food production and hospital food production which requires a system to produce large volumes of dishes from specialized menus have used this method of food production. However, other areas have now

A sushi conveyor belt system. Different colour plates determine the price of each item

introduced this concept such as the restaurant group Yo Sushi which incorporates a conveyor belt system inside each restaurant outlet as a means for customers to select and purchase their food.

Conveyor belts can be used successfully in all areas of a banqueting service. The advantage of using conveyor belts for plating starters, main courses and desserts for substantial numbers, is that every individual plate can be monitored for quality and consistency. A plated item that does not meet the required specification can simply be withdrawn from the system.

By purchasing a quality conveyor the head chef or food and beverage manager can eliminate the wandering round of tables by several chefs at a time, each with a different task to place on a plate to complete a dish.

When looking to purchase such a system you have to consider the size of your operation and choose a manufacturer who can build a conveyor to your specific requirements, with speed control, and photocell eye to control the belt and to stop it when a plate reaches the end of the line. Try to avoid mild steel, cast iron and painted units, it is much better to pay more at the beginning for a fully stainless steel unit including stainless rounded castors.

CLEANING AND CHECKING THE CONVEYOR BELT

Conveyor belts should be checked for damage, cleaned and sanitized using the following 7-Step cleaning process.

Step 1: Check for damage and dry clean

It is important that whilst dry cleaning the belt system signs of damage are looked for at the same time. Dry clean the conveyor belt and all associated equipment by removing large pieces of food from the belt's surfaces using a stiff brush. Also make sure compacted debris is removed from the sprockets, wheels and support rails. When cleaning the conveyor belt, work in a top-down, inside-edge-of-belt to outside edge-of-belt, ordered pattern.

Step 2: Pre-rinse

Pre-rinse the belt and support rails with hot water heated to a temperature of 52–54°C. Care needs to be taken to ensure floor drains are kept clear of debris to avoid flooding of water.

Step 3: Apply detergent

Apply an appropriate detergent mixture to the belt and support rails. The detergent can be allowed to remain on the belt for 10–15 minutes, but should not be allowed to dry, as dried chemical is often more difficult to completely remove and may support the growth of pathogens later on.

Step 4: Rinse and inspect

Flood rinse the belt and support rails with clean water at 52–54°C. After the rinse, inspect the belt and support rail components to ensure it is free of

An example of some airline food which has been assembled using the conveyor belt system

excess water and any residue foodstuffs. This inspection should be thoroughly conducted using sight, touch and smell.

Step 5: Pre-op the belt

Verify that all cleaning chemicals have been removed from the conveyor belt, sprockets and support rails. It is recommended that pH testing be used as an aid in determining that the belt is free of detergent. Run the conveyor belt slowly to help dry it and its supports, and remove any water from the floor.

Step 6: Inspect ready for sanitizing

Re-inspect the belt and support rails to detect the presence of dirt or foodstuffs. Sometimes in food processing units adenosine triphosphate (ATP) testing is used to verify the absence of bacteria. ATP is present in all animal, vegetable, yeast and mould cells. The detection of ATP indicates contamination by at least one of these sources.

Step 7: Sanitizing

Apply the appropriate sanitizers following the manufacturer's recommendations. Run the belt as the sanitizer is applied in order to ensure that all parts of the belt and support rails have been completely exposed to the chemical.

Worker on a conveyor belt system

Cautionary details whilst cleaning conveyor belts

Sometimes the use of a high pressure hose is recommended in the initial cleaning stages. It is important that water pressure should not exceed 300 psi at any stage of the cleaning process to avoid contamination resulting from overspray of water and chemicals.

A caustic wash may be necessary due to health or other safety requirements. It is recommended that caustic solutions should not be left on the belt or used in any stronger concentrations than necessary. Use of these products must strictly follow the manufacturer's directions.

Of special concern is the use of caustic or harsh chemicals on plastic belts and support rails, as these chemicals can soften plastic materials, which can lead to damage or failure of the belt and other components.

PREPARING AND STORING SUFFICIENT STOCKS

So that the required amount of ingredients and equipment are ready for the production line to begin, the correct menu needs to be selected for the day's operation. The ingredients should have been previously ordered from the suppliers and have been stored using the correct holding conditions.

In a typical large-scale catering operation, such as airline catering, all stock would be on a 48-hour holding rotation system. Raw materials will be held for no longer than 24 hours before being used in the production system.

All stocks should be systematically positioned for storage near the conveyor belt system avoiding cross-contamination and segregating the storage of each ingredient. Always ensure that the ingredients delivered are checked against the production menu for that day and if there is any discrepancy you should consult your line manager quickly.

For the service of in-flight meals and also in some hospitals, there will be a whole menu produced to be presented on a single tray. In this respect additional items will also be required to help with the customer satisfaction of the meal. These additional items can be:

- Condiments (salt, pepper, jams, confitures, sauces).
- Cutlery.
- Drinks.
- Napkins.
- Butter.
- Side plate for a bread roll.

 REMEMBER

Stock levels should be kept down to the level of what is required. Only order ingredients when they are needed to:

- Eliminate wastage.
- Maintain the freshness of ingredients.
- Maintain the quality of ingredients.

Service of a meal presented on a tray using the conveyor belt system

CHECKING THE SERVICE EQUIPMENT

The use of serving and catering equipment which is clean and correctly maintained is essential for the preparation and service of food using a conveyor belt system. Using the menu as a guide it is important before the commencement of service to collect all the relevant equipment required for the service operation.

Hospital kitchen using the conveyor belt system

Important equipment such as a bain-marie should be able to store hot food for up to two hours at an ambient temperature of 63°C and regular temperature checks should be taken to ensure its consistency. It is important to keep all cutlery and kitchen utensils clean and it is especially important to wash them thoroughly after using them with raw ingredients. If any equipment is damaged, this should be reported immediately to your line manager so that a replacement can be found.

Portion control

It is important to the success of the business that regulations for controlling the size and quantity of food to be served are adhered to. To help with this process certain items of equipment can be used on the conveyor belt system such as:

- Various sized scoops for mashed potatoes, mousses and ice creams.
- Various size ladles for sauces and soups.
- Fruit juice and wine glasses (75–150g).
- The use of individual pudding basins, dishes and stainless steel moulds.
- Various sized spoons for the service of vegetables.
- Measuring jugs and cups for liquids.
- Small sets of scales to weigh amounts of food per portion.

Equipment selected for use must be appropriate for the work it is intended to carry out. It should be of the correct capacity and situated in a convenient position, especially if it is a mechanical piece of equipment. All equipment

A selection of portion control utensils

must be properly maintained and staff using it should receive training in the correct usage and safety measures which need to be taken.

ASSEMBLING AND CHECKING THE TRAYS

All safe and hygienic practices should be followed when presenting food on to the trays using the conveyor belt system. Hazard Analysis Critical Control Points (HACCP) see Chapter 4, p. 56, is a system of food safety management that focuses on identifying the critical points in a process where food safety problems or hazards could arise and putting steps in place to prevent things going wrong. This is sometimes referred to as controlling hazards. Keeping records is also an important part of HACCP systems.

It is essential that all staff are fully trained in HACCP and understand the system of reporting any equipment failures, spillages or faults during work on the conveyor belt. The presentation of food and drink must be served using the trays on the conveyor system that are hygienic and suitable for use. Any conspicuous problems should be reported to your line manager.

To identify the production requirements each production line should follow the exact menu and dish specification. Usually each specification is given a pictorial guideline which illustrates exactly where each item should be placed on to a tray as it moves down the conveyor belt. Using this guide will give the staff and line managers the opportunity to regulate and check the standard of each tray as it passes down the line. One of the strong aspects of using

All production lines will have picture guidelines such as in this example

this method is that each staff member will have a specific task as each tray passes down the line so that large amounts of trays are prepared in an efficient manner.

The use of this particular specification sheet may also allow for dietary changes that need to be added to particular trays, such as vegetarian dishes to substitute any meat dishes. A clear and well-written specification sheet with photographic guidelines will always help with the preparation and presentation of the food and drink.

If during the production of dishes on the conveyor belt the ingredients that are being used to produce the dishes required either run out or are not of a sufficient quality, you should immediately notify the line manager or seek to temporarily halt the conveyor system until such time that normal service can be resumed.

Sushi presented onto trays

Assessment of knowledge and understanding

You have now learned about the responsibilities you have to work on a conveyor belt system and the importance of hygiene using this procedure.

To test your level of knowledge and understanding, answer the following short questions. These will help to prepare you for your summative (final) assessment.

Prepare the conveyor belt

1 State two reasons why it is important to have a safe and hygienic working practice for preparing the conveyor belt ready for use.

i) _____

ii) _____

2 State how you would dispose of waste ingredients hygienically.

_____

3 Identify why it is important to carry out food temperature checks during the process of production using the conveyor belt system.

_____

4 Explain the importance of maintaining food stock levels.

_____

Assemble the tray sets on the conveyor belt

1 State three reasons why safe and hygienic working practices for the assembly of tray sets on the conveyor belt are important.

i) _____ ii) _____

iii) _____

2 Describe how to report faults with equipment.

_____

3 Explain the importance of following exact production requirements and how this might be undertaken.

_____

4 Describe what you would do in the following unexpected circumstances:

a If the conveyor belt stops suddenly.

_____

b If some of the trays that are already on the conveyor belt system are not clean.

_____

c If you run out of certain ingredients during the production on the conveyor belt.

_____

INDUSTRY PROFILE

Name: **ROBIN ROWLAND**

Position: CHIEF EXECUTIVE OFFICER (CEO)

Establishment: YO! SUSHI

Current job role and main responsibilities:
Planning growth; managing existing position in the market; overseeing a team in five main areas of the business: operations, finance, people, properties and international.

How have you managed to develop the business and market the Yo! Sushi concept of dining to the British public?
Since 1997 when I started I have sought to make Yo! Sushi an affordable and aspirational brand and bring sushi, which is quite a niche market, to a much wider audience. The siting of the restaurants has played an important part in achieving this by placing them in malls, train stations and other busy public venues.

When did you realize that you wanted to pursue a career in the food service industry?
After managing a Michelin-starred restaurant I joined Whitbread as area manager and was involved with a portfolio of businesses as an operator of restaurants. I found the job very rewarding and loved working with passionate people in the industry.

Training:
I was a graduate and then a management trainee. I hold a degree in history and politics. I just love to work with great people and brands and that is why I pursued a role in hospitality management.

Experience:
Whitbread 1984–88; 1988–91 operational manager at New Orleans; regional director 1991–95 at New Orleans, Country hotels and central London restaurants. Then I became operations director with the restaurant group.

What do you find rewarding about your job?
Working with a great team and people who love the food. It's great to be able to be creative and not formulaic. I also love the international dimension to this industry.
I generally split my time between working with a close team and liaising with investors and banks.

What do you find the most challenging about the job?
The availability of great sites, the pressure on talent (there is a small pool of talent to choose from) and the increasing regulation in the industry.

What advice would you give to students just beginning their career?
Try and work for people with a product of which you are a customer, work for companies that are willing to invest in you and work hard!

Who is your mentor or main inspiration?
John Barnes who is a serial owner of some great restaurant companies. Ian Neill who is chairman of Wagamama, he's a top bloke.

What traits do you consider essential for anyone entering a career in the food and drink sector?
You've got to care about the products and customers and you've got to want to raise standards.

Can you give one essential management tip or piece of industry advice?
Work with people who you enjoy working with!

8

Clean and store crockery and cutlery

Unit 505 Clean and store crockery and cutlery

1GEN5.1 Clean crockery and cutlery

1GEN5.2 Store crockery and cutlery

What do I need to do?
- Know how to wash cutlery and crockery correctly by hand and machine.
- Know how to polish cutlery and crockery correctly.
- Know how to stack and store cutlery and crockery correctly.

What do I need to know?
- Why washing cutlery and crockery using the correct procedures is important.
- How to deal with broken or damaged cutlery correctly.
- The correct storage procedures for cutlery and crockery.

Information covered in this chapter
- How to clean cutlery.
- How to clean crockery.
- How to polish both cutlery and crockery.

KEY WORDS

Crockery
Plates, bowls and cups, generally made from porcelain or china.

Cutlery
Forks, knifes and spoons, used to eat with. May be made from stainless steel or silver-plated. Also known as silverware.

INTRODUCTION

In any food establishment crockery and cutlery are valuable and important assets that need to be looked after and stored well. When cutlery is laid on a table it provides an instant impression to customers of how an establishment is maintained and cared for. It is therefore important that both crockery and cutlery are washed, polished and stored correctly.

CROCKERY	CUTLERY
Plates	Forks
Soup bowls	Soup spoons
Tea and coffee pots	Knives
Dessert bowls	Tea spoons
Cups	Steak knives
Saucers	Fish cutlery
Sugar bowls	

Crockery

A steak knife

A fish knife

Soup bowl

Cutlery can be made from either stainless steel or can be silver-plated. Crockery can be made from porcelain, china, earthenware, or glass. These will affect how they should be cleaned and polished.

 TIP

If crockery and cutlery can only be washed by hand, ensure that rubber gloves are used and make sure that water is as hot as is physically possible.

CLEANING

Cutlery and crockery can be washed in one of two methods: either by using a machine or by hand. The same principles are applied to both methods although machine washing can be done at a higher temperature and therefore can reduce the amount of bacteria more effectively.

STAGES OF CLEANING

1 Rinse to remove debris.

2 Immerse in hot soapy water to clean.

3 Rinse in hot water to remove soap.

4 Air dry.

Dirty dishes stacked on a trolley

These stages of cleaning should be followed for both hand and mechanized cleaning, see also Chapter 10.

Cutlery that is silver-plated needs to be dipped in a silver cleaning solution regularly. This removes the tarnish and maintains the shine on it. After dipping, the cutlery will still need to be polished using the following method.

Both crockery and cutlery are polished before being used, as once cleaned watermarks can be left on them.

POLISHING CUTLERY

Cutlery is polished by immersing it in hot water, which has a dash of vinegar in it. The cutlery is then individually polished using a clean, dry tea towel. This also gives the employee an opportunity to check if the cutlery is damaged or bent and may need to be removed from service.

TIP

Try and handle the cutlery as little as possible. Use a tea towel to hold the cutlery.

Polishing cutlery

POLISHING CROCKERY

Prior to each service the head chef will decide which plates he will serve each of his dishes on. A quantity of these plates will be polished, to remove any watermarks in preparation for the service.

Crockery is polished by using a clean tea towel which has been lightly moistened with hot water and vinegar. The whole plate is wiped and then each plate is piled safely on top of one another. During this process the employee can check the crockery for cracks or chips and remove any damaged pieces.

STORAGE

Crockery and cutlery must be stored carefully, the reasons for this include:

- It could get damaged.
- It could be a hazard to employees or customers.
- It may need to be accessed quickly for service.
- The stock level may need to be counted.

TIP

Ensure that broken or cracked crockery is disposed of correctly and not just thrown in to a bin.

It must be wrapped up in cardboard before being disposed of.

Cutlery should be stored in cutlery trays. These are made from heavy duty plastic and should also be washed regularly. The cutlery should be sorted into its different types once polished, thereby being ready to use during service. If a particular type of cutlery is not being used for a period of time, it should be cleaned and polished and then wrapped in clingfilm and stored away from the service area.

Crockery, if not stored correctly, could get broken and become an expensive hazard. Some types of crockery need slightly different storage requirements.

Plates need to be stored on strong shelving. The shelving needs to be easily cleaned and not too high so that it can be accessed by all employees. Plates should not be piled up too high as they may over-balance. Care must be taken that only plates of the same size are stacked on top of each other and that plates are not placed too close to the edge of the shelves.

Cups and bowls can be stored in plastic racking which can be safely stacked. The rack can also be placed on trolleys to help if large quantities need to be moved.

Stored cutlery

 ACTIVITY

Look around your establishment and see how the crockery and cutlery are stored:

■ Could you recommend any improvements?

■ What is the procedure for disposal of broken cutlery?

Stacked crockery

STEP-BY-STEP: POLISHING CUTLERY

1 Using boiling water, malt vinegar and a clean tea towel

2 Pour a dash of vinegar into hot water

3 Dip first one end of the cutlery then the other into the water

4 Holding the cutlery in a cloth polish both ends well

5 Ensure that no part of the cutlery is handled

6 Place on a clean service plate

! REMEMBER

- Check for any bent or damaged cutlery and remove from service.
- Check for any broken or chipped crockery and remove from service.

Assessment of knowledge and understanding

You have now learned about the responsibilities of correctly cleaning and storing cutlery and crockery items. This will enable you to ensure your own positive actions contribute effectively towards the whole food service operation.

To test your level of knowledge and understanding, answer the following short questions. These will help to prepare you for your summative (final) assessment.

Preparing for assessment checklist

■ Ensure that you know the correct procedures for washing, polishing and storing crockery and cutlery.

Project

1 Draw a step-by-step diagram of how crockery and cutlery should be washed.

2 Write a list of what equipment is needed to polish cutlery.

3 In your establishment look at the different types of storage for crockery and make a list.

INDUSTRY PROFILE

Name: **STEPHANE PALLUAULT**

Position: FOOD AND BEVERAGE MANAGER

Establishment: ROYAL AUTOMOBILE CLUB

Current job role and main responsibilities:
Responsible for all bars, restaurants, lounges, service and products, financials, as well as recruitment, training and development of employees.

What is the most exciting thing about being a food and beverage manager?
The daily challenges of meeting or even exceeding our members' expectations as well as constantly looking at ourselves and the way we do things, to always try and improve. To develop the team of managers.

When did you realize that you wanted to pursue a career in the food service industry?
From a young age! At 15 and 16, I spent my summer months in a hotel, first in the restaurant, then in the kitchen. I loved it even though it was hard work! At first, I wanted to be a chef, but later on changed my mind for a more front-of-house role!!

Training:
Following my two summers in the hotel, I went to a catering school in La Rochelle (France) for three years and got the qualifications I was after. I then went to work straight away.

Experience:
I started at the 'bottom' and made my way up having worked in various 5-star hotels in Switzerland and the UK, The Lanesborough Hotel and One Aldwych Hotel to name a couple!

What do you find rewarding about your job?
To have our customers leaving the premises with only one thing on their mind: It was such a great experience, when can we come back?

What do you find the most challenging about the job?
Staff retention has always been a challenge in many places I have worked. Keeping your staff helps you with consistency of service. I think, nowadays, there are many challenges: from finding the right people, keeping them, exceeding customers' expectations (there is so much competition out there!) to meeting your financial targets and I could go on. I suppose this is not specific to our industry, but just a way of life and you need these challenges so you can become better at what you do!!

What advice would you give to students just beginning their career?
It's a tough industry but if you are passionate, just keep working hard and always ask more of yourself and your colleagues, and the 'rewards' will come. Listen, watch and learn from more experienced people.

Who is your mentor or main inspiration?
There have been several inspirational people along my various jobs. I have always tried to take what I considered to be their best qualities and apply it to my management style.

What traits do you consider essential for anyone entering a career in the food and drink sector?
You have to be a good leader. You are only as good as your team. You have to be passionate, have a good eye for details and always look at yourself. Listening to your team is also very important. If you need to implement changes, they will be more supportive if you have consulted them first on how to get the best results. They also often come up with the best ideas! Being financially acute will also help for future development!

A brief personal profile
I like to challenge myself, whether at work or in my private life. This year, I ran the London marathon. I was disappointed with my time (I did not meet my target) so I decided to run another one in September and actually bettered my previous time by 22 minutes!

Can you give one essential management tip or piece of industry advice?
Have a clear vision/identity of your products. Be a good manager and leader and the rest will fall into place.

9

Prepare, serve and clear areas for counter/ take-away service

What do I need to do?
- Set up the counter for take-away service.
- Maintain the counter during service.
- Serve customers.
- Break down and clear the counter area.

What do I need to know?
- Why setting up the counter correctly is important.
- What impact a clean and tidy establishment will have.
- The important factors in cleaning after a counter/take-away service.

Information covered in this chapter
- Preparing for a counter/take-away service.
- Activities during service.
- Clearing and cleaning after service.

KEY WORDS

Take-away service
Food produced in an outlet and sold for consumption elsewhere.

Disposable crockery
Plates, cups etc. that can be used only once.

Heat lamp
A light used to keep food hot during service.

Bain-marie
A water bath that is used to keep food hot during service.

A patisserie counter

INTRODUCTION

Take-away and counter service are provided to those customers who wish to purchase a meal or snack that they want to consume in another location. The service takes place at a counter and the food is either already prepared or prepared to order.

Take-away service can be offered as part of a normal restaurant function or can operate solely as a take-away. Take-away service can also operate on a temporary basis from a van, caravan or tent.

ESTABLISHMENTS THAT PROVIDE COUNTER AND TAKE-AWAY SERVICE INCLUDE

- Burger restaurants
- Fish and chip shops
- Pizza restaurants
- Kebab shops
- Sandwich bars
- Coffee bars
- Sushi restaurants
- Chinese restaurants
- Indian restaurants

Frying chips

ADVANTAGES AND DISADVANTAGES OF COUNTER/TAKE-AWAY SERVICE

ADVANTAGES	DISADVANTAGES
Fast service with a high volume of customers.	Limited food choices therefore specific dietary requirements may not be met.
Limited seating area therefore less cleaning between customers necessary.	Customers may not dispose of their litter properly outside premises impacting on environment.
Crockery and cutlery is disposable therefore less washing and cleaning up.	Use of disposable crockery and cutlery is not environmentally friendly.
Food items can be prepared on a different site and delivered to the establishment.	Food items may not be able to be modified to customer's choice.
Many large chains operate take-away establishments that customers know and trust.	Until recently many take-away establishments had a reputation for providing unhealthy, fatty and sugar-laden food items.

PREPARING A COUNTER/TAKE-AWAY SERVICE

As with all food service establishments there must be a close link between the food service employees and those cooking or preparing the items.

The counter may be set up by both sets of employees who may take responsibility for different areas of it. The following is a list of items that may need to be prepared:

- Napkins, bags, disposable cutlery and trays.
- Cups, sugar, milk and stirrers.
- Seasoning and sauces.
- Till items.
- The counter is clean and free from debris.
- Ensure that menu boards and promotional items are clean and up-to-date.
- Serving items, tongs, spoons and ladles are clean and in place.
- Heat lamps and bain-maries are turned on.
- Check temperatures of fridges and record.
- Ensure that the floor is clean and dry.
- Waste bins should be clean and empty with fresh bin liners.
- Put cleaning items in place for use during service.

Serving food

ORDER OF SERVICE FOR A COUNTER/ TAKE-AWAY

Customers arrive and can either read menus displayed on walls or collect items from refrigerated units.

Customers approach the counter, order and pay for items. All employees who are working at the counter must be fully aware of any special offers or deals that are being promoted.

> ✓ **TIP**
>
> Prior to taking an order the server must be aware of any deals or special offers being promoted.

These items will be prepared behind the counter. The order will then be gathered on to a tray or into a bag depending on what the customer has chosen.

If the items are being cooked to order, the customers must be given an accurate estimate of how long the order will take to be prepared.

Depending on the length of time necessary to prepare the items there may be a specific waiting area for customers. Otherwise customers can wait at the counter.

Some establishments may have seating areas where customers can take their items to eat.

Once customers have finished eating they must take their used items to a waste collection point.

 ACTIVITY

- With another member of staff or person in your group, use a take-away menu and practise taking orders from that menu.
- Take an order from a customer who is vegetarian.
- What drinks choices are there?

DURING SERVICE

The establishment must be maintained at all times during service. Even at its busiest, customers may always be passing and the cleanliness of the establishment will be an indication of how well it is run. During service the following may need to be done:

- Napkins, cutlery and trays are replenished.
- Seating area is tidied and tables are cleaned.
- Waiting area is tidied.
- Counter is kept free from debris.
- Check temperatures of refrigerators and of food under heat lamps and record.
- Check the outside of the premises for rubbish and litter.

 TIP

Especially during busy periods it is always good practice to 'clean as you go'. This will ensure that the premises remain tidy at all times.

CLEARING AFTER SERVICE

Once the establishment has closed the area must be tidied and cleaned in preparation for the next day.

Heat lamps and bain-maries should be turned off. Any food that has been held under them should be disposed of correctly. Waste bins must be emptied and washed out. Refrigerators should be emptied, cleaned and

TIP

Always clean the surfaces and counters using hot soapy water and sanitize after use.

A bain-marie

restocked. All refrigerated items should have their 'use-by' dates checked and any that date the following day should be discarded. Counters and surfaces should be washed down and sanitized. Floors should be brushed and mopped. Sauces and seasonings should be cleaned and refilled.

Heat lamps

Counter/take-away service is a quick and simple service which provides a fast meal or snack to its customers. Much of the speed of service is due to the preparation prior to service being carried out properly. During service employees should have a good knowledge of the menu and its items and be able to guide customers through the menu options. Once the establishment is closed it needs to be cleaned and cleared, not only to fulfil hygiene regulations, but also to ensure that it is ready for the next service.

Plastic forks

Drive-through pick-up

Assessment of knowledge and understanding

You have now learned about the responsibilities required for a counter service operation. This will enable you to ensure your own positive actions contribute effectively towards the whole team.

To test your level of knowledge and understanding, answer the following short questions. These will help to prepare you for your summative (final) assessment.

Preparing for assessment checklist

■ Check the set up procedures for your establishment.

■ Ensure that you know the menu items for your establishment.

■ Confirm that you are able to clear and clean the counter areas.

Project 1

1 Prepare a checklist for setting up and preparing your establishment.

2 What temperature records need to be kept during service? Where are these recorded?

3 What is the procedure for cleaning a spillage on the floor?

4 List the areas that get washed and sanitized after service has finished.

Project 2

1 What items are available on the menu for vegetarians?

2 What special offers or deals are available during the service?

3 What is the procedure when a product is running out?

4 What healthy options are available on the menu?

10

Prepare and serve areas for table service

Unit 606 Prepare and serve areas for table service

2FS1.1 Prepare service areas and equipment for table service

2FS1.2 Prepare customer and dining areas for table service

2FS1.3 Clear dining and service areas after table service

What do I need to do?
- Set up all the restaurant equipment.
- Set up tables for different types of service.
- Clear dining areas after service.

What do I need to know?
- Know and understand what the hazards are when preparing a restaurant.
- How to set up a table in preparation for different types of meal.
- How to clean and clear after table service.

Information covered in this chapter
- Preparing the restaurant or function room.
- Placing tables and chairs correctly.
- Setting tables.

KEY WORDS

Covers
The number of people at a table.

Still room
Area in a restaurant, normally, but not always, in the kitchen. The area is used to prepare bread items and hot beverages.

Waiter's stations
Sideboards within the restaurant that waiters use to prepare and store items for service.

Mise en place
French term for setting up the restaurant.

Table seating
The term used for an individual's cutlery and glasses on the table.

Tablecloths
The cloths used to cover a table.

INTRODUCTION

Setting up and breaking down a restaurant are as important activities as the actual service itself. Without setting up properly, the restaurant or food service establishment will not run correctly, will not meet hygiene or health and safety standards and will ultimately be a difficult place to work in.

To set up a restaurant first the room must be prepared, then the tables and chairs are set in place. After that the tables themselves are set up depending on the type of meal to be served and the style of restaurant. The other areas that need to be prepared are the waiter's stations and the still room.

After service has finished everything must be broken down and cleaned. This is important as the preparation for the next service will depend on everything being cleaned and ready to start again.

PREPARING THE RESTAURANT OR FUNCTION ROOM

Preparation is one of the most important tasks to be carried out in a restaurant. Ideally the entire room needs to be set up prior to each service. The preparation of a restaurant can also be referred to by the French term *Mise en place*, which can be shortened sometimes to MEP. The first task that needs to be carried out is to clean the entire room. This is either carried out by the waiters depending on the establishment, or there may be cleaners engaged to undertake this task.

 TIP

How a restaurant or food service establishment looks is vitally important to the whole operation as it is the first impression customers have.

A formal table setting

Cleaning schedule

AREA	CLEANING NECESSARY
Walls	Any marks removed and walls dusted.
Window sills	Washed and polished.
Floors	Brushed prior to service, brushed and mopped at the end of service.
Waiter's stations	All contents removed at least once a day, all areas washed.
Doors	Main door washed, all door furniture polished.
Ledges	Dusted.
Chairs	Soft seats vacuumed and all other parts washed and polished.
Windows and mirrors	Polished and any smears removed.
Tables	Washed and sanitized.

Putting tables and chairs into place

How tables and chairs are set out in a restaurant is very dependent on the style of establishment and the type of menu being served. As a general rule the more expensive and higher-class the restaurant the more space that the customers can enjoy.

✓ TIP

Check each table and chair for cleanliness or damage. Also ensure that there is no chewing gum stuck to the bottom of the tables or chairs.

In a Michelin-starred restaurant each table has space around it both for the waiters to work and for the customers to enjoy the comfort. The tables will be large and the chairs will be luxurious. In a brasserie-style restaurant there is less space around and between the tables, the tables will be smaller and the chairs less luxurious. In a mid-range chain restaurant the tables will be close together and the chairs will be functional, comfortable and easy to clean.

When setting out tables and chairs, there are a few basic guidelines to follow:

CHECKLIST

✓ Ensure that waiters are able to pass between the chairs without knocking into any of them.

✓ The tables should be spaced evenly around the room and not crammed into one end.

✓ The correct amount of chairs should be at each table, i.e. a table for four persons should have four chairs. Even if only three customers sit at the table it is always easier to reduce the amount of covers than increase them.

✓ Do not place tables of two near large groups as the smaller tables may not be able to hear what is being said at their table.

✓ Be aware of what guests may be able to see from each chair. Try and ensure that no-one is staring straight into the kitchen or bathroom.

✓ Try and space customers evenly around the table so they all may hear and see each other.

✓ Do not cram customers on to too small a table. They will be cramped and may not enjoy their meal.

✓ If customers are seated at too big a table they may feel 'lost' at it.

There are many different ways of placing seats around tables. It can impact on how customers enjoy their meal. The figure below shows two different methods of seating a table of two. The diagram on the right is an example of a formal setting where the customers may be having a business lunch. The diagram on the left is an example of a more informal setting where perhaps two friends may be enjoying a meal.

(a) Informal setting

(b) Formal setting

This figure shows different layouts for tables of four people. All layouts are dependent on the size and type of tables available. The top two are preferable as all the customers are spaced equally but this is dependent on the size of the tables.

Layouts for tables seating four people

The following figures show layouts for different styles of function. They can be used for different purposes of function. The figure below shows a top table with sprigs, which is frequently used at wedding breakfasts. The figure on the following page shows the more modern selection of round tables for a function.

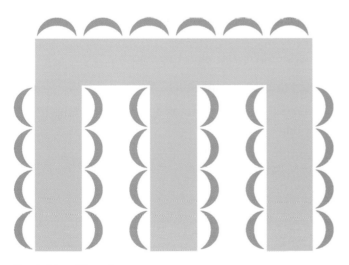

Top table with sprigs

Layout using round tables for a function

 ACTIVITY

- Draw a plan of your restaurant and state on each table how many customers can be seated at that table.
- Where would you seat a table of 15 persons?
- How would you accommodate 16 tables for two on Valentine's night?

Clothing up tables

Once tables are in the correct place they should next have their tablecloths put on. This is referred to as clothing up. See step-by-step on page 131 at end of chapter

There are certain rules that must be followed with tablecloths:

- Tablecloths should be handled as little as possible.
- When tablecloths are laundered they are folded and starched to ensure that they look good on the table.
- When they come from the laundry tablecloths should be folded in a concertina fold.
- When folded each size of tablecloth will be easily identifiable.
- The main crease on a tablecloth should run down the middle of the table.
- If a tablecloth is damaged or dirty it must be discarded immediately.
- Tablecloths should cover the legs of the table.

 TIP

Tablecloths should not have marks or tears. Send any marked or damaged cloths back to the laundry.

An a la carte set up

- Tablecloths should hang evenly on all sides.
- Tablecloths should never touch the floor.

Tablecloths must be stored carefully to ensure that they do not get damaged or dirty.

SETTING TABLES

Tables must be in place before they are set, so that once the cutlery is set on the table it is not moved or knocked out of place.

Chairs need to be set into place. If the table is clothed chairs should just touch the cloth, not be pushed in fully.

It is important that each table is consistently laid up. With all tableware laid correctly service will not be impeded because a customer does not have the correct cutlery or is missing an item of tableware.

Napkins

A lily napkin fold

Napkins can be made of many different materials including cotton and linen, or they can be disposable. Whichever napkin fold is to be used (see different step-by-step napkin folds) they must all be the same size, shape and height. Napkins should be handled as little as possible.

If the napkin is to be in the centre of the place setting then it should be placed on the table first. All napkins should be positioned in the same place on each setting. If a napkin is dirty or damaged it must be discarded.

 ACTIVITY

Refer to the step-by-step sections on napkin folding. Choose three different folds and practise folding them. Ensure that each time you fold a napkin it is the same size and shape. Check that you do not handle the napkins too much.

A waterlily napkin fold

A fan napkin

Cutlery

Cutlery must be polished prior to being laid on the table (see Chapter 8 polishing crockery and cutlery).

When cutlery is carried around the room it must be placed on a service plate, tray or held in a cloth. In some restaurants and establishments the waiters wear white gloves to set the tables to avoid getting finger marks on the cutlery.

When main-course cutlery is placed on the table it should be equidistant across the customer's place setting. There should be space for plates to be set down without moving the cutlery.

There are two main cutlery settings, 'a la carte' and 'table d'hôte'. For an a la carte setting each customer is given the same cutlery, generally a main-course knife and fork. Other cutlery is added depending on the customer's orders. The table d'hôte setting is one where the menu is set and all the cutlery can be placed on the table before the customers arrive.

In general, main-course cutlery is set first then each preceding course is laid outside it. The forks are on the left-hand side of the customer and the knives and soup spoon on the right. The side plate and butter knife are beyond the forks.

To ensure a consistent lay up each piece of cutlery should be the same space from the edge of the table. They should not be at the edge of the table as the customers could knock them off the table as they sit down.

Glasses

Glasses are polished and checked for fingerprints or watermarks. In an a la carte service a simple wine glass may be placed at each setting. At a function there may be different wines or drinks served with each course. The glasses for these may all be placed beside each setting.

TIP

Only lift cutlery by their handles. Do not ever hold on to the other ends as these have to go into the customers' mouths.

Clean glasses

Cruets

These are a vital part of any table setting. They should be full at all times, especially if they are glass and visible. They must be polished before being set down. Cruets should be set in the same place on each table.

Decorations

Table decorations can be very elaborate, for example at a wedding or function large flower arrangements may be placed in the centre of each table. Alternatively they could be very simple, perhaps a single flower stem or ornament. Either way they must be fresh, clean and appropriate for the meal. They should also not impinge on the diner's plates and customers should be able to see across the table to one another.

CHECKING TABLES

Once the room is set every table must be checked and the room as a whole must be looked at.

In particular look for:

Missing table items: each table must be inspected to ensure that nothing is missing.

Tables and chairs in correct position: this will prevent them having to be moved during service.

Debris on the floor: always brush the floor prior to each service.

✓ TIP

Checking the room after setting up is vitally important. It will ensure that the service runs smoothly.

PREPARING STATIONS AND STILL ROOMS

Waiters' stations are placed around restaurants and function rooms. Their purpose is to hold equipment that the waiters may need during service. They must be filled prior to service and kept restocked during service

ITEMS THAT SHOULD BE IN WAITERS' STATIONS	
✓ Cutlery	✓ Glasses
✓ Spare place settings	✓ Toothpicks
✓ Service plates	✓ Menus
✓ Trays	✓ Sugar bowls
✓ Clean napkins	✓ Ice buckets
✓ Crumbing plate	✓ Tablecloths

The still room is an area between the restaurant and kitchen that is used to prepare items that are needed for the restaurant. Traditionally this area was used to prepare bread, butter, tea and coffee, but over time its purpose has expanded and it can provide finger bowls and other accompaniments for service. During service cutlery is polished in the still room and is sent to the floor to refill the waiters' stations.

Within the still room the following equipment may be present:

- *Refrigerators*: Temperature should be checked and recorded prior to service.
- *Coffee machines*: Should be switched on and all equipment checked.
- *Hot water still*: Should be switched on.
- *Grill or small oven to heat bread*: Should be switched on.
- *Coffee and tea pots*: Restocked and polished ready for service.
- *Sugar bowls and milk jugs*: Polished and filled in preparation for service.
- *Bread baskets and butter dishes*: Bread baskets should have clean napkins placed in them and butter should be cut to the correct size.
- *Bread knife and board*: Located and put in place.
- *Equipment for polishing cutlery*: Vinegar, jugs and a good supply of freshly laundered tea towels should be prepared.
- *Salt and pepper cruets*: Filled and have spares ready.
- *Sauces*: Prepared and put into fridge.

Prior to each service the following items may need to be requisitioned from the stores. The amounts will depend on how many customers are expected.

Items that need be ordered in each day:

- Milk
- Butter
- Sauces
- Bread or rolls
- Lemons

CLEARING AND TIDYING A RESTAURANT AFTER SERVICE

AREA	ACTION
Tables and chairs	Once all customers have left the establishment all tables should be cleared of settings. The chairs should all be placed on top of the tables.
Floors	Should be brushed and mopped.
Waiters' stations	Should be cleared down and washed.
Crockery and cutlery	Should all be washed up and as much as possible polished.
Glasses	Should be washed up and as many as possible polished.
Debris, empty bottles	Should be placed into bins.
Dirty napkins and tablecloths	Should be counted and bagged to be sent to the laundry.

STEP-BY-STEP: NAPKIN FOLDING – THE CONE

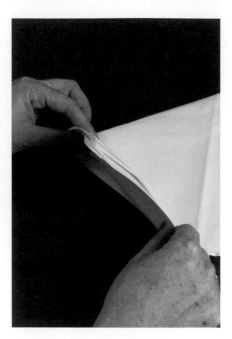

1 *Take a clean, freshly laundered napkin. Fold the napkin in half to form a rectangle*

2 *Pick up one corner of the napkin and wrap the entire napkin around your hand*

3 *Fold the end point back on itself*

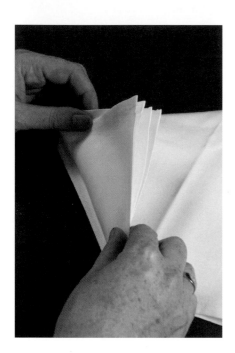

4 *Open the napkin to stand up*

STEP-BY-STEP: NAPKIN FOLDING – THE BISHOP'S MITRE

1 *Take a clean, freshly laundered napkin*

2 *Fold one corner up*

3 *Fold the other corner down*

4 *Fold the entire napkin in half*

5 *Bring the ends together and tuck under one another*

6 *Pull out into the final shape*

STEP-BY-STEP: NAPKIN FOLDING – THE LILY

1 *Take a clean, freshly laundered napkin*

2 *Fold in half into a triangle*

3 *Bring both points of the triangle up to the centre point*

4 *Then fold the top fold back in half again*

5 *Fold a small edge up*

6 *Turn the napkin over*

7 *Tuck one end into the other*

8 *Set upright and tuck the leaves into the band*

9 *Final result*

STEP-BY-STEP: NAPKIN FOLDING – THE WATERLILY

1 Take a clean, freshly laundered napkin

2 Fold each corner into the centre

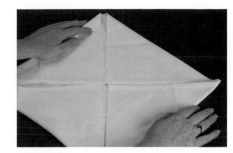

3 Repeat once again

4 Turn the entire napkin over and fold each corner into the centre again

5 Place a glass in the centre of the napkin

6 Pull out the edges from under the napkin

7 This fold can either be used on a plate by itself or in a bowl or basket

STEP-BY-STEP: NAPKIN FOLDING – THE FAN

1 *Take a clean, freshly laundered napkin*

2 *Fold in half to form a rectangle*

3 *Starting at one end concertina the napkin*

4 *Fold the whole napkin in half*

5 *Set upright and tuck the remainder underneath itself to balance it*

STEP-BY-STEP: NAPKIN FOLDING – THE WAVE

1 *Do not unfold a freshly laundered napkin*

2 *Open each end once*

3 *Roll each end into the centre twice*

4 *Crease the outside fold*

5 *Turn the napkin over and fold back on itself*

STEP-BY-STEP: NAPKIN FOLDING – THE PRINCE OF WALES FEATHERS

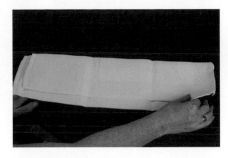

1 *Take a clean, freshly laundered napkin*

2 *Fold one point up to about 5 cm below the other point*

3 *Bring the left hand corner up to beside the lowest point*

4 *Fold the second edge up to beside the lowest point*

5 *Fold the bottom half of the napkin up to the lowest points*

6 *Flip the bottom half back on itself*

7 *Turn the napkin over*

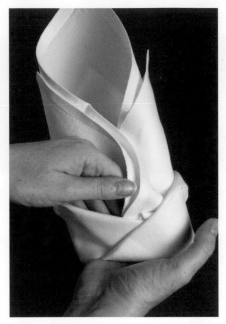

8 *Tuck the ends in*

9 *Bring the points down*

10 *Final result*

STEP-BY-STEP: CLOTHING A TABLE

1 *Use the correct size of cloth for the table*

2 *Open cloth across the table, so that the large fold is at the top*

3 *Lift the large fold with your thumb and forefinger*

4 *Lift the next edge of the cloth with your little finger. Flick the other edge slowly across the table*

5 *Once the far edge is in place release your thumb and forefinger and pull the other edge into place*

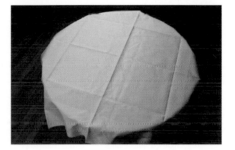

6 *Check that the cloth is undamaged and unmarked and that the main crease is running in the correct direction*

Assessment of knowledge and understanding

You have now learned about the responsibilities for planning and setting tables. This will enable you to ensure your own positive actions contribute effectively towards the whole team.

To test your level of knowledge and understanding, answer the following short questions. These will help to prepare you for your summative (final) assessment.

Preparing for assessment checklist

■ Write a list of all the different duties that need to be completed to set up your establishment.

Project 1

1 Write a step-by-step list of how a table of two covers, three covers and four covers is set in your establishment for restaurant service.

Draw a diagram of the waiter's station, list all the items that need to be set up in preparation for a restaurant service.

2 Why does everything need to be cleaned out of the waiter's station at the end of each service?

3 Why is it important that the floor be kept clean and free of debris before, during and after service?

Project 2

1 A function of 25 people are booked into your establishment this evening for a birthday dinner. The menu has been agreed. Draw a table plan of how you would organize the room.

2 Design a table for the above function. Which cutlery and settings would you use? Don't forget to include table decorations.

Mary's Birthday Dinner

Potted Shrimps

Beef Wellington with roasted potatoes and a selection of vegetables

Crème Brulee

Name: **RICHARD HARDEN**

Position: CO-PUBLISHER

Establishment: HARDEN'S LIMITED

Current job role and main responsibilities:
Co-publisher, with brother Peter, of Harden's London and UK restaurant guides. Main jobs – general management, survey analysis, restaurant reviewing, website editing, guidebook writing.

What is the most exciting thing about working at Harden's?
For better or worse, we are the only UK business which does what we do the way that we do it.

When did you realize that you wanted to pursue a career in the food service industry?
I didn't, it's an accident really. And I'm really a publisher/journalist – the link with food service is almost incidental.

Training:
Qualified as barrister.

Experience:
With brother Peter, pioneered concept in UK of basing restaurant reviews on user-generated content (USG).

What do you find rewarding about your job?
It has been fascinating to track, and in a tiny way contribute to, the development of the restaurant business over nearly 20 years.

What do you find the most challenging about the job?
The media environment is economically very challenging for operators of all sizes, and we are a very small operator.

What advice would you give to students just beginning their career?
Go and eat out, as real customers, at the best places you can afford. You'll learn nothing if you go along to your mates' restaurants, even if it is cheaper/free, as the experience is not authentic.

Who is your mentor or main inspiration?
We were inspired to believe that there might be scope in the market for survey-driven restaurant guides by the success of the Zagat guides in the US, and the Marcellino's guides in Germany.

What traits do you consider essential for anyone entering a career in the food and drink sector?
I don't think you can generalize.

A brief personal profile
I qualified as a barrister and worked in the City of London for eight years before setting up Harden's, with my brother Peter, in 1991.

Can you give one essential management tip or piece of industry advice?
Remember the customer.

11

Serve food at the table

Unit 607 Serve food at the table

2FS2.1 Greet customers and take orders

2FS2.2 Serve customer orders and maintain the dining area

What do I need to do?

- Identify customers' requirements and provide them with assistance when they arrive.
- Ensure that customers have access to the correct menu and you can answer any questions that they might have with confidence.
- Assist customers in making their choice and ensure that they have sufficient information for their needs.
- Provide customers with correct table items and have the necessary service equipment for their meal.
- Remove and replace table items in accordance with the customers' requirements.
- Understand the necessity for every customer to be served to a consistent standard.

What do I need to know?

- Know and understand how to greet customers.
- How to communicate positively, professionally and confidently.
- How to take customers' orders correctly.
- How to organize customers' tables in accordance with their food order.

Information covered in this chapter

- Reservations, guest arrivals and seating.
- Taking customers' orders.
- Adjusting cutlery.
- Serving dishes.
- Crumbing down.
- Billing.

KEY WORDS

Covers
A word used to describe the quantity of customers at a table.

Mise en place
Literally means to put in place, or do the preparation for.

Position number
The number given to each seat at a table, in order to identify them.

INTRODUCTION

How food is served at a table to a customer differs depending on the type of establishment. This chapter will cover the main topics which are essential to food service in any establishment: greeting customers, giving them menus, taking their order accurately, preparing their table, serving and clearing the dishes. Finally, taking their dessert and coffee order then giving them the bill.

One of the most important things to remember is that customers come to a restaurant to enjoy the food, ambience or company of others. They do not expect to be entertained by the waiting staff, therefore service should be hospitable and unobtrusive.

 TIP

Even if you are busy with another customer, acknowledge new guests as they arrive, by looking them in the eye and smiling.

GUEST ARRIVAL

From the moment that guests arrive in a restaurant their first impression is often the one that will set the tone and standard for the rest of their stay. Therefore it is vital that they are greeted in a manner appropriate to the establishment.

A smiling receptionist

It is good practice to look each customer in the eye and smile as they arrive. The wording that is used to greet a customer is important, a salutation can often be forgotten, so greeting 'good morning/afternoon or evening' is a pleasant start to the interaction. Too often guests are greeted immediately upon arrival with the question 'Do you have a reservation?' If a customer does not have a reservation they can feel unwelcome.

Ideally when customers arrive they should be greeted with a smile, eye contact and 'good morning/afternoon/evening, how may I help?'

ACTIVITY

Consider how you are greeted in a variety of different situations e.g. train stations, hairdressers, cafes and restaurants.

- ■ What questions are asked and how are they worded?
- ■ Does the person look at you and smile?
- ■ How does this influence the rest of your transaction?

Customer reservations

Once the customers have arrived in a restaurant and have been greeted, the next step is to check if they have a reservation. Reservations are not an exact science, frequently customers book tables for more or less guests than they actually arrive with. Although this could have financial implications on the restaurant, if managed correctly this can be alleviated.

After the customers have been welcomed, the name of the reservation should be asked for and the amount of guests checked. It is at this point that the table could be adjusted or changed to suit the needs of the party. For example, if a table is reserved for five people and only three of the party are actually going to sit, then it is worth sitting the party at a smaller table and the larger table can then be sold to another group of customers.

 TIP

If you cannot find a customers' reservation do not make them feel more uncomfortable by interrogating them, if you have a table available for them sit them down, or ask them to have a drink at the bar while you organize something for them.

Brasserie Reservations   Date: _____

Time	No. of covers	Name/Telephone Number	Table No.	Notes
12.00pm				
12.15pm				
12.30pm				
12.45pm				
13.00pm				

Example of a reservation sheet

Seating customers

Customers should be guided to their table and during any interaction between reception employees and waiting staff, the customers should never be referred to as their table number but as the name of their party.

For example, as the Smith party are shown to their table, they should never be referred to as 'table number 5', but *always* as the 'Smith party'.

A table reservation sign

A table being pulled out

As the customers are shown to their tables either their chairs are pulled out for them or if it is banquette seating their table is pulled out to ease their access.

The first impression of the laid table is another indicator that gives the customers an idea of the restaurant's standard.

Menus

The menu is a vital part of any restaurant and it can come in many different forms. It is essential that the menu is accurately worded and priced and that the items stated are available. How a menu is presented represents the establishment.

Menus must be:

1 Clearly laid out with each course or part of the menu easily legible.

2 Clean and fresh, not stained or torn.

3 Spelt correctly.

4 Indicate exactly what is in each dish.

It is the waiter's responsibility to be able to confidently talk about the menu and answer any questions that a customer may have regarding the dishes. Waiters must also be able to identify which dishes contain which ingredients and be able to guide customers who may have food allergies or intolerances.

TRADE DESCRIPTIONS ACT

The Trade Descriptions Act 1968 makes it a criminal offence to apply a false description to goods, or to supply goods that have been falsely described.

In recent years some establishments have been prosecuted for stating on their menus that they are using only organic products but when investigated it was discovered that they had not been.

TAKING THE ORDER

In any restaurant it is important that the customers' orders are taken accurately to ensure that they get their dishes from the kitchen as quickly as possible. This ensures that the dishes are given to the customers without having to ask them again what they have ordered.

Traditionally, the order-taking procedure that has been used is called 'the triplicate docket system'. Recently this has been superseded by computerized systems, but it is important to be able to use and understand a manual system.

COMPARISION BETWEEN COMPUTERIZED ORDERING SYSTEM AND MANUAL ORDERING SYSTEM

COMPUTERIZED SYSTEM	MANUAL SYSTEM
Order gets to kitchen quickly.	Order can be delayed on its way to kitchen.
Electronic system may not work correctly.	Order can be written down incorrectly.
Customer bill calculated at time of ordering.	Customer bill needs to be manually calculated.
System needs to be reprogrammed when menu is changed.	Price changes are easily facilitated.
Order still needs to be written down prior to being entered onto the system.	Once the order is written down it does not need to be replicated.

Taking an order

The manual ordering system

Although there are many different types and shapes of docket on sale at present the following ordering system should be used on blank dockets.

Each docket written has three copies each used for a different purpose. The top copy is to be given to the kitchen for the chefs to cook from. The second docket is given to the reception desk to calculate the bill and the third remains on the waiter's station.

The docket should be divided into three sections. The top of the docket is where the starters are written, the middle of the docket is where the main courses are written and the bottom of the docket is where the side orders are written.

As each item that a customer orders is written clearly in the middle of the section, the correct position number of the person should be written on the right-hand side of the item. Once the order is complete the amount of each item ordered is recorded in the right-hand column. All changes to an item must be recorded clearly and accurately.

 TIP

It is very good practice for all waiters in an establishment to write their dockets using the same style. This avoids confusion and mistakes can be easily spotted.

 TIP

Each place setting at the table will have a position number. Make sure that you are aware of these before your guests arrive.

PRIOR TO WRITING A FOOD ORDER DOCKET IT IS ESSENTIAL TO INCLUDE:

✓ The table number.

✓ The number of covers.

✓ The time the order was taken.

✓ The initials of the person taking the order.

Order taking etiquette

Rather than asking if the customers are ready to order and making them feel rushed, a waiter can ask if they would like any help with the menu.

Any ladies should have their orders taken first, then gentlemen, and finally the host. The waiter should take the order for the first course and the main course at this point.

As each customer gives their order, the waiter should write their chosen dish clearly on the docket. At the same time the waiter should repeat the chosen item back to the customer to ensure that they have the correct order. If a customer chooses not to order a course this

2	Soup	②	4
1	Salad		1
1	Melon		3
1	Steak		4
1	Chicken		1
1	Venison		3
1	Veg Tart	②	
12	4	TS	

An example of a written docket

needs be indicated on the docket, in order to avoid confusion in the kitchen. If the waiter is unclear about what a customer has ordered then he must ask them there and then to repeat themselves. *Never guess an order!*

All dockets must be written to the same format so mistakes can be easily spotted. The writing must be clear and legible to ensure that they can be easily read in the kitchen and by other floor staff.

 ACTIVITY

Using a sample menu practise taking and writing down orders, whilst helping customers with their choices.

■ Check the writing is legible.

■ Ensure that the correct item has been requested.

■ Can the docket be easily read by a busy chef?

 TIP

Cutlery should only be carried around a restaurant on a service plate or a tray. Never in your hand.

ADJUSTING THE CUTLERY

Once the order has been placed in the kitchen, the customers' cutlery may need to be adjusted to ensure that they have the correct eating utensils for their meal. Different establishments have differing standards as to when this should be carried out but in an effort to ensure that the guests are interrupted on the least amount of occasions and to ensure that the waiting staff are as organized as possible, it should be recommended that this is carried out as soon as the order has been placed in the kitchen.

To carry out any changes to the cutlery the waiter should first prepare the cutlery at his station. The cutlery that is to be changed should be laid out on a service plate. It is advisable to change the cutlery for both the starter and the main course at this point.

When approaching a customer's table try to do so with the minimum of impact. Do not lean over customers and ensure that they do not have to move.

BASIC CUTLERY NEEDED FOR DISHES

DISH	CUTLERY	ACCOMPANIMENTS
Soup	Soup spoon	
Pasta dishes (as a starter)	Side fork and dessert spoon	Parmesan cheese
Fish starter dishes	Fish fork and fish knife	Lemon wedge
Non-fish starter dishes	Side fork and side knife	Dressing as required
Main course dishes	Large knife and large fork	
Steak dishes	Steak knife and large fork	
Dessert dishes	Dessert spoon and side fork	

A waiter changing cutlery

A table laid up for a function

SERVING THE DISHES

When the kitchen has completed cooking or preparing all the dishes for each course they will send them to the restaurant to be served. It is a waiter's responsibility to ensure that each of his customers receives the dish that they selected.

This information is written on the docket and once the waiter has the correct dishes, he should serve them in the following manner:

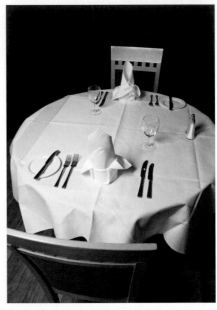

A table laid up for two people

■ All dishes should be served to the left-hand side of the customer.

■ Ladies should be served first, then gentlemen and finally the host.

■ Dishes should never be served unless they are all present.

■ As dishes are placed in front of guests state what they are to avoid the customers being confused.

 ACTIVITY

Using the dockets that you wrote for the previous activity adjust the cutlery at a place setting.

■ Ensure that you are not stretching over a customer in order to do so.

■ Try the same activity for a three-course meal.

Dishes to be served to customers

A plate being held correctly

Clearing a table

Tables should be cleared of dirty plates when every customer at the table has finished. The only exception to this would be if a guest indicated that they had finished with their dishes and wanted them removed.

Main away

The term 'main away' is used to tell the kitchen when the customers are ready for their main course to be served. Depending on the type of establishment and the type of menu being served this is carried out at different stages. For example, if a meal is being served in a brasserie-style establishment where the customers are expecting a fast service, then the 'main away' is called prior to the first course being served. In a fine dining establishment where the pace would be slower, then the 'main away' would be called after the first course has been cleared completely.

A table being cleared correctly

After clearing the table each cover must be checked to ensure that they have the correct cutlery for the next course.

Serving main courses

PRIOR TO SERVING THE MAIN COURSE CHECK:

✓ The starter dishes have been cleared.

✓ The main course cutlery is correct.

✓ Ensure that the correct dishes have been ordered.

The main course should be served to the customers from the left-hand side, starting with the ladies at the table first, then the gentlemen, and finally the host. Once again the plates should be lifted and carried without putting thumbprints on the rim.

Sometimes the incorrect order is sent or an order has been wrongly taken. If this occurs, take the dish back to the kitchen and get an accurate time of when the dish will be ready. Ensure that the head waiter or restaurant manager is aware of the mistake.

If customers are sitting at a table watching their companions eating, it can make them feel uncomfortable. A head waiter or restaurant manager may resolve this by offering the customers a taster or intermediate course while waiting for their ordered dish to arrive. Alternatively all the dishes may be returned to the kitchen and cooked afresh in order to ensure that the customers enjoy their meal together.

 TIP

If a customer has a problem let your supervisor know as soon as possible. Do not try and hide a problem as you may not be able to resolve it yourself.

Crumbing down using a napkin and brush

Crumbing down

Once the main course has been finished by all the customers, the table is then cleared (see clearing a table, p. 145). After the main course all the plates, including side plates, bread baskets and cruets are removed. The table is then 'crumbed down' to remove any debris which may be left on the table top. This can be done using a variety of implements.

Once the crumb down is complete the customers should be offered the dessert menu. It is advisable not to ask the customers if they would like to see the dessert menu but to give it to them and offer them a few minutes to look at the menu. If customers have eaten two courses and are asked if they want to see the dessert menu they generally will say no, but if given the menu they may be tempted by some of the dishes.

Dessert orders

The customers should not be left for too long to contemplate the dessert menu, but they should be given a chance to read it. As with the main course, the order must be written down clearly. In some establishments the tea and coffee order can be taken at this point. Once the order has been given to the kitchen then the dessert cutlery must be laid on the table.

At this point the customers could be offered the alternative of a savoury dish instead of a dessert, to have before their dessert. These dishes range from a traditional cheese plate to herring roes on toast or Welsh rarebit. The cutlery needed for this would be a small knife and fork and the cruets would need to be returned to the table.

Dessert settings

> **✓ TIP**
>
> Please ensure that the sugar bowl is placed on the table prior to the coffee and tea being served.

A pot of tea and cup

Tea and coffee service

The customers may want to have their coffee with their dessert or after it. It is important not to serve the coffee too early to the customers as they may feel that they are being pushed out or rushed through their meal. The coffee and tea should be freshly made when served. The cups should be placed on the top right-hand side of the customer with the handle pointed to the right and the teaspoon pointing from the top to under the handle of the cup.

Coffee and tea service is covered in greater detail in Chapter 23 and Chapter 24.

Billing

When customers ask for the bill it is important that they are given it as quickly as possible. The waiter must check the bill to ensure that the correct items are on it as it would be embarrassing for the customers and the establishment if they were being over-charged. It would likewise be damaging for the establishment if the customer was being under-charged as the restaurant would lose money. It is important that the waiter is aware of the payment methods that the establishment uses so that payment can be processed as quickly as possible.

Guests leaving

As the guests leave the establishment it is good manners for each member of staff to say goodbye and thank you, once again body language plays a part in this and even making eye contact and smiling as a guest leaves will leave a good impression with them.

> **❗ REMEMBER**
>
> Giving the customer the bill is the final part of the service, the bill must be delivered promptly and it must be accurate.

STEP-BY-STEP: CLEARING A TABLE

1 Look at the plates on the table and decide which order is the most practical to clear.

2 Always clear dirty plates from the customer's right-hand side.

3 With your back to the customer, bend your knees and lift the first plate and transfer to the other hand.

4 Keep the plate away from the customers and holding the knife firmly with your thumb, tuck the fork under it.

5 Move to the right of the next customer, lift the next plate and place firmly on top of your thumb and little finger of your other hand.

6 Scrape any debris onto the bottom plate and secure cutlery under the knife.

7 Continue collecting plates from each customer.

8 Once all large plates have been cleared, clear side plates and any other plate from the table.

9 Ideally each waiter should, after practise, be able to clear a table of four customers in one movement.

! REMEMBER

When clearing a table it is important to ensure that the customers are not splashed or anything is dropped on them.

STEP-BY-STEP: CARRYING PLATES

1 Before lifting a plate it is important to envisage what way it needs to be placed in front of the customer.

2 When a plate is placed in front of a customer the main constituent of the dish should be directly in front of them. Lift the plate so that it can easily be set in front of the customer.

3 Lift the plate by placing your fingers under the rim.

4 Place your thumb along the edge of the plate.

5 Never put your thumb on to the rim of the plate.

6 When carrying two plates in one hand, rest the plate on your bottom three fingers and put your thumb and little finger above the plate.

7 Rest the second plate on top of your thumb, little finger and the palm of your hand.

8 Ensure that the plate is secure before moving.

9 If either of the plates move or any of the foods drop, return immediately to the chef.

> **! REMEMBER**
>
> It is important that the dish is given to the customer presented in the same way as it leaves the chef.

STEP-BY-STEP: SERVING DISHES TO CUSTOMERS

1 When a plate is placed in front of a customer the main constituent of the dish should be directly in front of them.

2 When the order is taken the position number of each dish should be given.

3 The first dishes to be placed should be to the ladies of the party.

4 The last dish to be set should be to the host of the table.

5 The plates should be set before the guests to their left-hand side.

6 If a guest is seated on a banquette or their seat is inaccessible, try not to lean over them but as unobtrusively as possible place their dish in front of them.

7 Any side dishes or accompanying sauces should be set near the guests.

8 Try and ensure that the customers do not feel cramped by large amounts of dishes.

> **! REMEMBER**
>
> Although it is important to know and use the correct etiquette for table service, it is more important to be as unobtrusive as possible when serving customers.

Assessment of knowledge and understanding

You have now learned about the responsibilities in the service of food using efficient and effective procedures. This will enable you to ensure your own positive actions contribute effectively towards the whole team.

To test your level of knowledge and understanding, answer the following short questions. These will help to prepare you for your summative (final) assessment.

Project 1

1 Using a copy of a menu from any restaurant, state what checks must be done before it is given to a customer.

2 Identify which items on the menu, if any, are suitable for vegetarians.

3 Take a starter and main course order for a table of four from the menu; write it clearly on a docket.

4 Include as many variations in the menu as possible, for example dishes with no sauce, substituting one garnish for another.

5 Prepare the cutlery at a table for that order, include any sauces that may be needed as accompaniments to the dishes.

Project 2

1 Carry three empty main course plates correctly while walking around. To increase the difficulty place an orange in the centre of each plate and move about a room without the orange rolling off the plate.

2 Practise serving plates to a table.

3 Set up and clear a table of four covers, who have finished their main course. Try and include as many different sizes and shapes of plates as possible.

THE MODERN PANTRY

INDUSTRY PROFILE

Name: **ANNA HANSEN**

Position: CHEF PROPRIETOR

Establishment: THE MODERN PANTRY, CLERKENWELL, LONDON

Current job role and main responsibilities:
I am Head Chef at my restaurant as well as General Manager. This involves writing menus, managing my kitchen crew and teaching them how to recreate my ideas, making sure I get good GPS. I have a General Manager who takes care of the front of house but spend many hours with her developing ideas and ways to constantly improve the running of The Modern Pantry and keep our existing clients happy whilst encouraging new clients to come and try us out.

When did you realise that you wanted to pursue a career in the food service Industry?
When I was 16 but at that stage I was still at school and my mother encouraged me to finish my education which I did. I studied business management. I then travelled to the UK where I began dishwashing at a restaurant and soon rediscovered my love of food. I began training as a chef and have never looked back.

Experience:
My first job was at The French House Dining Room in Soho with Fergus Henderson where I became sous chef. I went on to work with Peter Gordon at The Sugar Club where I was head pastry chef and junior sous chef and in Melbourne at the Richmond Hill Café and Larder with Stephanie Alexander where I was a chef de partie.
I worked in many other restaurants along the way but those have been the greatest influences in my cooking career. I also set up a catering company and then in 2001 opened my first restaurant with Peter Gordon and partners in Marylebone, London called the Providores and Tapas Room. I left there to develop The Modern Pantry which opened in August 2008.

What do you find rewarding about your job?
I love the satisfaction of creating a meal for someone that they love. I love the creative aspect, coming up with new dishes, discovering new ingredients and finding ways of using them.
Working so closely with my chefs and front of house has created a great family atmosphere, almost like a home from home.

What do you find the most challenging about the job?
Managing a restaurant is a constant challenge. I have around 35 staff and being a good boss to all of them and getting the most from them is my biggest challenge.

What advice would you give to students just beginning their career?
It is a tough industry but the only thing you need to have when you start is drive and a good work ethic. That means being able to work as a team, respecting the people you work with and understanding that learning involves a lot of mistakes and critique from those who are teaching you. This is sometimes hard to take but if you can overcome the urge to take it personally you will go far.

Who is your mentor or main inspiration?
Fergus Henderson and Peter Gordon are my mentors and my inspiration comes from the world of food around me. My travels, walking through China Town, talking to people about the food they love etc. I was also greatly influenced by my Danish Grandmother. Her cuisine was typically 'immigrant' in her skill at adapting a recipe by replacing unavailable ingredients with something else. Her understanding and respect for an ingredients flavour was amazing.

What traits do you consider essential for anyone entering a career in the food and drink sector?
Honesty, as I said earlier, a great work ethic and a real love of the industry as this is what keeps you on your feet for all those long hours!

A brief personal profile
Born 26.01.70, Montreal, Canada. Moved to Auckland, NZ with my mother and older brother 1972 where I remained until I was 22.
1991 – Completed a diploma in Business Management and Commerce
1992 – Travelled to the UK where I now live in North London
Shortly after my arrival in London I found a job dishwashing at The French House Dining Room which had recently opened and was headed by chefs Margot Clayton (now Henderson) and Fergus Henderson. It was here my relationship with food blossomed and I discovered the sheer joy of 'nose to tail eating'. Fergus was my mentor. I now work at my new restaurant 'The Modern Pantry' in Clerkenwell which opened in August 2008. In January we were awarded a 'Bib Gourmand' by the Michelin Guide.
Previously I was part owner and joint head chef of The Providores in Marylebone, London with Peter Gordon, another of my mentors. We won several accolades including: Square Meal 'Best New Restaurant' award, Autumn 2001; New Comer of the Year' award 2003 at the Catey's; AA Rosette Award for Culinary Excellence – we were awarded two rosettes in 2002, 2003 and 2004.
Whilst at the Providores I also I played a major role in the setting up and operation of 'PUBLIC' restaurant in New York, 'PUBLIC' won its first Michelin star this year.

How do you keep yourself and your staff up-to-date with any changes to your menu and wine lists?
Prior to each service all staff get together for a briefing about menu changes and wine lists. As our menu contains some less well known ingredients it's vital that front of house staff can explain them to customers.
We also hold post service debriefings to discuss any problems that may have arisen during service.

Can you give one essential management tip or piece of industry advice?
Just be nice. It will take you far.

12

Provide a silver service

Unit 608 Provide a silver service

2FS3.1 Silver serve food

2FS3.2 Clear finished courses

What do I need to do?
- Make sure that service equipment is clean, undamaged and ready for service.
- Portion, serve and arrange food items using correct service techniques.
- Clean plates and debris from customers' tables.

What do I need to know?
- What health and safety and food hygiene regulations apply to silver service.
- What health and safety and food hygiene regulations apply to clearing tables.

Information covered in this chapter
- When silver service is used.
- Equipment necessary.
- Different silver service techniques.
- Crumbing down.

KEY WORDS

Silver service
The name applied to the service of food on to an individual's plate using cutlery.

Soup tureen
A dish used for serving soup.

Crumbing down
The action of removing crumbs and debris from table either using a crumber or a napkin.

INTRODUCTION

Silver service is a style of service used by waiting staff to place food on the plate of customers while they are at the table. Silver service is a very traditional style of service that is becoming popular again in some establishments. It is a method of serving food onto the customer's plate from silver dishes, in front of them, using service forks and spoons.

Silver service if not done correctly can lead to food being cold when it is served or food items being dropped or spilled on customers. These issues can make customers wary of being served in this style and can also lead to staff being nervous. It is important that waiters do not silver serve unless they are confident that they can carry it out.

The chefs can have a great impact on the style of service and many chefs prefer to put the food items on a plate themselves. Silver service gives them more control on how the food items look.

Silver service is a skill which can be used on many different occasions. Even simply lifting a food item from one plate to another can be done quickly and effectively using silver service techniques. It is a skill that many waiters have and, although they may not need to use it regularly, it is nevertheless a very useful skill.

✓ TIP

Silver service can also be used on many different occasions and makes waiters look professional when they need to move food from one plate to another.

WHEN IS SILVER SERVICE USED

Silver service can be used to serve at:

- Large functions.
- Buffets and carveries.
- Formal restaurant tables.

Large functions

Prior to beginning silver service at large functions, the kitchens need to be informed of the sizes of the tables. They will then portion the items on to the service 'flats' or dishes. To ensure that the service is carried out quickly each table needs to have all the items served without delay. This needs to be done by a team of two or three waiters, who will work in relays. One waiter will set the plates in front of the customers, a second will serve the meat dish, a third may serve the potatoes. The first waiter will return and serve the vegetables, the second will serve the sauce. It is essential that each table is completed by the team before they move on to a second table. It is also important that the food is served quickly as it will start to cool.

Buffets and carveries

Silver service skills are used to help customers who are being served from a buffet or carvery. As the customers make their choice the waiter uses a spoon and fork to serve the item.

A formal dining room

Formal restaurant tables

Within a restaurant, meals can be silver served to each customer. Customers can choose their own dish and it can be served to them individually. The food items will be brought from the kitchen to a sideboard or service trolley where the items can be kept warm on a hot plate. This is the service that can really show the skill of the waiter as each item needs to be served quickly.

ADVANTAGES AND DISADVANTAGES OF SILVER SERVICE

ADVANTAGES	DISADVANTAGES
Large groups can be served from the kitchens relatively quickly.	Food may not be as appetizing when placed on the plate.
Customers can choose which items they want.	If staff are not correctly trained then the service can be slow and ineffective.
The chef has more control over the look of each dish as it leaves the kitchen.	Food may not be as hot as it should be when served.
Is an indication that staff within an establishment are highly trained and skilled.	Customers may not get offered all items.
Food items can be portioned before leaving the kitchen.	Some customers may be given larger portions than others.

EQUIPMENT NEEDED FOR SILVER SERVICE

EQUIPMENT	PREPARATION	REMEMBER
Flats or dishes to serve from.	These need to be polished prior to service. They need to be warmed before service.	A wide selection of flats and dishes need to be available.
Under-plates for the serving dishes.	The smaller dishes need to be placed on cooler under-dishes. These need to be polished prior to service.	
Plates for the customers.	Plates and bowls for service need to be polished and checked for damage.	Any chipped or damaged crockery needs to be discarded in the correct manner.
Service cloths.	A selection of cloths needs to be folded and available to lift and carry plates and dishes.	Cloths with marks and drips on them will convey a negative image to the customers.
Soup tureens and ladles.	Soups tureens and their lids need to be polished and warmed. Ladles need to be polished and placed ready for service.	
Cutlery to serve.	Service cutlery includes spoons, forks and ladles. Need to be polished before service.	It is important to ensure that plenty of cutlery is available during service.
Sauce boats and ladles.	To serve sauces, these need to be polished.	

ETIQUETTE FOR SILVER SERVICE

✓ Serve to the left-hand side of the customer unless it is inconvenient or could be a hazard to the customer.

✓ Try and serve each table moving in a clockwise direction.

✓ Serve ladies first.

✓ Ensure that customers are made aware of any hot items.

✓ Do not start to clear until all customers at the table have finished.

✓ When approaching the table do not lean over the customers but approach the table sideways.

Silver serving bread

How to silver serve bread

Bread should be silver served onto the customer's side plate and can either be sliced from a larger loaf or individual rolls. There may be different types of bread for the customers to choose from. Once the customers make their choice the bread will then be lifted out of the basket or tray and placed on the customer's side plate. The waiter will lift the roll using two forks with the prongs facing each other.

 TIP

Unless carefully held, bread rolls can roll off the service cutlery and onto the floor.

Butter should already be on the customer's table.

How to silver serve soup

Prior to the soup being brought out from the kitchen, hot soup bowls should be placed in front of each customer. The kitchen must let the waiters know what the portion size should be. Soup should be ladled from the tureen carefully out into the customers' bowls. The ladle should be poured into the bowl away from the customer to prevent the customer being scalded. Sometimes the soup may be served from the kitchen in individual tureens. Depending on the style of service, these tureens may be poured directly into the customers' bowls.

Once the soup is in the bowl any garnish, for example croutons, may be served into the bowl.

How to silver serve main courses

Hot main course plates should be placed in front of each customer. The first item that should be offered is the meat or main protein of the meal. This should be placed at the 6 o'clock position, nearest the customer. It is vitally important that care is taken with the service dish so that it is not held near the customer or his neighbours. Once the meat or main protein is in place, the potatoes and vegetables can be served. The potatoes must be placed at 11 o'clock, the top left-hand side of the plate and the vegetables at 1 o'clock, the top right-hand side of the plate. Once all the main parts of the meal are on the plate, any sauces or dressings can be offered. These can be spooned or poured from sauce boats.

Serving food

Serving items from a buffet

How to silver serve pies and tarts

Depending on whether the pie is to be served either hot or cold, a hot or cold plate should be placed in front of the customer. The pie or tart should be pre-cut. The waiter can either use a cake slice or two fish knives to lift each slice of pie or tart onto the customer's plate. Sauces may be offered by a following waiter.

How to silver serve puddings

Dessert bowls should be placed in front of the customer. Using a serving spoon a portion of the pudding should be lifted from the serving dish and placed in the customer's bowl. The spoon should be rolled to produce a round egg-like shape of the pudding. Any sauce or cream should be offered by a following waiter.

How to silver serve cheese

Cheese is served from a board. Side plates are set in front of the customers who are asked to choose which cheeses they would like. As they make their selection a slice is cut from the larger block of cheese using a cheese knife and placed on to their plate. Biscuits or bread are served using a spoon and fork.

 ACTIVITY

Practise with service cutlery lifting the following items:

- A tissue.
- An orange.
- A plastic bottle.
- A small book.

Practising with these items will increase your skill and confidence at silver service.

- Check that you know the procedure if something falls on to the floor while silver serving.

- Ensure that customers do not trip or slip on any debris on the floor.

- Some establishments have a rule that if something is dropped, a member of staff should stay with it to warn customers while another member of staff brings a dustpan and brush to clean it up.

CLEARING PLATES

Once all the customers have finished eating, their plates need to be removed from the tables. In a busy restaurant environment it is important that this is done quickly and efficiently. The most efficient method is for the waiter to carry as many of the plates as is possible.

Plates should be cleared from the right-hand side of the customer. Clear the largest plates or ones with most debris first and the smallest plates and vegetable dishes last.

Use the first plate picked up for cutlery keeping the fork under your thumb to secure all cutlery under it and scrape further plates discreetly on to it. Do not pile the plates too high and ensure you are always comfortable.

Do not be afraid to make two trips to clear a table, use a tray for finger bowls and small dishes if necessary.

After clearing all the plates and bowls the table should be crumbed down.

 ACTIVITY

Using clean plates and cutlery practise clearing a table. Start with two covers and then as your skill increases clear three and four covers. Practising will increase your skill and confidence at silver service.

Crumbing a table

Crumbing a table is usually carried out after the main course and is done to remove the light debris from the table. Traditionally this was the time when the guests would be able to place their arms on the table.

■ Immediately after clearing a table use a clean folded napkin or a crumber to remove any breadcrumbs and debris from the table.

■ Brush debris on to a clean side plate.

■ When the table is clear of debris offer dessert menus or move dessert cutlery down.

■ Always remember when crumbing a table to be careful not to knock anything over.

Clearing a table

1 Approach customers from the right-hand side.

2 Lift plate from front of customer and step back from the table.

3 Transfer plate from one hand to the other

4 Secure cutlery.

5 Move to next customer and lift their plate, step away from the customers.

6 Place second plate on top of fingers above first plate.

7 Scrape debris from top plate on to bottom plate.

8 Move to next customer and repeat.

> **! REMEMBER**
>
> Do not scrape the plates next or near to customers as debris could be dropped on to them.

STEP-BY-STEP: CRUMBING A TABLE

1 *Once the main course plates, cutlery and side plates have been cleared, crumb down either using a crumber or a napkin and a side plate.*

2 *Ensure that you pull the debris away from the customer.*

STEP-BY-STEP: SILVER SERVICE

1 *Hold the spoon and fork between your thumb and forefinger. Ensure that the ends are tightly in the palm of your hand.*

2 *There are two ways to lift items. The first method is to use the spoon and fork like tongs.*

3 *The second method is to lift the items underneath with two forks. This method cannot be used if there is a sauce.*

4 *The meat or main protein of the meal should be served on the bottom of the plate, nearest the customers.*

5 *Potatoes need to be served first, they can be lifted individually.*

6 *The potatoes should be positioned at 11 o'clock on the plate from the customer.*

7 *Vegetables should be served next.*

8 *Vegetables should be placed at 1 o'clock on the plate.*

9 *Sauces can be carefully poured on to the plate for the customer.*

10 *Alternatively the sauce may be carefully spooned on to the plate.*

! REMEMBER

Be very careful not to drip or splash customers as you silver serve.

Assessment of knowledge and understanding

You have now learned about the responsibilities you have to work effectively in silver service. This will enable you to ensure your own positive actions contribute effectively towards the whole team.

To test your level of knowledge and understanding, answer the following short questions. These will help to prepare you for your summative (final) assessment.

Make sure that you keep this for easier referencing and along with your work for future inclusion in your portfolio.

Preparing for assessment checklist

■ Practise silver serving a three-course meal to an a la carte table of four covers.

■ Clear the table correctly after each course.

Project 1

1 List the service cutlery that should be prepared prior to serving the following meal.

Restaurant Menu

Leek & Potato Soup

Roast Beef with Yorkshire Pudding, Roast Potatoes, Glazed Carrots and Gravy

Sherry Trifle

Cheese and Biscuits

2 Describe how the soup would be served.

3 What hazards could occur when serving the above meal?

4 Which plates would be used to serve the cheese and biscuits?

Project 2

1 List three ways you can ensure that customers do not get splashed when tables are being cleared.

i)_____ ii) _____ iii) _____

2 What are the advantages of being able to clear a table correctly?

3 What action must be taken when a piece of food falls on the floor during service?

INDUSTRY PROFILE

Name: **ALAIN KERLOC'H**

Position: GENERAL MANAGER

Establishment: DEANES RESTAURANT, BELFAST

Current job role and main responsibilities:
I am responsible for all aspects of the daily smooth running of the restaurant including staff training, customer care and sourcing new products or services for our customers. I also ensure that we are fully compliant with all health and safety and hygiene requirements.

What is your favourite element of your role as restaurant manager at Deanes?
Coming from a large French family, I am a natural entertainer and love it when a customer has had a great night out at Deanes. Of course I am also passionate about good food and wine, so hospitality was a logical career choice for me!

When did you realize that you wanted to pursue a career in the food and beverage service industry?
I undertook my first 'stage' at age 16 in a Michelin Star restaurant called 'Le Jeanne d'Arc' in Ste Marine in Brittany and it was here, under the direction of the head sommelier, that the love of fine wine was instilled in me. My passion for the profession was propelled from there.

Training:
I did a 4-year course at Chaptal catering college in Quimper Brittany where I was taught everything from the principles of cooking though to service and the business side of the industry.

Experience:
1990–92: Hotel de Goyen, Audierne Brittany, France. Commis waiter – supervisor; 1993–94: Military Service; 1994–95: Sommelier at Nuremore Hotel, Carrickmacross, Co. Monaghan, Ireland; 1995–97: Head sommelier in Dromoland Castle, County Clare, Ireland (1-star Michelin at time); 1997–99: Restaurant manager The Tea Room, Clarence Hotel, Dublin; 1999–2001: Restaurant manager at Restaurant Michael Deane, Belfast, Northern Ireland; 2001–2006: Restaurant manager L'Arpège, Paris (3 star Michelin); 2006/2007: I opened Restaurant Mirazur in partnership with head chef; April 2007–present: Restaurant manager at new Deanes Restaurant, Belfast, Northern Ireland.

What do you find rewarding about your job?
There's nothing more rewarding than a sincere thank you from a customer. Obviously, recognition from respected guides such as Michelin and AA are rewarding although, to me, it is the customer who is the most important judge!!

What do you find the most challenging about the job?
The long hours and physical nature of the job can be very demanding. It is essential that you always remain composed, friendly and professional at all times even if you have been on your feet all day! In an industry renowned for its high turnover of staff it can also be difficult to attract and retain good staff and its often difficult to maintain consistency in a fluctuating staff base. This makes regular and continuous training an absolute necessity.

What advice would you give to students just beginning their career?
I would advise young people to be humble as this is an ever changing industry with so much to learn. I would also advise young people to travel the world with their skills as there is no better way to build upon your existing knowledge and experience. Be ambitious – do not hesitate to apply for work in the very best restaurants where you will push yourself to the height of your ability.

Who is your mentor or main inspiration?
I have worked with many inspirational leaders throughout my career such as: Mark Nolan from Dromoland Castle in County Clare who was a great promoter of team work and an inspirational motivator, Alain Passard at Arpège in Paris for his creativity, humility and passion and of course Michael Deane of Deanes in Belfast for his encouragement and trust in others' capabilities

What traits do you consider essential for anyone entering a career in the food and drink sector?
The most obvious is to have a desire to work with people, as a customer orientated approach is integral to this business. You also have to be a good team player, capable of training and leading others and delegating tasks.

A brief personal profile
I feel that my greatest achievement to date is my promotion to restaurant manager at L'Arpège, Paris in 2002. This promotion within a 3 star Michelin restaurant was a significant new challenge for me and I was honoured to be the ambassador of Alain Passard's food. In March 2006, I opened Mirazur Restaurant in Menton on France's Cote d'Azur. In November 2006, the restaurant was awarded best newcomer in France in the National 'Gault-Millau' guidebook and was awarded a Michelin star after just ten months!

Can you give one essential management tip or piece of industry advice?
Try to see your profession as a challenge and an enjoyable pursuit. View service as an exciting adrenalin rush rather than a stressful experience.

13

Provide a carvery/buffet service

Unit 609 Advise and consult with clients

2FS4.1 Prepare and maintain a carvery/buffet display

2FS4.2 Serve and assist customers at the carvery/buffet

What do I need to do?
- Set up a buffet/carvery table.
- Prepare table items and service items for a buffet/carvery.
- Arrange and display food items on a buffet/carvery.
- Replenish buffet as required.

What do I need to know?
- Why preparing a buffet correctly is important.
- Why portion control is needed in buffet service.
- Why it is important to maintain safe and hygienic working practices.

Information covered in this chapter
- Different types of buffet.
- What a carvery is and how its service works.
- Service from a carving trolley.

KEY WORDS

Buffet
A type of service where the customers can help themselves to the dishes they require, with little or no assistance.

Carvery
A specialized type of buffet where a roast meat is served to the customer.

Carving trolley
A classical service where the roast meat dish is brought to the customers' table and carved to their specifications in front of them.

INTRODUCTION

Buffets and carveries are a form of service where the customer can see the food items that are being offered. The customers can then either help themselves or waiters serve the items from the buffet.

STYLES OF BUFFET

- Finger buffet.
- Fork buffet.
- Hot buffet.
- Cold buffet.

Buffets can be used to serve three-course meals or they may be used to offer just one course.

 TIP

Ensure that there is a supply of cleaning cloths, service cloths and a dustpan and brush when the buffet is set up. This will help with cleaning up if there is spillage during service.

Buffet and plates

In many hotels breakfast is served from a buffet and this enables the hotel to offer a wide selection of hot and cold items. If the items are set up correctly and the buffet is kept well it can run for a long period so that the hotel guests can eat when they desire.

Preparing a buffet

One of the advantages of buffets is that they are a very flexible form of service. They can be served from permanent fixed counters or can be set up in an empty room.

Prior to setting up a buffet table the amount and type of dishes need to be agreed with the chefs preparing the food for the buffet. The types of serving dishes and the amount of people to be served will indicate what length of buffet table to put up.

Portion control is a vital part of buffet service. Buffets will be prepared for a fixed amount of customers. If customers are left to help themselves they can sometimes take too much leaving little for those who follow.

The tables that the customers can sit at can either be set up as for any other table service (see Chapter 11) or the customers can bring their cutlery from the buffet.

TIP

It is essential that each item on the buffet has its own service cutlery. This prevents one dish from contaminating another.

A buffet set up

Set up the buffet table

1 Set up required amount of trestle tables.

2 Trestle tables need to be clothed or covered.

3 Plates and bowls need to be checked and polished.

4 Cutlery and napkins need to be polished and laid out.

5 Serving cutlery needs to be polished and set out where they will be used.

6 Side plates need to be prepared to put serving cutlery on during use.

7 Sauces and accompaniments need to be prepared and placed into sauceboats.

8 Nearer the time that the customers are to be served, the food is to be brought from the kitchen.

TIP

Always check the floor around the buffet area for debris as items can be easily dropped or spilled during service.

A hot buffet/chaffing dishes

DISHES AND THEIR ACCOMPANIMENTS

DISH	ACCOMPANIMENT/SAUCE
Roast beef	Horseradish sauce
Boiled beef	Caper sauce
Roast mutton	Redcurrant jelly
Roast pork	Apple sauce/apple jelly
Roast goose/duck	Apple sauce
Roast turkey	Cranberry sauce
Roast chicken	Bread sauce
Boiled fish/fish stew	Rouille
Deep fried fish	Tartare sauce
Poached fish	Hollandaise sauce
Pasta dishes (except fish dishes)	Parmesan cheese
Salads	Vinaigrette
Cold poached fish	Mayonnaise

A served buffet

The customers arrive and can choose their tables. At this point their starters may be served or alternatively the customers may choose their starters from the buffet.

A waiter may be needed to explain how the service works and to guide the customers through the meal. At this point the customers may be offered drinks which would be served by the waiter.

The customers may then visit the buffet and choose items. There may be one or more waiters working behind the buffet who will help serve the items to the customers. In some cases the waiters will serve using a spoon and fork in the style known as silver service. Otherwise they will use tongs to serve the customers.

As the customers choose their items the serving waiters will pass their plate along the buffet giving a portion of each item. It is important that the serving waiters know how much of each item is in a portion, but they must also listen to the customer and acknowledge how much they require.

Customers may have special dietary requirements and it is essential that waiters working at the buffet are aware of the content of each dish. It is also important that the serving cutlery is not swapped around on dishes to prevent contamination. Once finished serving food the waiter will hand the plate to the customer.

Customers must take their plates back to their table. Depending on the style of buffet, the customers may return to the buffet for a second helping of dishes.

During the time that the customers are eating, the buffet should be replenished and tidied up by the waiters working behind it. Some items may need to be changed completely, others may simply need setting on to a different plate.

Once they have finished their items the waiter will clear the plates and may then direct them to the buffet for the next course. Alternatively the next courses may be ordered from a menu.

When the customers finish they can leave either paying on the way out or the bill will be brought to their table.

Self service items

Self service buffets require fewer waiting staff. There is more preparation required to ensure that the customers have everything that they need to serve themselves.

As the customers arrive they can pick up a tray to put their items on. They can make a selection from a variety of hot and cold items. There may still have to be waiting staff available to maintain and replenish the buffet, and possibly help serve hot items.

The items may well be portioned on to plates or dishes to ensure that the correct portion is given.

Hot buffet/hot lights

The customers may have to pay for the items that they have chosen. After that they may be required to pick up cutlery items, napkins, and any sauces and accompaniments.

When there are no customers at the buffet the waiters should use the opportunity to tidy and replenish the buffet.

Once the customers have chosen and paid for their items they can then choose their seats. If at any point they feel that they need more items or require additional courses they can help themselves again from the buffet.

 ACTIVITY

Ten customers are attending a lunch, which is to be a cold buffet. Write a list of the preparation that you need to do to set up before their arrival.

■ How would you set the buffet table up?

■ How many plates do you need?

Remember to set up the tables for the customers to sit at.

CARVERIES

Carveries are a form of buffet that became popular in the 1980s. The customers can choose from a selection of roast meats, which are carved in front of them at the hot part of the buffet.

The preparation for the carvery is much the same as for the rest of the buffet, except that the meat is carved on a heated carving dish. This dish or plate needs to be heated before the meat is placed on to it. A carving knife and fork need to be prepared for service, the knife must be sharp to avoid accidents. It is important, especially with roast meats, that a selection of the accompanying sauces are available and are replenished during service.

During service customers can choose a specific part of meat: if it is chicken they may prefer a leg rather than a slice of breast. They may be able to choose whether roast beef is served rare, medium or well-done or may be able to have a small selection of each item.

 TIP

It is important that all hot items have their temperatures checked. They need to remain above the danger zone 5–63°C.

Slicing ham at a carvery

Carving roast turkey

CARVING TROLLEY

Carving trolleys are a very traditional form of service where a roasted or baked meat or dishes are served to customers from a trolley. The customers order the items as they would in an a la carte restaurant. Rather than the items being served and plated in the kitchen, they are carved from the trolley beside the customers at a table.

As the trolley is brought to the customer it must have everything on it necessary for their meal. The trolley must be polished and prepared prior to service. A selection of service cutlery including a carving knife and fork must be polished prior to service.

Customers place their order and when it is ready to be served a hot plate, vegetables and potatoes should be brought out from the kitchen. The trolley is then wheeled over to the customers' table where the items are shown to the guests prior to being carved.

The waiter can interact with the customers, if appropriate, discussing which piece of the food item they would like or how much sauce they prefer. Once all items have been served on to the plate, the plate is set in front of the customer by the waiter.

Assessment of knowledge and understanding

You have now learned about the responsibilities you have to work effectively in a carvery operation. This will enable you to ensure your own positive actions contribute effectively towards the whole team.

To test your level of knowledge and understanding, answer the following short questions. These will help to prepare you for your summative (final) assessment.

Preparing for assessment checklist

■ Ensure that you know how to prepare all the areas of the buffet/carvery.

■ Write a checklist of your duties during buffet/carvery service

Project 1

1 Write a list of items needed to prepare a carvery serving roast beef and roast chicken.

2 What duties are performed by the waiter behind a buffet?

3 What are the portion sizes for each dish on the buffet?

4 What is the procedure if a customer asks for another portion of an item from the buffet?

Project 2

1 What is the correct procedure if a buffet runs out of an item?

2 How should spillages be dealt with?

3 Why is it important that each different item on a buffet has its own serving cutlery?

4 If two platters of sandwiches are half-finished on a buffet and there are more customers to come, what should the waiter's actions be? What must be checked?

INDUSTRY PROFILE

Name: **VINCENT MICHAEL McGRATH**

Position: DIRECTOR OF FOOD AND BEVERAGE (F&B)

Establishment: THE SAVOY HOTEL – FAIRMONT HOTELS AND RESORTS

Current job role and main responsibilities:

Director of food and beverage for the Savoy Hotel, Fairmont. Annual turnover of £24 million. Responsible for the entire day-to-day operations of the division and long term strategy planning. The hotel is closed at present for a £100 million renovation project, due to reopen in summer 2009. Working on all new F&B concepts, menu design, FF&E and recruitment for the entire F&B Team. Responsible for a team of over 240 employees working between two bars, restaurant, in-room dining, banqueting, lounge, kitchen and stewarding.

What is the most exciting thing about working at the Savoy?

The history of such an iconic hotel and the attention to detail we strive to achieve.

When did you realize that you wanted to pursue a career in the food service industry?

From an early age at school, I always had an interest in cooking and experimenting and it was the only thing I wanted to do.

Training:

Cauldon College – Staffordshire three years; City and Guilds, HCIMA, Wine and Spirits; three-month practical experience in Aviemore Scotland; casual work at the North Stafford Hotel whilst studying; first job full-time: Four Seasons Hotel, London, as a commis waiter.

Experience:

Four Seasons Hotel, Park Lane, London, 5 Star Deluxe: commis waiter, server, headwaiter, supervisor, kitchen commis, room service night manager. *Hyatt Regency Hotel*, Birmingham, Pre-opening team, 5 Star: assistant restaurant manager, assistant catering ops manager, director of catering. *Dorchester Hotel*, Park Lane, London 5 Star Deluxe: deputy food and beverage manager. *Conrad International Hotel*, Dublin, Ireland 5 Star: director of food and beverage. *Four Seasons Hotel*, Park Lane, London, 5 Star Deluxe: director of food and beverage. *Four Seasons Hotel*, Hampshire: Pre-opening team, 5 Star Deluxe: director of food and beverage.

What do you find rewarding about your job?

The guest experience: meeting and exceeding expectations turning moments into memories. Working with the most talented and passionate team members.

What do you find the most challenging about the job?

Every day is different: you need to be prepared for the unexpected – today will be unlike any other day in the world of hospitality. A challenge but also an achievement.

What advice would you give to students just beginning their career?

Training – learn as much of the technical aspects of the job and treat one another with respect and dignity.

Teamwork – work together to achieve your goals, and enjoy – it's a great industry to be part of.

Who is your mentor or main inspiration?

There have been two great mentors throughout my career: Mr Gemelli the restaurant manager at the Four Seasons, Park Lane, when I started my career as a commis waiter. I learnt so much from his experience, determination and the important fundamental parts of service and guest experience. John Stauss, regional VP and GM Four Seasons, London, always pushing you to exceed and achieve, inspiring and motivational hotelier.

What traits do you consider essential for anyone entering a career in the food and drink sector?

Energy and determination and willing to achieve and stand on your own two feet.

A brief personal profile

My biggest achievement has to be where I am today within the industry. My love for the industry lies in F&B, every day is a different day. I am a member of the Champagne Academy and Alsace wine association. Travelling is also a great interest of mine.

Can you give one essential management tip or piece of industry advice?

Determination! Never give up, as long as you have the right attitude, personality, passion and drive you will be successful.

14

Maintain and deal with payments

Unit 502 (1GEN2) Maintain and deal with payments

1GEN2.1 Maintain the payment point

1GEN2.2 Deal with payments

What do I need to do?

■ Know how to use the correct procedures for handling payments.

■ Know how to handle errors and problems.

What do I need to know?

■ How to set up your payment point.

■ How to operate the payment point correctly.

■ How to collect the contents of the payment point and who to hand over payments to.

Information covered in this chapter

■ Legislation.

■ Points of sale.

■ Methods of payment.

■ Different systems for effective running of point of sale.

■ Avoiding walkouts.

KEY WORDS

Cashier
A cashier is a person responsible for totalling the amount due for a purchase, charging the consumer for that amount, and then collecting payment for the goods or services exchanged.

Credit
Money available for a customer to borrow during the duration of their stay/visit. Arrangement for deferred payment for goods and services.

EPOS
Electronic Point of Sale. Data recorded at checkout and used for forecasting and stock control.

Float
An amount of money placed in a till/EPOS at the start of the shift and used to provide change for cash transactions. The float is always kept at the same value and is the first thing to be placed in the till at the start of the shift and the first amount of money to be removed from the till at the end of shift, prior to reconciliation taking place. It may be removed in change for reuse during the next shift.

Payment
In return for goods or services a customer/guest is required to provide monetary value through cash, cheques or credit cards.

PDQ
'Process Data Quickly'. Usually used in reference to PDQ terminals – these are the terminals used by businesses to manually swipe or input customer card details in order to take payments.

PIN
'Personal Identification Number'. A number you choose and use to gain access to various accounts or to provide authorization for charges to a credit/debit card. This information should be kept by the customer and is private.

Promotional offer
A method of increasing sales of merchandise through advertising; any activity designed to enhance sales.

Redeem
To pay off, buy back, or to clear a debt by payment.

Voucher
A voucher is a bond which is worth a certain monetary value and which may only be spent for specific reasons or on specific goods.

Walkouts
When a customer walks out of the establishment/organization without providing payment for goods and/or services received during their stay or visit.

INTRODUCTION

Nearly every organization these days will have a till point. It is very likely that this will be electronic. In its simplest form it will calculate the bill as a total, but in its most complex form it will be able to give details about what customers purchased, break these down into sales mixes, evaluate how they paid the bill and communicate with the credit card companies to track any fraudulent transactions. This chapter will look at the types of payment made by a customer, the methods of taking payment and the importance of ensuring that all customers pay their bill.

LEGISLATION

When a customer enters your establishment and orders your services, providing a tariff is displayed, they automatically enter into a contract whereby you supply the service and/or goods and they are expected to pay in return for receiving those services/goods.

The key legislation in regard to the remainder of this topic includes:

- Sale and Supply of Goods Act 1994 – a customer can refuse to pay if:
  - The goods supplied do not correspond with the description.
  - A displayed item is not what it seems.
  - The goods are inedible.
- The Trade Descriptions Act 1968/1972 makes it a criminal offence to mis-describe goods or services. Care should be taken with:
  - Wording wine lists.
  - Describing menu items.
  - Describing conditions.
  - Describing the service provision.
- Price lists – Price Marking (Food and Drink Services) Order 2003 – price of food and drink must be clearly illustrated and displayed.
- Service, cover and minimum charges – Part III of the Consumer Protection Act 1987 – it is an offence to mislead price information and such offence authorizes the issue of a code of practice.
- Data Protection Act 1998
  - Personal data shall be processed fairly and lawfully.
  - Personal data shall be obtained only for one or more specified and lawful purposes, and shall not be further processed in any manner incompatible with that purpose or those purposes.
  - Personal data shall be adequate, relevant and not excessive in relation to the purpose or purposes for which they are processed.
  - Personal data shall be accurate and, where necessary, kept up-to-date.
  - Personal data processed for any purpose or purposes shall not be kept for longer than is necessary for that purpose or those purposes.

- Personal data shall be processed in accordance with the rights of data subjects under this Act.
- Appropriate technical and organizational measures shall be taken against unauthorized or unlawful processing of personal data and against accidental loss or destruction of, or damage to, personal data.

■ Customer property and customer debt – Hotel Proprietors Act 1956 –

- Establishments have liability for guest's property for those who have booked overnight accommodation.
- If customers are unable to pay, no right of lien exists except for inns – i.e. the right to hold property against non-payment of an account.

METHODS OF PAYMENT

Tills through the ages...

A nineteenth-century till

Tills originally worked off a form of calculator where buttons were pressed to remind the cashier of what was spent. Initially they were large and clumsy but also considered a work of art. Many were elaborate and you can find some of these still in antique shops. Towards the end of the twentieth century tills became neater, quicker, and smaller and provided more information. In the mid-1980s supermarkets started using bar codes and scanners as tills in order to track stock control as well as monitor more carefully what customers were purchasing. This technology has continued to develop and they still use the fundamental basics of bar codes.

A twentieth-century till

A twenty-first-century till

In hospitality outlets however touch-screen tills have become commonplace, making it easier and quicker to enter a customer's order. These tills communicate with the kitchen informing the chefs about what to cook. They also track and monitor what guests order and can group these into relevant information that the managers can then use to help:

- Design menus.
- Track popular dishes.
- Track less popular dishes.
- Consider guest's preferences.
- Look at consumption of drinks – wines, beers, soft drinks, etc. as well as considering the more popular of each of these from the menu.
- Monitor sales on a daily basis and compare with budget.
- Stock control – take into consideration what was sold to the customer versus what was purchased by the outlet.
- Monitor how payments were made – cash, cheque, credit card, sales ledger (see table at bottom of page).
- Reconciliation of payments made and when they entered the bank account.
- Monitor individual staff sales.

Equipment needed to set up a payment station or till point

- Till/Point of Sale (POS).
- Electric sockets (to plug in electric till).
- Telephone line (for the credit-card system).
- Hand-held credit card machines (PDQs).
- Spare till rolls.
- Notepad.
- Pens/pencils.
- Float.
- Check pads/order pads.

TYPES OF PAYMENT

METHOD OF PAYMENT	DETAILS	EXAMPLES
Cash	Payment is made, change may be given. Money is banked daily and immediately credited to the outlet's bank account.	This includes notes and coins.

METHOD OF PAYMENT	DETAILS	EXAMPLES
Cheque	This form of payment is rapidly going out of fashion. Cheques used to be taken instead of cash and were considered a safe form of payment. The owner of the cheque would also be required to present a cheque guarantee card that was issued by the bank and guaranteed that the cheque would be honoured (paid) by the bank up to a certain limit (normally £50 or £100). The money to the value of the cheque would be paid to the outlet on presentation of the cheque and taken out of the customer's bank account. On average it would take between 3 and 5 days for the cash to go into the bank account.	
Credit cards	The customer presents their credit card as a form of payment. The card is placed into a PDQ and the customer is then asked to enter their PIN number or sign a piece of paper (receipt). The money is paid into the outlet's bank account between 1 and 4 days after the transaction. The customer receives a monthly statement detailing their transactions on the credit card and is then required to pay the credit card company.	Credit card companies include Visa, MasterCard, American Express and Diners Club.
Debit cards	The customer presents their debit card as a form of payment. The card is placed into a PDQ and the customer is then asked to enter their PIN number or sign a piece of paper (receipt). The money is paid into the outlet's bank account between 1 and 4 days after the transaction. The money for the transaction is immediately taken out of the customer's bank account.	Debit card companies include Maestro and Solo.
Vouchers	A voucher is a piece of paper or card that has been given to the customer either as a gift or as part of a promotional offer. This voucher is redeemed against the final bill and thereby reduces the amount the customer needs to pay by cash or credit/debit card. The outlet then needs to claim the money back from the supplier of the voucher – either head office or an independent company.	This may include luncheon vouchers, promotional vouchers and gift cards.

METHOD OF PAYMENT	DETAILS	EXAMPLES
Account	An account is very commonly found in hotels. The guest checks in with reception and automatically an account is set up against their room number.	
	Reception will previously have taken a deposit and credit amount via one of the previously mentioned forms of payment to use against transactions placed on account.	
	At the end of the guest's stay, the account will be paid either by cash or credit account or transferred to a sales ledger account.	
Sales ledger	Sales ledger accounts are set up as a form of credit for larger companies who wish to settle several bills centrally.	
	These accounts will be set up through the accounts department, who will consider the company's credit worthiness and amount of credit provided.	
	The organization will be sent a statement of all bills from that outlet at the end of each month (or once a month) and payment will be expected within 30 days of the date of the statement.	
Prepaid	It is possible that the bill has been prepaid by deposit for a special occasion or event. The organizer must determine the exact number of customers prior to the event and track the numbers that attend. Prepayment/deposit is offset against the final bill.	
	Any balance will need to be settled by the guests present (using any of the above forms of payment) or billed to the organizer through the sales ledger.	

DIFFERENT TYPES OF SYSTEMS USED FOR PAYMENT

In most hospitality outlets there are two forms of 'system' used to obtain payment from the customer.

The first is where an organization will use a central cashier. Features of this include:

- One central cashier for the whole outlet. This may even include the reception desk in a hotel or a cashier in a restaurant
- Each department (in a hotel) will put through a variety of transactions based on the facilities used by the guest – these will go through to the guest's room account and is done using electronic key cards or signatures from the guest.

■ Alternatively a waiter or bar person may put transactions through to a table number.

■ Once the guest is ready to leave the outlet or hotel a bill will be generated by the cashier and the guest will either go the cashier to make payment, or the bill will be taken to the guest and payment obtained.

■ Why use a cashier?

   – It can help to avoid walkouts – see below.

   – In a busy outlet it means there is one person whose main role is to ensure that all guests have paid their bills, thereby leaving the rest of the team to focus on customer service skills and quality of service and product.

■ Why not use a cashier?

   – It can be one more salary to consider – expensive.

   – Deferral of responsibility from the staff to the cashier which can lead to blame if mistakes are made, e.g. 'It's not my fault!'

Taking orders using an electronic device

THE CASHIER'S ROLE

✓ Issue check pads to the waiting staff prior to a meal period.

✓ Check the pricing of each menu item and ensure that the point of sale is kept up-to-date in relation to this information.

✓ Receive and check money or credit, to gain signatures for payment.

✓ Ensure each transaction/table/check is paid for and generate a missing checks list that the staff can monitor and ensure payment is taken.

✓ Complete the sales control sheet that details the revenue received is recorded under headings that include cash, cheques, credit card transactions, etc. Check that the revenue matches sales taken in terms of food, beverage, etc. May also include information in relation to number of covers, average spend.

✓ Complete the necessary paying-in slips for cash and cheques, either direct to a bank or through the head cashier's office.

The second system is where the individual member of staff is responsible for gathering payments for all transactions. This is the norm and most commonly found in bars and restaurants. How does it work?

■ The member of staff takes the customer's order.

■ Delivers their order.

■ Generates the bill once the customer has requested it.

■ Ensures safe payment is made for the transaction.

PROBLEMS IDENTIFIED WITH USING A MANUAL SYSTEM/INDIVIDUAL MEMBERS OF STAFF:

✓ Number of transactions taking place on a daily basis.

✓ Control of the operation.

✓ Poor handwriting on checks can lead to incorrect order/incorrect prices.

✓ Poorly presented bill.

✓ Human error can lead to wrongly calculated bill, wrong prices charged, incorrect service charge and taxes.

✓ Communication between departments has to be done physically and takes the frontline staff away from providing the best possible customer service.

✓ Manual systems don't provide quick management information.

✓ High cost of labour involved to provide the same level of management information.

Cashing up the till at the end of the shift/day

Before the money is banked at the end of the day, the till must be 'cashed up'. This means that sales must be reconciled (matched) with payments. If not enough actual money has been taken for the sales reported, then this can mean one of several errors has taken place:

1 Not all the cash has been collected from paying customers.

2 Not all the credit card payments have gone through the till/credit card machine (PDQ).

3 Too many sales have been recorded and not voided.

Process to follow when cashing up the till

1 Print out a 'z' report/reading – this will detail all the sales for that shift/day, plus how the sales were received in terms of payment, i.e. cash, cheque, credit card, sales ledger accounts.

2 Remove the float from the till – if you have a float of £100 to start the day then this should be taken out of the till before you begin any further reconciliation.

3 On a pre-prepared form that should list what the 'z' reading says in one column, followed by a further column that reads what you actually have, you should now count all your monies.

4 First, count the remaining cash after the float has been removed. Compare this to the 'z' reading and record any discrepancies in the third column.

5 Next, check the credit card readings from the PDQ machine. Compare these to the 'z' reading and record any discrepancies in the third column.

 ACTIVITY

What other reasons can you think of to explain why sales may not match to payments?

 TIP

You should use as much change as possible to make up the float at the end of the day/shift. This will save you ordering more change from the bank or being short of change for the next shift.

6   Count your vouchers next and record these. Again, compare these to the 'z' reading and record any discrepancies in the third column.

7   Record your sales ledger total from the 'z' reading, and then add up the signed receipts you have from those who requested to pay on their account. Receipts should match the 'z' reading.

8   Now add up your totals from the 'z' reading in column one, add up the totals from actual payments, add up the discrepancies.

9   Your company will have given you a guideline to what an acceptable discrepancy is, if you are outside this boundary then you will need to go back through your cashing up. Where should you look for the discrepancies?

  a   Check you counted the float correctly.

  b   Check you counted the remaining cash correctly.

  c   Check the till drawer to make sure no money was left in there or is trapped in the workings of the till.

  d   Check your credit card readings.

  e   Check your sales ledger readings again.

10 If you still can't find the discrepancies, ensure the duty manager is aware of the discrepancy and ask him/her to check. Then ask the accounts department to come and help or leave a message for them to check it the next day.

TIP

If signed receipts don't match the 'z' reading, this could imply that payment was incorrectly recorded. It could also mean that if the company queries the amounts posted to the sales ledger account and there isn't signed proof, then they could refuse to pay for that item on the statement.

TIP

When you cash up at the end of a shift, you are often tired. It can be difficult to find the discrepancies then. At this stage, leave a message for the finance team to check it for you.

When they come in the next day they can usually find the mistakes very quickly and easily, because they are trained to look for them.

They can also check with the bank to make sure you counted the cash correctly.

Cashing Up Slip Dated _____

Employee Name: _____
Shift: AM/PM

Cheques & Cash:		
Cheques	_____	
100 Pounds	_____	
50 Pounds	_____	
20 Pounds	_____	
10 Pounds	_____	
5 Pounds	_____	
2 Pound coins	_____	
1 Pound coins	_____	
50 pence coins	_____	
20 pence coins	_____	
10 pence coins	_____	
5 pence coins	_____	
1 & 2 pence coins	_____	
Total Cheques & Cash	_____	POUNDS
Less Starting Float	(_____)	POUNDS
(A) Cheques & cash to Deposit	_____	POUNDS
Cash Receipts	_____	POUNDS
(Discrepancies) Cash Over (Short)	_____	POUNDS

(B) Credit Card charges – TOTAL:	_____	POUNDS
(C) Credit Card tips – TOTAL:	_____	POUNDS
Declared tips – TOTAL	_____	POUNDS
SALES TOTAL (A + B) :	_____	POUNDS

BANK DEPOSIT:		
Cheques & Cash to deposit **(A)** – TOTAL:	_____	POUNDS
Less Credit Card tips **(C)** – TOTAL	(_____)	POUNDS
DEPOSIT TOTAL (A - C) :	_____	POUNDS

Employee Signature _____

A cashing up sheet

ACTIVITY

In a work environment that you are familiar with, ask if you can watch them cashing up a till.

■ Note the procedures they follow and how they may differ from the example above.

■ Ask what they do in a case where there may be discrepancies.

■ Ask how they bank the money – i.e. do they use a security firm or do they bank the money themselves at the local bank? What security measures do they have in place to secure the banking of the money?

■ Now you have viewed how they do it, ask if you can have a go at cashing up a till, while they watch you.

Watch out for forged notes!

AVOIDING 'WALKOUTS'

Walkouts are when customers leave the outlet without having paid their bill.

Why does this happen? There are three types of walkout:

■ Premeditated: the customer came in to the organization, used the facilities and never had any intention of paying the bill. They will have come up with a plan for leaving the organization without paying, either before they came in or during their visit.

■ Accidental: the customer didn't mean to walkout without paying, they just did. Maybe they forgot, e.g. elderly people, stressed people, distracted people, etc.

■ Chancers: the customer came into the organization with every intention of paying the bill but found an opportunity to be able to walk out without paying – maybe because the service staff were distracted, too busy to monitor, or because the customer wanted the thrill of trying to avoid payment.

 ACTIVITY

What are the signs that the customer may be considering not paying their bill??

They all go off to the toilet in penny numbers and take their bags/coats.

Now think of some other examples.

HOW CAN YOU AVOID WALKOUTS?

✓ Keep alert to the customer and their behaviour.

✓ Keep alert to the customer towards the end of the meal.

✓ Don't look as though you are stressed or too busy.

✓ Make it your business to keep an eye out for payment.

✓ When they have asked for the bill and it has been presented, keep an eye on them for making payment, putting a card down ready. Do not get distracted. How many times have you gone for a meal and then had to wait ages to sort out payment when you are ready to leave or need to be at the next place, e.g. theatre or nightclub?

✓ Bars frequently take your credit card and lock it up securely as part of your 'tab', to ensure you go back and settle the bill.

1 *A bar tab system*

2 *Remove drawer from stack*

3 *Open up and slot card in*

4 *Close drawer and pull out ticket*

5 *Hand ticket to customer*

Assessment of knowledge and understanding

You have now learned about the types of payment available for paying bills, some of the security issues relating to payments and handling cash and the set-up of cashier systems and payment of bills.

To test your level of knowledge and understanding, answer the following short questions. These will help to prepare you for your summative (final) assessment.

Project 1

1 How can you avoid walkouts?

_____

2 How should you set up your payment point in the outlet where you work?

_____

3 What is the correct procedure for handling payment?

_____

4 What should you do if there are any errors with payments? For example, what should you do if the credit card cannot be accepted or is rejected by the PDQ?

_____

5 What other types of problems might you come across while receiving payment for a bill?

_____

6 How should you handle these?

_____

7 For example, what should you do if a customer is contesting the fact that they did not eat or drink some of the items that are detailed on the bill?

_____

8 What might happen if you don't report errors to your supervisor or manager?

_____

Project 2

You should now ask your assessor to evaluate you based on completing the following tasks.

1 Enter information into the payment point correctly.

2 Tell the customer how much they have to pay.

3 Acknowledge the customer's payment and validate it where necessary.

4 Put the payment in the right place according to your organization's procedures.

5 Give correct change.

6 Carry out transactions without delay and give relevant confirmation to the customer.

15

Prepare and clear the bar and drinks service area

Unit 513 Prepare and clear areas for drinks service

1DS1.1 Prepare customer and service areas

1DS1.2 Clear customer and service areas

1DS1.3 Clean and store glassware

Unit 611 Prepare and clear bar area

2DS1.1 Prepare customer and service areas

2DS1.2 Clear customer and service areas

2DS1.3 Clean and store glassware

What do I need to do?

- Set up the bar area for service.
- Clean and set up the customer areas for service.
- Ensure that all the glassware is prepared and safely stored.

What do I need to know?

- The different types of stock needed within a bar.
- The different service equipment needed within a bar.
- The different types of electrical equipment that would be behind a bar.
- How to clean and handle glassware correctly.

Information covered in this chapter
- ■ Types of bar
- ■ Equipment needed
- ■ Glasses
- ■ Fridges and ice machines

KEY WORDS

Bar
A place where alcoholic and non-alcoholic beverages are sold and served.

Draught
A drink that is dispensed directly from a tap.

Spirits
A generic term for alcohol that is typically 37 to 50 per cent alcohol per volume.

Cocktail
A term used for a drink mixed from two or more alcoholic beverages.

INTRODUCTION

There are many different types of bar, each contains slightly different equipment depending on what and who they serve. As with all other types of food and beverage establishment the better prepared a bar is prior to service the better and faster it can dispense drinks. It is important that all areas are set up and broken down correctly and that all equipment and accompaniments are prepared correctly.

DIFFERENT TYPES OF BAR

There are several different types of bar from which drinks are sold and served:

- ■ Public bar or pub: In which customers are served across a counter.
- ■ Lounge bar: In which customers are served by waiting staff.
- ■ Cocktail bar: In which alcoholic drinks are mixed to order for customers.
- ■ Wine bar: Where the bar specializes in offering a wide selection of wine served both by the glass and in bottles.

A typical bar

■ Dispense bar : Which prepares drinks for waiters to serve in a restaurant environment.

DRINKS STOCK

Bottled stock

Bottled stock includes bottles of beer, wines and pre-mixed alcoholic and non-alcoholic drinks. When produced, all except for wine will have a sell-by date on the label or cap. When restocking a bar with these products it is important that the closest date is served first. This means that during restocking, all existing stock must be taken off the shelf and the new stock put at the back of the shelf.

All stock that is sold in bottles or cans must be wiped with a clean damp cloth prior to being put on a shelf. This is not only to ensure that any visible dust or dirt is removed, but also to make sure any chemical or bacterial contaminants are removed.

The majority of bottled stock should be stored in refrigerators to chill them prior to service. In order for the stock to chill sufficiently for service it is advisable to restock the fridges either as early in the morning as possible or at the end of the evening shift.

 TIP

If any bottled stock has leaked or had its cap removed or interfered with, do not serve it.

Give it to the manager to return to the wholesaler.

Draught stock

Draught stock includes beers, ciders and some soft drinks. The alcoholic drinks are sold in measures of pints or half-pints.

Drinks served by optics

In public houses the drinks served from the optics are generally the house brands, those which are most commonly served. Some bars do not use optics but prefer that all their spirits are poured.

Drinks served by measures and pourer

This depends on the type of bar. In a cocktail bar spirits are generally 'free poured' whereas in a public house, wine bar or lounge bar the spirits and wines are all measured.

STOCK ROTATION

At the beginning and end of each shift or service the bar stock will have to be replenished from a store. This is to ensure that as each service commences all the items on the bar list and wine list are available for the customers to order.

Rotation of stock is the term used to ensure that the stock is used in order and that which is sold is fit for consumption. On all bottled products and cartons there will be a 'sell-by' date which is used to identify which items must be used first. In order to successfully rotate stock the original stock must be taken off the shelves, the new stock should then be placed at the back of the shelves. Then the original stock is put at the front of the shelves ready for use first.

SERVICE EQUIPMENT

The cocktail shaker

Shakers are used when it is necessary to really mix ingredients well. To use, place the ice into the shaker, add the ingredients, place the parts together and shake. When shaking drinks, ensure that two hands are used and that the shaker is held so that all parts are in contact to stop the shaker coming apart during shaking and the contents coming out.

A cocktail shaker

A Boston shaker

There are two basic types of shaker:

Boston shaker

Consists of two cones, one which is placed inside the other. These shakers are quick and easy to use. Usually one cone is made of glass, the other of stainless steel.

Standard shaker

Three-piece utensil, usually made entirely of stainless steel. The top part has a strainer 'in-built' into it (a Hawthorn strainer can still be used if the lid and middle part are removed and the Hawthorn strainer placed over the base part).

Mixing glasses

The mixing glass

This is like a glass jug with no handle. It is used for mixing clear drinks which do not contain juice or cream.

The strainer

The most popular is a Hawthorn strainer. This is a flat, spoon-like utensil with a spring coiled round its head. Used in conjunction with a cocktail shaker and mixing glass to hold back ice after the drink has been prepared.

The Hawthorn strainer

Bar spoon

This is a long-handled spoon with a twisted shaft and a flat muddler end. The muddler end can be used to crush sugar, mint, etc. when making cocktails.

The bar spoon

Bar liquidizer or blender

There is a wide range of these available. Variable speed controls can be useful. Liquidizers are best used for preparing drinks that require fruit to be puréed. These are used for blended cocktails.

Bar trays: These can be either made of stainless steel or plastic. All drinks should be served on trays and all glasses should be carried on trays.

A blender

IMAGE COURTESY OF WWW.DRINKSTUFF.COM

Bar equipment

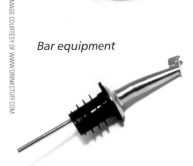

Ice crusher: This is used to crush ice for cocktails.

Ice buckets: These are in a variety of sizes, some are used to contain ice that go into drinks from behind the bar. Some are used to keep white wine cold during service.

Jugs and pitchers: These can vary in size depending on what is required. Large pitchers may be used for jugs of Pimms, small jugs would be needed for a customer to add water to their whisky.

Pourers: These are placed on top of bottles to control and direct how much is poured into a drink.

Speedrails: These are attached to the bar and hold the main spirits that are used during the service.

Bar mats: These are placed on the bar and can be made of rubber, plastic, metal or cloth. They are used to soak up any drips or minor spills that may occur.

Condiment holder: This can vary in size and shape and is used to hold lemon slices, lime wedges and any other condiments that are needed.

Muddler: This is used to crush fruit or ice for specific cocktails.

Glass rimmer: This contains sugar or salt to stick around the rim of a glass.

Swizzle stick: A stick served in a drink for the customer to stir their own drink.

Drip trays: These are normally held under beer pumps to catch drips from pouring drinks.

Tip trays: In some bars these are used to give the customers their bill and their change.

Till, printer and credit card machine: In order to process orders accurately and count bills it is essential that these are in full working order and are maintained through the service.

Zester: This is used to remove small amounts of citrus peel for garnish for cocktails.

DRINKS ACCOMPANIMENTS

Traditionally there are accompaniments that must be served with certain drinks. More recently with the upsurge in cocktail bars and less traditional public houses, drinks accompaniments have become more sophisticated.

DRINKS ACCOMPANIMENTS

GARNISH	SERVICE
Lemon slices or wedges	These should be placed into the glass prior to pouring the drink on to it as their purpose is to enhance the flavour of the drink.
Orange slices	These should be placed into the glass prior to pouring the drink on to it as their purpose is to enhance the flavour of the drink.
Olives	A single olive can be added to a martini.
Onions	Onions skewered on a cocktail stick can be added to a martini.
Lemon/orange peel	Some cocktails ask for orange peel or lemon peel, this is made by using a small sharp knife and taking a small slice from the very top layer of peel.
Lemon/orange/lime zest	Using a zester a thin strip of peel is removed and used as a garnish in a cocktail.
Coffee beans	Some cocktails.
Ice	Drinking or potable water that has been frozen into either blocks or chips to help chill drinks.
Cherries	Maraschino cherries are used to garnish some cocktails.

GLASSES

There are many different sizes and shapes of glasses which are used in bars. Some are used to improve the flavour or aroma of a drink, for example a brandy balloon helps the aroma of the brandy to be appreciated by the drinker. Some glasses are specific sizes to ensure that the size of the measure is correct, this can be seen by pint and half-pint glasses where the glasses themselves are a legal measure for beers and ciders.

Various glasses

> **! REMEMBER**
>
> If a glass breaks it is imperative to ensure that it is swept up and disposed of safely. Never put broken glass in a plastic bin liner, always place it in a cardboard box, and seal it before placing it in the bin.

A glass washer

IMAGE COURTESY OF WWW.KCM-CATERING-EQUIPMENT.CO.UK

Glass washers

Glass washers can vary immensely in size depending on the size and type of operation. They work by first rinsing the glasses then using commercial glass wash and hot water in excess of 80°C to wash and rinse them. The glasses are then steamed dry.

In order for glass washers to work effectively they need a good supply of water and the correct quantities of glass wash need to be used. They should be emptied and cleaned at the end of every session.

Once the glasses have been washed they need to be polished as watermarks will have been left on the glass during the drying process.

> **✓ TIP**
>
> Always use a plastic container for boiling water, as you are less likely to burn yourself and the glasses are less likely to get chipped.

Glasses need to be washed after use and polished prior to use. Glasses can either be washed by hand or by machine.

CHECKLIST FOR POLISHING GLASSES

✓ Fill plastic jug or container with boiling water.

✓ Using a clean dry cotton glass cloth, lift glass by the base or stem and hold over steam for a few seconds.

✓ Wipe entire glass including base and stem.

✓ Hold glass up to light to check for smears or marks left.

✓ Place glass on tray or shelf in readiness for service.

Storing glasses

Glass is a delicate substance and it is important to store glasses correctly. Not only can they break and perhaps injure either a member of staff or a customer, they can also be expensive to replace.

Racks

There are several different methods of storing glassware for use in a bar:

- *Shelving*: These need to be made of a non-porous material. On top of the shelving plastic mesh is used to prevent the glasses becoming chipped or cracked. Glasses need to be stacked or placed carefully on shelves.
- *Racks*: These are square plastic crates that are divided into sections so that tall glasses can be held up. The crates can then be stacked up one upon another and can be stored like this.

 ACTIVITY

Have a look at the different types of glasses in the photograph on page 195 and consider how they should be stored safely.

REFRIGERATORS AND ICE MACHINES

Bar refrigerators are used to chill drinks items. Many drinks have their flavour improved by being chilled. It is important to remember that it can take several hours to chill bottles of wine, therefore restocking should be done at the end of the previous shift rather than at the beginning of a shift.

Bar refrigerators are specifically made to hold bottles safely and to ease service. Some refrigerators fit under the counter and are accessed from the front. Some are accessed from on top and others are full height. Items that need to be chilled include white wines, beers and many soft drinks including bottled water.

Bartender – complete bar

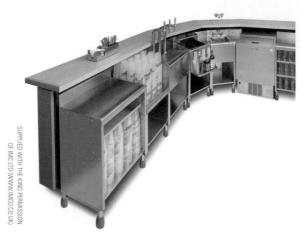

Bar (with glasses)

Bar refrigerators need to operate at about 8°C. If they are too cold the liquids in the bottles could freeze and expand and the bottle could become damaged. If the refrigerator becomes too warm this will affect the drinks and they will not be served at the correct temperature.

Refrigerators need to be kept clean internally and if not emptied and cleaned regularly a build-up of dirt can form, which may cause damage internally. The outside of refrigerators must be kept free of dust and there must be good ventilation to ensure that there is adequate air supply to the vents.

Ice machines also differ in size and shape. Ice machines can produce different amounts of ice per hour and different sizes and shapes of ice. How much ice an establishment needs will determine what size of machine is present.

Ice machines need to have a supply of clean drinking water to produce ice. The also have a space in the bottom of the machine for the storage of ice cubes. It is essential that this area is kept clean and only plastic scoops are used to get ice out of the machine.

Ice machines

SERVICE AREAS

Prior to service the bars need to be set up to ensure that during service the bartender is prepared. These areas need to be kept clean as they are considered as food preparation areas under the Food Hygiene Regulations 2006.

AREAS THAT NEED TO BE CHECKED PRIOR TO SERVICE

✓ All the shelving and counters need to be wiped down using a damp cloth.

✓ The garnishes need to be prepared and stored in preparation for service.

✓ All glassware should be checked for cracks and chips and be polished ready for use.

✓ Bin liners need to be put in bins.

✓ Fill up ice containers.

✓ Prepare napkins, straws, cocktail sticks.

✓ Make sure that optics and measures are ready for service, this is vital not only for service but also for compliance with the Weights and Measures Act 1985.

✓ Prepare all equipment for use.

✓ Wipe the bar trays.

The bar must look professional at all times and it is imperative that no debris is left on top of the bar. From a customer's perspective how a bar looks is a reflection of the service that is given.

STEP-BY-STEP: POLISHING GLASSES

1 *Use boiling water and a clean tea towel*

2 *Hold the glass over the water until it fills with steam*

3 *Wipe glasses vigorously with the clean tea towel to remove any marks*

CUSTOMER AREAS

Customer service areas need to be kept clean. Floors should be swept, vacuumed or washed daily. All tables and chairs should be cleaned and tables should be polished. All drinks and bar menus should be clean and checked.

Assessment of knowledge and understanding

You have now learned about the responsibilities you have to prepare and clear customer service areas and to clean and store glassware. This will enable you to ensure your own positive actions contribute effectively towards the whole team.

To test your level of knowledge and understanding, answer the following short questions. These will help to prepare you for your summative (final) assessment.

Preparing for assessment checklist

■ List the different types of bar.

_____

_____

Project 1

1 Choose a type of bar and write a checklist on the duties that need to be carried out prior to opening the bar.

_____

_____

2 Write a checklist for the closing duties for that bar.

_____

_____

Project 2

1 What actions would need to be taken if a glass is broken?

_____

_____

2 List the actions to take if a refrigerator full of bar stock breaks down prior to service.

_____

_____

16

Serve alcoholic and soft drinks

What do I need to do?

- Learn about the different products available in a bar.
- Understand how to take a drinks order.
- Know how to measure alcoholic beverages correctly.
- Prepare a range of alcoholic and soft drinks.
- Maintain the drinks area during service.
- Serve customers in the correct manner.

What do I need to know?

- Understand the law regarding the sale and service of alcohol.
- Understand the different methods of how alcohol is made.
- The main different types of alcoholic beverages.

Information covered in this chapter

- Licensing legislation.
- Alcohol awareness.
- How alcohol is made.
- Description of different spirits, liqueurs and beers.
- Mixers and soft drinks.
- Taking drinks orders.
- Common drinks orders.
- Accompaniments and garnishes.

KEY WORDS

Weights and Measures Act
The legislation concerning the size of drinks that can be poured and the alcoholic strength.

Liqueurs
Sweetened alcoholic beverage.

Alcohol
A beverage that is intoxicating.

Spirits
A liquid that has a strong alcoholic content as it has been distilled.

INTRODUCTION

Many people think that working or running a bar is an ideal job, combining work and a social life. When working in a bar there are many things to learn and remember, first the law concerning the sale of alcohol which is very strict and needs to be adhered to at all times.

A bartender or bar manager needs to remember that they have a moral responsibility to their customers to ensure that they do not harm or injure themselves. Therefore awareness of how people react to alcohol is important.

Then there are the bar products themselves. A bartender needs to understand how the drinks that he will sell are made and have a good working knowledge of the stock that he has available, both alcoholic and non-alcoholic.

Finally, the bartender must be able to take an order effectively and prepare the drinks for the customers.

LEGISLATION

Weights and Measures

Measures are government-stamped and conform to legal requirements regarding weights and measures legislation. The Weights and Measures Act 1985 is a piece of consumer legislation that determines the size, weight and quantity of specific alcoholic beverages.

When serving standard drinks, measures must be used (these are currently 25 ml for a standard spirit, or multiples thereof – for example, a double measures 50 ml). When making cocktails or mixing drinks, it is not always necessary to use measures but a specific licence is needed for this.

All alcoholic drinks must be served in appropriate measures. These are:

Thimble measures

- ■ Spirits are sold in 25 ml measures (or multiples thereof e.g. 50 ml).
- ■ Liqueurs are sold in 50 ml measures.
- ■ Liqueur wines/fortified wines are served in 50 ml measures.
- ■ Vermouths are sold in 50 ml measures.
- ■ Wines are usually sold in 125 or 175 ml glasses.
- ■ Draught beers are sold in pints or ½ pints.

To measure accurately use a single measure and to give a double, pour two measures into a glass or use a double measure. Always ensure that the measure is full to the top (failure to do this would mean that the guest would not receive the full measure and this contravenes the Weights and Measures Act 1985). Do not, however, over-fill the measure as this will lead to using too much drink stock and will also contravene the Weights and Measures Act 1985.

 TIP

If you are in any doubt about the size of a measure to give a customer, check with your supervisor first.

Do not guess!

TYPE OF ALCOHOLIC BEVERAGE AND ALCOHOLIC CONTENT

TYPE OF ALCOHOLIC BEVERAGE	ALCOHOLIC CONTENT
Spirits	The alcohol level of spirits can vary, but they are typically 37 to 50 per cent alcohol per volume. This means that for any given amount of the drink, 37 to 50 per cent of the drink is alcohol.
Liqueurs	Typical alcohol levels are 17 to 45 per cent alcohol per volume. Although the alcohol level is less than most spirits, liqueurs are served in larger 50 ml measures, or multiples thereof.

TYPE OF ALCOHOLIC BEVERAGE	ALCOHOLIC CONTENT
Liqueur wines (fortified wines)	The correct European Union (EU) term for these wines is liqueur wines. These are in fact wines that have been fortified by the addition of alcohol. The alcohol level of these is typically 18 to 35 per cent volume.
Wine	The alcohol level of wine is from 8 to 15 per cent volume (most wines are 10 to 13.5 per cent volume). The measure to be used is 125 ml or 175 ml.
Beers and lagers	These are served from bottles or draught and must be chilled. The typical alcohol levels of beers and lagers are 2 to 8 per cent volume.

Various bottles

Licensing legislation

There are legal restrictions concerning the age that people can be on licensed premises and served alcoholic drinks. Following are some key points that must be borne in mind when serving drinks. The most recent piece of legislation, The Licensing Act 2003, made the law surrounding the sale of alcohol clearer.

WHO MAY BE SERVED ALCOHOL INCLUDE

✓ 16 years and older: May purchase beer, porter, cider or perry with a meal in an eating area on licensed premises.

✓ Under 18 years old: May not purchase or be supplied with or consume alcohol in a bar on licensed premises during permitted hours.

✓ Over 18 years old: May purchase alcohol on licensed premises during permitted hours.

Other responsibilities

Under The Licensing Act 2003 a licensee and/or his/her representative, such as an employee carrying out his duties as part of his/her employment, has responsibilities such as:

■ Taking reasonable care to ensure that persons buying alcoholic drinks are 18 years of age or over.

■ Ensuring that the licensed premises are not used by working prostitutes.

■ Taking reasonable precautions to ensure that alcohol is not misused and that no-one who is drunk is served.

■ Taking all appropriate steps to ensure that drugs are not sold on licensed premises.

■ That there must be a licence in place prior to any alcohol being served or sold.

■ The Act also, in some instances, removed the need for specific closing times to be adhered to.

 ACTIVITY

If you were working behind a bar how would you ask someone to leave who had consumed too much drink?

Trade Descriptions Act 1968

Under the Trade Descriptions Act 1968, drinks must be described appropriately to guests. For example, if a guest requests a gin and tonic, then the house gin and tonic can be served. If a guest requests a specific brand of gin and tonic, then this must be the one served. Where the type of gin and tonic requested by the guest are not sold in that establishment, then the guest must be made aware of this and offered alternatives.

The above list is not exhaustive but merely identifies some of the major responsibilities of bar staff on licensed premises.

ALCOHOL AWARENESS

What is alcohol?

Alcohol is obtained from a natural process called fermentation. Yeasts feed on sugars in the beverage and convert them into alcohol and carbon dioxide (for most drinks the carbon dioxide is allowed to escape).

The sugars in the beverage that the yeast converts into alcohol are derived from a variety of sources including grapes, apples and berries, sugar cane, agave (tequila) as well as cereals and grains such as wheat, maize and barley.

Safe consumption levels

Medical advice from the government gives the following levels of consumption for men and women:

- Men 21 units per week
- Women 14 units per week

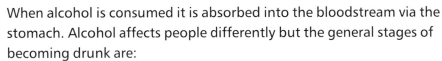

A UNIT OF ALCOHOL IS EQUIVALENT TO:

✓ Half-pint (284 ml) of ordinary strength lager, beer or cider, generally 3.5 per cent volume.

✓ 25 ml spirit (40 per cent ABV).

✓ 175 ml glass of wine at 9 per cent ABV.

ABV = alcohol by volume

Sensible appreciation of alcohol

When alcohol is consumed it is absorbed into the bloodstream via the stomach. Alcohol affects people differently but the general stages of becoming drunk are:

- Stage 1: Happy (relaxed, talkative and sociable).
- Stage 2: Excited (erratic and emotional, movement and thinking affected).
- Stage 3: Confused (disorientated, loud, out of control).
- Stage 4: Lethargic (unable to stand, talk or walk).

It is the legal and moral responsibility of licensees to ensure that guests do not become drunk whilst on their premises. It is important to look out for signs of drunkenness and to deal with them accordingly.

Dealing with drunken guests

Prevention is the best way of dealing with drunkenness!

TIP

Different wines, beers and spirits have different levels of alcohol percentages. It is important to consider the alcohol level when serving different drinks to guests and also when using them as part of cocktails. Always check the label for the ABV.

TIP

Look out for the following signs of drunkenness:

Aggression
Carelessness with money
Drowsiness
Slurred words
Clumsiness
Vacant expression and loss of train-of-thought

DEALING WITH DRUNKEN GUESTS:

✓ Be aware of how much drink guests have consumed.

✓ Tactfully and politely engage guests in conversation to assess their level of mental alertness.

✓ If a guest seems drunk, notify your manager immediately.

✓ If directed by your manager to not serve any more drinks then ensure that this is communicated to the guest in a polite and tactful manner. Expressions such as 'You are drunk' are best avoided as they can be perceived as confrontational.

✓ Always inform your manager if you are having difficulties with guests.

✓ Always stay in control and do not argue with the guest.

✓ If the guest is part of a group it may be possible to enlist the help of others in the group.

HOW ALCOHOL IS MADE

Alcohol is made by converting sugar to ethanol in a liquid using yeast. It is a chemical process and when being produced for public consumption needs to be controlled.

Alcoholic drinks are made by three different methods:

- Beer is made by a method called brewing.
- Wine is made by a method called fermentation.
- Spirits are made by a method called distillation.

How beer is made – brewing

Brewing is the process by which starchy substances can be turned into alcohol. The raw material, usually barley, is steeped in water then allowed to germinate. This is called malting. The malt is then boiled, sometimes with hops, this is the brewing part of the process. The 'wort' as it is known is then fermented using yeast, this creates the alcohol. The beer can then be left in casks or tanks to mature, prior to bottling. The alcoholic strength of beer is about 5 per cent alcohol by volume (ABV).

Wine making – fermentation

Grapes are crushed to extract their juice. The juice is then fermented to produce alcohol. Fermentation occurs when sugar and yeast react in a liquid, with a little warmth, to produce alcohol and carbon dioxide, which is released. In order to control this process extra yeast can be added to create a stronger wine. By law, wine is only allowed to be between 8 per cent and 15 per cent alcohol by volume (ABV).

Making spirits – distillation

Distilled drinks are stronger than ordinary fermented drinks. To distil a drink, a fermented mixture is heated to a temperature between 70°C and 100°C, the alcohol vaporizes while the water remains liquid. This alcohol vapour is re-condensed (through cooling), to form a liquid high in alcoholic strength.

Distilled liquor is usually made from natural sugars such as honey, ripe fruit, sugar cane or any starchy substance, e.g. barley, which can be easily converted to sugar. Distilled drinks produce higher strength drinks than purely fermented drinks, and much of the original flavour is removed from the drink during distillation.

 ACTIVITY

Look through the list of spirits described in the following pages and identify which are distilled from:

- Barley
- Wheat
- Sugar
- Grapes

 TIP

If you taste dried juniper berries, this is the taste of gin.

Gin

Spirits

Gin

Gin is an alcoholic drink distilled from grain into which are infused aromatic plant products particularly oil of juniper. The two basic types are Dutch and British. Dutch gin (Genever), directly stems from medicinal compounds, evolved in the Netherlands in the sixteenth century. It is heavily aromatic and usually drunk neat and chilled. British dry gin, the universal style, originated in London in the 1870s. Much lighter in style and more popular than Genever it is used essentially as a versatile mixing spirit or in the classic martini cocktail.

Pastis/Pernod

Pastis is an aniseed-flavoured drink very popular in France. Originally these aperitifs contained wormwood, where the infamous absinthe got its drug-like properties and tendency to cause serious damage to the nervous system. After they were banned the producers switched the flavouring to aniseed and kept production going. The name *pastis* is from a French dialect word meaning 'confused' or mixed, a reference to the cloudy appearance of the drink when diluted with water.

Rum

A white or dark distilled spirit produced from sugar cane. Largely produced in the West Indies, Puerto Rico (Bacardi) and Jamaica are the predominant producers. All rums are distilled colourless, brown and dark rums are adjusted to their final colour by using caramel. Certain premium rums are matured in oak casks long enough to acquire some natural tint from the woods. Colour is, however, principally a matter of style as it has nothing to do with taste and only marginally with quality. White rum is best used in cocktails and punches with the daiquiris being the most common of all cocktails.

Tequila

This spirit is made in several Mexican states from the plant *agave tequilana*, a variety of cactus. The pulp of the plant is chopped up and baked to extract the sap. It is then shredded and pressed so that the juice runs out and begins to ferment. Some tequila is aged in wood, gaining colour. Tequila is drunk generally with salt and lime/lemon or in the margarita cocktail.

Tequila

Vermouths

These are aromatized wines made wherever wine is produced although commercial production began in Turin, Italy in the eighteenth century. A base wine is made and then this is fortified and flavoured with herbs and spices. Most often used as aperitifs or as an ingredient in cocktails but also very popular in cooking as it contains many different herbs suitable for adding flavour in sauces or even for poaching fish.

The following are different types of vermouth:

■ Martini: Can be Bianco (white), red (Rosso) or dry.

■ Noilly Prat: Bone dry.

■ Cinzano: Sweet white vermouth.

■ Dubonnet: Strong bitterness with contrasting sweetness.

■ Punt e Mes: Similar to Dubonnet with balanced sweetness and bitterness.

■ Lillet: Produced in Bordeaux and is a blend of fruit juice and a base wine and herbs.

Vodka

Vodka

A clear alcoholic drink made from grain, molasses, potatoes or various other vegetables that are available for distillation. It probably originated in Poland although the Russians dispute this and is now made in many countries including the UK. Vodka, a Russian word derived from *voda* (water) is a neutral spirit, basically has neither taste nor smell, although in recent years the British market has been offered premium brands such as Ketel One and Grey Goose which are made with a prominent flavour. There are also vodkas that have flavours added to them such as the Absolut vodkas made with lemons or pepper.

Blended whisky

Blended whiskies are a mixture of whisky made from malt and whisky made from corn. The higher the percentage of alcohol in malt whisky, the better the quality of the blend. Often the blend contains whisky from 50–60 different distilleries, and also whiskies which are different ages. Any which are produced purely in Scotland are referred to as Scotch, but it is also produced in America and Canada.

Whisky (blended)

Whisky (blended)

Malt whisky

Malt whiskies are made by steeping barley in water until it starts to sprout and then drying it, usually over peat, to give it a smoky flavour. The term single malt indicates that it is the product of one distillery. Single cask bottling indicates that all the whisky in that bottle has been matured in an individual barrel. Malt whiskies come from specific regions of Scotland: the Highlands, Lowlands, Islay and Campbelltown.

Malt whisky

Irish whiskey

It is thought that as Ireland contains the oldest distillery in the world, the Irish may have been the first to make whiskey. Whether this is true or not may never be confirmed, but there are two main whiskey-producing areas in Ireland, County Cork, where Jamesons is distilled, and County Antrim, where Bushmills is produced.

Irish whiskey

Rye whisky

An American whisky, produced and consumed mainly in Pennsylvania, Maryland and Canada. It is made from non-malted rye and barley or rye malt. It is not matured for as long as Scotch or Bourbon and it is most famous for being used as the main ingredient for the internationally popular Manhattan cocktail.

Bourbon

An American whisky named after Bourbon County in Kentucky. Bourbon is distilled from maize corn and malted rye and barley are added in varying quantities.It is aged in charred wooden barrels for at least two years before being bottled. Straight Bourbon has not been blended.

- Blended straight: A mixture of several bourbons.
- Blended: A mixture of straight bourbon and neutral alcohol.

Although most bourbon is drunk in south and west USA, it is gaining popularity in Europe and the UK.

Cognac/brandy

To be a cognac, a brandy must come from the region of Cognac, just north of Bordeaux, in France. Cognac is made from grapes, the residue of skins and stalks from the wine-making process. They are matured in oak barrels and all are blended. The cognac industry has a strict labelling system. Three-star or VS on a bottle means that the cognac has been matured in old oak barrels for at least two years. A label stating VSOP implies that the brandy has been matured for four years. The XO is a brandy which has been matured for over six years.

Armagnac

Armagnac is similar to brandy and is produced from grapes in the Armagnac region south-east of Bordeaux. Armagnac is rich and pungent in comparison to cognac and is generally produced from the Folle Blanche grape. Armagnac is matured in oak barrels made from young wood.

Eau de vie

A French term meaning 'water of life', it is the generic French term for all brandies. Cognac and Armagnac are produced in specific areas, and the same method of production is employed all over France, Germany and Switzerland. Eau de vie's are distilled from a variety of fruits.

Calvados

The most well-known eau de vie is Calvados which is distilled from apples and originates from Brittany and Normandy in Northern France.

Marc and grappa

Marc is the name for a brandy that has been distilled outside the regions of Cognac and Armagnac in France. Most wine-producing regions produce marcs and they have a more delicate flavour. The Italian version of marc is grappa and it is generally made by individual winemakers to avoid wasting any of the grape pulp. Good-quality grappa comes from a single grape variety and is matured in glass to retain its lightness and fruitiness.

Sherry

Sherry is a classic liqueur wine that is made in and around Jerez in the south of Andalucia. Sherry is a wine that has been fortified with alcohol during fermentation. There are many different styles and sub-styles of sherry of which fino, amontillado, manzanilla, oloroso and Pedro Ximenez, are included.

- Fino sherry is the finest and most delicate of all sherry styles.
- Amontillado sherry is an aged fino and is therefore darker with a dry, nutty flavour.
- Manzanilla is a style of sherry that is not produced in Jerez but aged in nearby Sanlucar de Barrameda. Manzanilla is extremely dry, almost bitter and has a very delicate bouquet.
- Oloroso is a style of sherry, and is very dark and sweet. There are further developed oloroso sherries, which have been slightly sweetened.
- Pedro Ximenez is a dessert wine from Jerez, which is made from sundried grapes. It is very dark and sweet and has a high sugar content with a concentrated grapey flavour.

Port

Port is fortified wine made from adding brandy to a wine to stop the fermentation of grape pulp and juice. The resulting wine is both sweet and high in alcohol. Although port-style wines are made in places as far apart as South Africa, Australia and California, European law restricts the use of the term 'port' to wines from the closely defined area in the Douro Valley of Northern Portugal.

- White port: Is made from white grapes which are generally golden in colour. They are non-vintage and are sold at about two to three years old. It is normally sold as an aperitif and served chilled.

- Late bottled vintage: Is a wine from a single year, bottled between the fourth and sixth years after harvest. The traditional style is bottled without filtration or treatment, so that like a vintage port it will throw a sediment.

- Tawny port: The word tawny is applied to a confusingly wide range of different styles of port. In theory tawny implies a wine which has been aged in wood for so long, much longer than a ruby, that it loses colour and the wine takes on an amber brown or tawny hue.

  Aged tawny port is a port that has been left to age in wooden casks for six or more years, begins to take on a tawny colour and a soft silky character. Most of these tawny ports are bottled with an indication of age on the label. The terms 10, 20, 30 or over 40 years old seen on the labels are, however, approximations as tawny ports are blended from a number of years' produce. Aged tawny ports are made from the very best wines of the highest quality. They can also be drunk chilled.

- Vintage port: This is the most expensive style of port, it accounts for hardly one per cent of all port sold, yet it is the wine that receives probably the most attention and is one of the world's simplest wines to make. Wines from a single year, or vintage, are blended and bottled after spending between two or three years in wood. The quality of the fruit used in vintage port is one of the highest and 'quintas' only declare vintages when they feel that they have a sufficient quantity of the wine.

Port

Madeira

Madeira is a fortified wine from the island of the same name, off the Atlantic coast of North Africa. In addition to being fortified with brandy, madeira is heated for four or five months to create a wine of great character with a caramel tang.

Marsala

Marsala is a fortified wine produced in the Sicilian port of Marsala. It has a burnt sugar taste and is used predominantly in cooking.

Beers and stouts

Lager

Lager

The word lager is taken from the German word 'to store', and is a term used to describe any bottom-fermented beer. A bottom-fermented beer is one that is stored in casks, after its first fermentation, where the yeasts are left to work a second time. All pils and lagers are bottom-fermented; it makes the product softer and has more sparkle than traditional ales.

Pilsner means 'from Pilsen', which is a town located in Hungary. Pils is brewed in the same method as lager but uses a different type of malt to produce a lighter-coloured beer than a lager.

Ale

Ale is a type of beer brewed from barley malt with a top-fermenting brewer's yeast that ferments quickly, giving a sweet, full body and a fruity, and sometimes butter-like, taste. Most ale contains some herb or spice, usually hops, which imparts a bitter, herbal flavour and balances the malt sweetness. As an appellative ale means any top-fermented beverage made from malt. Traditionally ales are made in England and are served at room temperature rather than chilled like other beers.

Stout

Stout is a top-fermented beer made with highly roasted, malted barley and unmalted barley. The most well-known stout is Guinness which has a strong acrid, malty flavour and is thick and very dark. Draught Guinness is served by the can which has a release system to give it the pressure to form its creamy thick head.

Non-alcoholic lager

This product has been developed in recent years. Some contain small amounts of alcohol while others are completely alcohol-free.

Other spirits and liqueurs

Advocat

A liqueur made with beaten egg yolks, sugar and brandy served both before and after meals. The best-known brands are made in the Netherlands and are sometimes used in mixes, especially the Snowball when it is combined with lemonade.

Amaretto Di Saranno

An Italian liqueur flavoured with almonds, apricots and aromatic extracts.

Anisette

The flavour of the many liqueurs known as anisette or anise varies according to which seeds are used, aniseed or star anise. Well-known in France are the anisettes of Bordeaux (especially that of Marie Brizard), but most liqueur houses make a version of anisette.

Akvavit

A grain-based spirit flavoured with cumin, aniseed or fennel which has been manufactured in Scandinavia since the fifteenth century. Its name comes from the Latin 'aqua vitue' (water of life). It has a high alcoholic content, should be served very cold and can be stored in a freezer.

Archers or peach schnapps

A popular sweet drink made from a base spirit which is flavoured with peaches. It is an ingredient of the popular Bellini cocktail.

Apricot brandy

Apricot brandy is produced by infusing a brandy spirit base with apricot fruit.

Baileys

An Irish whiskey cream liqueur. Manufactured in Ireland from the late 1970s and usually served over ice.

Baileys

Benedictine

An amber-coloured herby French liqueur used primarily as a digestive. Dom Bernado Vincelli, an Italian Benedictine monk from the Old Abbey of Fecamp is accredited with first producing it. As homage to the monks he called it Benedictine and printed DOM (Deo Optimo Maximo, To God, most good, most great) on the bottle. Benedictine is based on 27 different plants and spices which are incorporated in what is still a secret formula at the distillery at Fecamp in Normandy.

Cachaça

A Brazilian spirit, distilled from sugar cane used almost solely for making Caiphini cocktail. (See Chapter 17, cocktail descriptions.)

Campari

This distinctive bitter drink is produced in Italy and has a wide range of uses in cocktails. It is generally drunk as an aperitif with soda or orange juice. It is also used in the famous Negroni cocktail. (See Chapter 17, cocktail descriptions.)

Curaçao

A liqueur based on sweet or bitter oranges. It was originally made from dried peel of the bitter oranges from the island of Curaçao on the west coast of Venezuela. It is now made by many liqueur houses and is often sold as triple sec. Curaçao is used in various cocktails and also in cooking, most notably in crepe suzette.

Chartreuse

A herb liqueur made according to a very ancient recipe by the Carthusian monks at Voiron, near Grenoble. The composition of Chartreuse is a secret but it is known that it is prepared from various plants and herbs, including balm, hyssop, angelica leaves, cinnamon bark, mace and saffron. It is produced as either green or yellow.

Cherry brandy

Cherry brandy is the term normally applied to cherry liqueurs and is produced by infusing the base spirit with cherries.

Cointreau

Very similar to curaçao and triple sec but has evolved to become one of the most popular liqueurs in the world. Made exclusively from oranges from the island of Bali it is usually drunk over ice or used in cocktails.

Cremes

Cremes are a sweet liqueur with a syrupy consistency. Cremes are obtained by soaking various substances in brandy or spirit containing sugar syrup i.e. blackcurrants, bananas etc. Some popular cremes are Bananes (banana), Cacao (white and brown), Cassis (blackcurrant), Framboise (raspberry), Menthe (mint, white and green), Mure (blackberries).

Drambuie

A scotch whisky-based liqueur that can be drunk anytime. Its formula is the property of the Mackinnon family, who keep it a secret. The origin of the name apparently comes from the Gaelic expression *an dram buidheach* (the liqueur that satisfies). Drambuie although not known in continental Europe is very popular in the US.

Frangelica

A sweet aromatic liqueur made from hazelnuts from Italy.

Fernet Branca

A strongly flavoured Amaro/digestive from Italy. It is made from herbs, flowers and spices and is reckoned to aid digestion.

Galliano

This liqueur is golden in colour and tastes flowery, spicy with a tinge of vanilla. Galliano was named after an Italian war hero. It most commonly features in a Harvey Wallbanger cocktail. (See Chapter 17, cocktail descriptions.)

Grand Marnier

A cognac-based liqueur flavoured with oranges that has been produced and marketed by the Marnier-Lapostolle family since 1880. Traditionally drunk after dinner and should always be served in a brandy balloon.

Kahlua

A coffee liqueur originating from Mexico. It is used in many cocktails or as an after dinner drink.

Kummel

A liqueur flavoured with caraway seeds probably first made in Holland in the sixteenth century. Today kummel is the speciality of Northern European countries. Some versions are served rather sweet and therefore on the rocks to make them more refreshing.

IMAGE COURTESY OF DIAGEO PLC

Pimms

Pimms

This is a uniquely English drink which is a gin-based drink called Pimms no 1. Pimms no 6 is a vodka-based version which is occasionally used.

Sambucca

A colourless Italian anisette. It is very popular in Rome where it is drunk 'con la mosca' (with the fly) meaning coffee beans are floated on top and lit releasing the coffee flavour through the drink.

Tia Maria

A coffee-flavoured rum liqueur from Jamaica. Normally served over ice.

✓ TIP

When first working in a bar try and learn what the most frequently asked for drinks are.

Triple Sec

An orange-flavoured liqueur very similar to Curaçao. It is used mostly in cocktails including the famous Margarita.

Soft drinks, juices and mixers

The term soft drink refers to drinks, often carbonated, that do not contain alcohol. 'Soft drink' specifies a lack of alcohol. Beverages like colas, sparkling water, iced tea, lemonade, squash and fruit punch are among the most common types of soft drinks, while hot chocolate, hot tea, coffee, milk, tap water, alcohol and milkshakes do not fall into this classification. Many carbonated soft drinks are optionally available in versions sweetened with sugars or with non-caloric sweeteners.

Juice is a liquid naturally contained in vegetable or fruit tissue. Juices may be supplied in concentrate form, often in tetrapaks or bottles and have a noticeably different taste from 'fresh-squeezed' versions. Juice should not be confused with a squash, which is usually an artificial juice to be diluted with water.

Popular juices include but are not limited to apple, orange, prune, lemon, grapefruit, pineapple, tomato, carrot, grape, strawberry, cherry, cranberry and pomegranate. It has become increasingly popular to combine a variety of fruits into single juice drinks and sell them in bars. Often combinations of freshly squeezed juices and carbonated drinks are used to form non-alcoholic cocktails.

TAKING DRINKS ORDERS

Within a bar or restaurant it is important that the customers can place their drinks orders quickly and that the drinks served are exactly what they asked for. One of the key areas for any successful bar employee is that they have good product knowledge prior to coming into contact with any customers. Before taking a drinks order the bartender or bar waiter must be aware of any beverages that are not available.

TAKING AN ORDER BEHIND A BAR

✓ If the bartender is busy with another customer he/she should make eye contact with the customer to acknowledge them.

✓ It is important when asking customers for their drinks orders that appropriate language is used.

✓ When the order is taken the bartender should repeat any queries that he may have.

✓ At this point the customers may be made aware of any special offers or deals that the establishment may be running. Alternatively the bartender could suggest or offer samples to the customer to encourage them to buy different products or brands.

✓ Once the order has been placed in full the bartender should put together the drinks order. The sequence that some of the items need to be made may need some consideration, for example if a draught beer with a head is left to sit while a cocktail is made the quality of the beer may be affected by the time the cocktail is complete.

✓ After the order is given to the customer the bill should be totalled up and the customer made aware of it.

✓ There may be different methods of payment that can be used and the bartender should be aware of them.

 ACTIVITY

Have a look on-line at some bar and restaurant drinks lists:

■ Which drinks do you know how to make already?

■ What products have you not heard of before?

TAKING AN ORDER FROM A CUSTOMERS' TABLE

✓ The procedure is similar to the one above but the bar waiter takes the order and relays the order to the bartender to produce the drinks specified.

✓ The bar waiter then brings the drinks ordered to the customers' table and serves each one individually to the customers.

✓ Sometimes the billing for this procedure can be done by the customer opening a 'tab' or an account behind the bar, often this is guaranteed using a credit card.

Common drinks orders

The drinks listed below are examples of drinks that can be frequently asked for in bars and restaurants. Often a bartender needs to clarify what the customer expects, therefore they will need to ask some questions prior to preparing a drink.

Rather than asking which brand customers would like, giving the customers the choice of brand can lead to them choosing a more expensive brand than they would have normally chosen.

FREQUENTLY ASKED QUESTIONS USED BY BARTENDERS

DRINK	FREQUENTLY ASKED QUESTIONS
Gin and tonic	Ice and lemon?
Half or pint of lager	Which brand?
Glass of white wine	Which grape? Which country?
Glass of red wine	Which grape? Which country?
Scotch	Ice and water?
Mineral water	Sparkling or still?
Vodka and tonic	Which brand?
Orange juice	Ice?
Glass of champagne	Which brand?
Glass of sherry	Dry or sweet?

Accompaniments and garnishes

Ice: Ice should be freshly made from clean fresh water. In cocktails crushed ice is used but in general bar drinks ice cubes are used.

Slice of lemon, orange or lime: These should be freshly sliced each day.

Twist: A long zest twisted in the centre and normally dropped into a cocktail.

Zest: A small thin piece of citrus peel with as little pith as possible. The essential oil is squeezed on top of the drink and it is optional whether the zest is then dropped into the drink.

Frosting or rimming: A glass is 'frosted' or 'rimmed' by rubbing the rim with a piece of moist fruit and dipping the moistened rim in the frosting substances.

Spiral: The complete peel of a fruit cut in spiral fashion.

STEP-BY-STEP: MEASURING SPIRITS USING MEASURE

1 *Take clean single measure and clean glass*

2 *Hold the measure over the glass and carefully pour in the alcohol*

3 *Transfer the alcohol to the glass. Wash the measure after use*

 REMEMBER

Do not exceed measure or under measure as this could contravene the Weights and Measures Act 1985.

STEP-BY-STEP: MEASURING SPIRITS IN ICE USING MEASURE

1 *If the customer requires ice place the ice in the glass first*

2 *Hold the measure over the glass and carefully pour in the alcohol*

3 *Transfer the alcohol to the glass. Wash the measure after use*

STEP-BY-STEP: MEASURING SPIRITS USING OPTICS

1 *Fill the glass with ice, if the customer requires it*

2 *Push glass under the optic and hold it there until all the liquid passes into the glass*

 REMEMBER

Always check that the optic is full before you pour, especially if it is busy.

STEP-BY-STEP: MEASURING SPIRITS USING FREE-POURING METHOD

 REMEMBER

Never use the free pouring measure without training and practise first.

STEP-BY-STEP: POURING LAGER FROM A KEG

1 Take a clean dry pint or half-pint glass.
2 Place at a 90° angle to the spout of the pump.
3 Pull down pump handle fully.
4 As the glass fills up straighten up the glass.

 REMEMBER

Lager should have a head of bubbles on the top about ¾ cm deep.

STEP-BY-STEP: POURING REAL ALE

1 Take a clean dry pint or half-pint glass.
2 Place glass directly below the pump.
3 Pull down pump handle fully and release.
4 Repeat until glass is filled.

 REMEMBER

Real ale should have a head of bubbles on the top about ½ cm deep.

STEP-BY-STEP: POURING LAGER FROM A BOTTLE

1 Take a clean half-pint glass.
2 Hold glass at a 45° angle and bottle at similar angle.
3 Pour liquid slowly into glass.
4 Leave some liquid in bottle and present the bottle beside the glass.

 REMEMBER

If you pour the lager or beer too quickly it will overflow and the customer will lose some of the drink.

STEP-BY-STEP: POURING STOUT

1 Take a clean dry pint or half-pint glass.

2 Place at a 90° angle to the spout of the pump.

3 Pull down pump handle fully.

4 Fill the glass until ¾ full.

5 Leave stout to settle until the head has separated.

6 Finish pouring drink by holding upright under the tap and pushing the tap back.

> **! REMEMBER**
>
> Stout will always take longer to prepare than any other drink, so pour it first.

Assessment of knowledge and understanding

You have now learned about the responsibilities of serving alcohol and soft drinks. This will enable you to ensure your own positive actions contribute effectively towards the whole team.

To test your level of knowledge and understanding, answer the following short questions. These will help to prepare you for your summative (final) assessment.

Preparing for assessment checklist

Practise taking drinks orders and work out in which order you would prepare them.

Project 1

1 Design a bar list for a small local bar in your area.

_____

2 Which drinks would you include and why?

_____

_____

3 Would you include a small wine list or a cocktail list, if not why not?

_____

4 Include some non-alcoholic drinks in your selection.

_____

Project 2

Imagine you are working behind a bar:

1 Someone you suspect to be under-age asks you for an alcoholic beverage. What would you do?

_____

2 A customer asks for a gin and tonic. What questions could you ask them to ensure that they get what they want?

_____

3 Choose three different brands of vodka, how would you describe them to a customer?

_____

_____

_____

17

Prepare and serve cocktails

Unit 613 Prepare and serve cocktails
2DS3.1 Prepare service area and equipment for serving cocktails
2DS3.2 Serve cocktails

What do I need to do?
- Set up and maintain the cocktail bar area.
- Ensure that cocktail making equipment is clean and ready to use.
- Prepare and store cocktail ingredients.
- Prepare and store cocktail accompaniments and garnishes.
- Prepare alcoholic and non-alcoholic cocktails.

What do I need to know?
- Understand the law regarding licensing, weights and measures legislation.
- How to accurately describe a variety of alcoholic and non-alcoholic cocktails to customers.
- The different cocktail making techniques.
- How to measure alcohol accurately.

Information covered in this chapter
- Positions within a cocktail bar.
- Weights and measures legislation.
- Sensible appreciation of alcohol/Dealing with drunken guests.

- Cocktail bar set up and breakdown.
- Cocktail bar equipment.
- Cocktail accompaniments and garnishes.
- Cocktail making techniques.
- Classic alcoholic and non-alcoholic cocktails.

KEY WORDS

Mixology
The art of cocktail making

Flair
The art of entertaining customers while making cocktails, by juggling and throwing cocktail equipment, glasses and bottles.

Cocktails
Drinks containing two or more alcoholic beverages.

Virgin
Cocktail containing no alcohol.

INTRODUCTION

The word 'cocktail' was first defined in print as a 'mixture of spirits, sugar, water and bitter' in an American magazine in 1806.

Generally, the term 'cocktail' is accepted today as a generic name for all mixed drinks. The cocktail bartender, however, understands a cocktail to be a relatively short drink, a larger volume drink would be called a 'mixed drink' or a 'long drink'.

Within this chapter we will look at the different positions that could be needed for the bar to run effectively. When working in any licensed premises it is important that the employees be aware of the licensing laws and be aware of what effect alcohol has on the body and how to deal with it.

POSITIONS WITHIN A COCKTAIL BAR

Cocktail bars vary in size and the staff needed within them will change accordingly. The position of cocktail bartender is a specialized one which the individual needs to train for.

Cocktail bartenders

A cocktail bartender or barman is responsible for serving drinks behind a bar. Their responsibilities include:

Cocktail bartender

- Setting up and breaking down the bar and ensuring that all the glassware, equipment and garnishes are available.
- Stocking and maintaining the beverages for the bar and ensuring that they are secure.
- Having an extensive knowledge of the ingredients and preparation of a wide variety of cocktails.
- Taking customers' orders and preparing their drinks to the correct standard.
- Taking payment for the customers' drinks.
- Liaising with customers and understanding what they want and suggesting other drinks.

Cocktail waiter

In many cocktail bars or lounge bars the customers are served their drinks at the table by cocktail waiters. These may be persons training to become cocktail bartenders. Their duties include:

- Setting up the bar seating area.
- Ensuring that there is a good supply of trays and coasters for service.
- Making sure that the glassware is ready for service.
- Having a good depth of knowledge of the cocktails available, and be able to guide the customers to help them make their order.
- Taking orders and dealing with customer's payments.
- Ensuring that the bar seating area is kept clean and tidy at all times.

Flair bartenders

Flair bartenders are a specially trained type of bartender who combine making cocktails with juggling bottles, glasses and cocktail equipment to entertain the customers. They provide a show at the same time as producing the cocktails requested. It takes a great deal of skill and experience to be a successful flair bartender.

There are a great many competitions between flair bartenders and these are interesting to watch. The skills that they use will have been practised many times.

TIP

Do not attempt to juggle bottles or cocktail equipment in the confined space behind the bar unless you are competent at it already.

WEIGHTS AND MEASURES

Measures are government-stamped and conform to legal requirements regarding weights and measures legislation. The Weights and Measures Act 1985 is a piece of consumer legislation that determines the size, weight and quantity of specific alcoholic beverages.

When serving standard drinks, measures must be used. These are currently 25 ml for a standard spirit or multiples thereof, for example, a double measures 50 ml. When making cocktails or mixing drinks, it is not always necessary to use measures but a specific licence is needed for this.

When making cocktails it is important to know the quantities and proportions of the spirits to be used. A good cocktail is one which has strong alcohol content but one with balance and flavour.

TIP

Do not be tempted when making cocktails to pour large measures into the glass, remember it is illegal to let someone get drunk on your premises.

SENSIBLE APPRECIATION OF ALCOHOL

When alcohol is consumed it is absorbed into the bloodstream via the stomach. As cocktails are generally strong and have much of the alcoholic content masked by fruit juices or sugary drinks, often customers do not realize how strong they are.

Alcohol affects people differently but the general stages of becoming drunk are:

- Stage 1: Happy (relaxed, talkative and sociable).
- Stage 2: Excited (erratic and emotional, movement and thinking affected).
- Stage 3: Confused (disorientated, loud, out of control).
- Stage 4: Lethargic (unable to stand, talk or walk).

It is the legal and moral responsibility of licensees to ensure that guests do not become drunk whilst on their premises. It is important to look out for signs of drunkenness and to deal with them accordingly.

TIP

Look out for the following signs of drunkenness:

Aggression

Carelessness with money

Drowsiness

Slurred words

Clumsiness

'Vacant' expression and loss of train-of-thought.

DEALING WITH DRUNKEN GUESTS

Prevention is the best way of dealing with drunkenness!

DEALING WITH DRUNKEN GUESTS

- ✓ Be aware of how much drink guests have consumed.
- ✓ Tactfully and politely engage guests in conversation to assess their level of mental alertness.
- ✓ If a guest seems drunk, notify your manager immediately.
- ✓ If directed by your manager not to serve any more drinks then ensure that this is communicated to the guest in a polite and tactful manner. Expressions such as 'You are drunk' are best avoided as they can be perceived as confrontational.
- ✓ Always inform your manager if you are having difficulties with guests.
- ✓ Always stay in control and do not argue with the guest.
- ✓ If the guest is part of a group it may be possible to enlist the help of others in the group.

COCKTAIL BAR SET UP

When setting up a cocktail bar each bartender will have a 'station'. This is dependent on the size of the bar and its business. Some bars may have only one station some will have four or five. Ideally each bartender will prepare the cocktails in front of the customers, therefore all the equipment that he needs will be arranged in front of him.

CHECKLIST FOR PREPARING A COCKTAIL BAR

- ✓ Fill ice wells up with fresh ice.
- ✓ Ensure that all spirits and liqueurs are available.
- ✓ Check that there is sufficient glassware.
- ✓ Fill up all juice containers and clearly mark use-by date on each pourer.
- ✓ Check that all parts of the blender are in working order.
- ✓ Check that fridges and freezers are in working order.

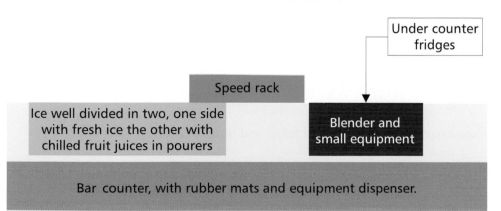

A bar counter with rubber drip mats and equipment dispenser

Martini-Style Cocktails

. . .

The Classic Martini
Extra-Chilled Gin or Vodka perfumed
with a few drops of Dry Vermouth

. . .

Apple Martini
Vodka, Pomme Verte Liqueur & Fresh Apple Juice

. . .

Raspberry Martini
Stoli Razberi, Raspberry Liqueur & Fresh Raspberries

. . .

Chocolate Martini
Vodka, White Cacao & White Mint Liqueurs

. . .

French Martini
Vodka, Chambord Liqueur & Pineapple Juice

. . .

Blueberry Martini
Stoli Vanilla, White Crème de Cacao & Blueberry Liqueur

. . .

Wasabi Martini
Vodka, Wasabi Paste, Lime Juice & Sugar Syrup

. . .

Rose Petal Martini
Bombay Sapphire, Lanique Rose Petal Liqueur,
Lychee Juice & Peychaud Bitters

. . .

Orange Cosmopolitan
Grey Goose Orange, Cointreau,
Cranberry Juice & Fresh Lime Juice

. . .

Mitch Martini
Zubrowska Vodka, Fresh Apple Juice,
Peach Liqueur & Passion Syrup

. . .

Some bars will have promotional material to highlight or advertise the selection of cocktails available. These menus could also show special deals or seasonal offers. Menus may contain a mixture of classic cocktails and speciality cocktails for the premises. There is an expectation by the customers of cocktail bars that a trained bartender will have a good working knowledge of a wide range of classic cocktails.

Example of a cocktail list you might find at The Ritz

COCKTAIL BAR BREAKDOWN

It is just as important to clean down and tidy the bar correctly after service as it is to set it up prior to service. There are two reasons for this: first, it leaves the bar ready and in a professional manner for the next member of staff; second, by ensuring that the bar is cleaned thoroughly and regularly it adheres to Food Hygiene and Health and Safety Legislation Act 2006.

CHECKLIST FOR BREAKING DOWN A COCKTAIL BAR

✓ Empty ice wells and dry.

✓ Ensure that all bottles are sealed and pourers are cleaned.

✓ Wash and polish all glassware.

✓ Wipe down all shelving and surfaces.

✓ Check use-by dates on all juices and discard as appropriate. Wash out pourers.

✓ Breakdown all blenders and leave all parts ready for next day.

✓ Empty and turn off glass washers.

✓ Check that fridges and freezers are in working order.

COCKTAIL BAR SERVICE

In some bars the customers will order at the bar and in other bars there may be waiter service where a waiter takes the order at a table.

When the customer orders a selection of cocktails the bartender will produce all the drinks without compromising the quality and ensure that they are all served in the best possible condition. For example, if the drinks order includes a frozen margarita and a B52 then the frozen margarita will be made first as the B52 is comprised of layers of liqueurs which will sink if left for a period of time.

As the bartender mixes the drinks he will either place them on a tray to be served or on to coasters on the bar in front of customers. Once the cocktail order is complete the bill will be totalled for the order. See Chapter 14 for billing and payment.

TIP

Always serve drinks from a tray to a table.

EQUIPMENT

A cocktail bar needs slightly more specialist equipment than a regular bar. Within a busy cocktail bar there will be larger quantities of each piece of equipment.

The cocktail shaker: Shakers are used when it is necessary to mix ingredients really well. To use it, place the ice into the shaker, add the ingredients, place the parts together and shake.

There are two basic types of shaker:

Boston shaker: Consists of two cones, one which is placed inside the other. These shakers are quick and easy to use. Usually one cone is made of glass, the other of stainless steel.

Standard shaker: Three-piece utensil, usually made entirely of stainless steel. The top part has a strainer 'in-built' into it (a Hawthorn strainer can still be used if the lid and middle part are removed and the Hawthorn strainer placed over the base part).

The mixing glass: This is like a glass jug with no handle. It is used for mixing clear drinks which do not contain juice or cream.

The strainer: The most popular is a Hawthorn strainer. This is a flat, spoon-like utensil with a spring coiled round its head. Used in conjunction with a cocktail shaker and mixing glass to hold back ice after the drink has been prepared.

Bar spoon: This is a long-handled spoon with a twisted shaft and a flat muddler end. The muddler end can be used to crush sugar, mint, etc. when making cocktails.

A cocktail shaker

Boston shaker

Standard shaker

IMAGE COURTESY OF WWW.DRINKSTUFF.COM

A blender

A zester

Bar liquidizer or blender: There is a wide range of these available, the blades should be much stronger that those for a kitchen as they have to break up ice. Variable speed controls can be useful. Liquidizers are best used for preparing drinks that require fruit to be puréed.

Bar knife and chopping board: These should both be fairly small and the knife should have a serrated edge. The chopping board should be made of either wood or plastic and should be easy to clean.

Grater: A small hand-held grater can be used to freshly grate spices and some fruit.

Zester: This is a small hand-held piece of equipment used to remove thin strips of peel from citrus fruit.

Pourers: these can be inserted in bottles of spirits to control how quickly the liquid is poured.

A grater

Juice pourers: Fresh juices are stored in these in preparation for service. They can be colour coded, for easy identification of the contents.

Muddler: A baton either made from wood or plastic which is used to crush herbs or fruit into drinks.

A condiment dispenser

Condiment dispenser: These have different sections in which to store fruit cut for service.

Equipment dispenser: This is normally stationed on top of the bar counter and has a range of service items in it. This could include bar napkins or coasters, straws, and swizzle sticks.

Ice crusher: This is a small hand-held device in which ice for a single drink can be crushed. In larger cocktail bars ice machines which produce crushed ice would be used.

Salt/sugar glass rimmer: Some cocktails have salt or sugar around the top of the glass, this can be done either by using a saucer or this specific piece of equipment.

Speed rack: These are attached to the bar to hold bottles. The bartender can quickly mix drinks by having easy access to the ingredients. Speed rack generally contains the proprietary spirits.

CHECKLIST FOR MAINTAINING BAR EQUIPMENT

CHECKLIST FOR MAINTAINING BAR EQUIPMENT

- ✓ Clean each piece of equipment thoroughly after use.
- ✓ Check for damage and discard or replace if item is damaged.
- ✓ Ensure that each piece of equipment is properly set up prior to service.
- ✓ Check that all staff can use each piece of equipment correctly.
- ✓ Store all equipment in a safe and secure place.

Cocktail shakers

GLASSES

Glassware is an important part of the presentation of a cocktail. As some of the drinks are 'short' and contain few ingredients, they need to be served in small glasses. Those drinks which are 'long' are mixed with juices or soft drinks and are served in longer glasses.

Glassware needs to be clean and polished in preparation for service, see Chapter 8 for cleaning and polishing glassware. To ensure that the drink remains cold after it is served often the glasses are stored in the freezer. It is important to check that the glasses are not cracked or chipped when they are removed from the freezer as they can be easily damaged when frozen.

Highball: A highball glass is a glass tumbler which holds between 8 and 12 fluid ounces.

✓	**TIP**

Drinks should never be served in glasses which are chipped or cracked. These should be discarded immediately.

A highball glass

Collins glass

Martini glass

| ✓ | **TIP** |

Never lift a glass by putting your finger inside it. Always lift it from the bottom outside or the stem.

Collins: A Collins glass is a glass tumbler, holding 8–12 fluid ounces, used to serve mixed drinks. The Collins glass is somewhat narrower than a highball glass.

Martini: A martini glass or cocktail glass is a glass with a cone-shaped bowl on a stem above a flat base, used to serve cocktails, predominantly martinis. As with other stemware, the stem allows the drinker to hold the glass without affecting the temperature of the drink.

Hurricane: These are large stemmed glasses in the shape of a hurricane lamp, used for tropical cocktails and blended drinks.

Margarita glass: A tall stemmed glass with a rounded bottom, used for margaritas.

Rocks glass: The rocks glass or old-fashioned is a short tumbler used for serving drinks over ice, or short cocktails. They hold approximately 8–12 fluid ounces.

Hurricane glass

Margarita glass

Rocks glass

Shot glass: This is a small glass designed to hold or measure 1–3 ounces of liquor, to be poured into a mixed drink, or drunk straight from the glass.

Champagne glass: This is a tall stemmed glass which slows the fizzy beverage from becoming flat.

Wine glass: This is a stemmed glass with a rounded bowl.

ACTIVITY

Have a look in your bar and see if you can identify the different glasses that are used.

- Which would you serve an alcoholic cocktail in?
- Which would you serve a non-alcoholic cocktail in?

Shot glass

Champagne glass

Wine glass

ACCOMPANIMENTS AND GARNISHES

Cocktail garnishes are decorations or ornaments that can add character to a drink. A large variety of cocktail garnishes can be used, some are edible and some inedible. Certain drinks require specific garnishes, some are at the discretion of the establishment or bartender.

Many rum-based cocktails tend to be decorated with tropical-themed garnishes, parasols or slices of fruit. Tequila-based drinks favour limes and other citrus fruits. Gin and vodka-based drinks tend towards olives, onions, or possibly a citrus twist or a single maraschino cherry. Whisky and brandy-based drinks tend towards minimal garnishes.

Twist: A long zest twisted in the centre and normally squeezed then dropped into the drink.

Zest: A small thin piece of citrus peel with as little pith as possible. The essential oil is squeezed on top of the drink and it is optional whether the zest is then dropped into the drink.

Frosting or rimming: A glass is 'frosted' or 'rimmed' with sugar or salt by rubbing the rim with a piece of moist fruit and dipping the moistened rim in the frosting substances.

Spiral: The complete peel of a fruit cut in spiral fashion then wound around a spoon to form a spiral.

 TIP

Always make sure that garnishes are fresh, do not store them for more than one day!

A sugar rim

Umbrellas

Grated: A small hand grater is used to finish a drink with fresh cinnamon, nutmeg or chocolate.

Wedge: A cut of citrus fruit, melon or pineapple, cut and slid on to the side of the glass.

Sticks: Sticks of carrot or celery which can be used as stirrers for drinks.

Single jewels: Single cherries, olives, cocktail onions or berries used to decorate a short drink.

Sprigs or leaves of herbs: The leave of fresh herbs used to flavour and enhance a cocktail.

Cocktail umbrellas: A small cardboard umbrella that can be used to garnish some drinks.

A zest spiral

Jewels decorating a drink

Drinking straws: These come in various sizes and colours and can be used by the customers both to sip drinks and to stir or mix drinks.

Fire: Some drinks can be lit before being served. This can be very dangerous as the glass could crack and the flaming liquid may burn the customer.

Sparklers: Some drinks may be decorated with flags for dramatic effect.

Swizzle sticks: These are generally made of plastic or wood and are placed in the glass to enable customers to stir their own drinks.

✓	**TIP**

Before placing a garnish in a glass, ensure that the customer can actually drink the cocktail. It might be too big for the glass!

A sparkler

Swizzle sticks

ACTIVITY

Practice the following skills until you can consistently make them to the same standard.

■ Make a lemon wedge.
■ Cut a spiral of orange peel.
■ Frost a glass with salt.

 TIP

Practice these techniques until every drink that you produce is of a consistent standard.

COCKTAIL MAKING TECHNIQUES

There are specific methods and techniques that are used in cocktail making. A fully-trained cocktail bartender will be able to carry out all these techniques quickly and professionally. See the step-by-step guide to each technique towards the end of the chapter.

COCKTAIL MAKING TECHNIQUES

TECHNIQUE	METHOD
Blend	Put the ingredients into the electric blender; add crushed ice if required by the recipe, and blend until the required consistency is achieved. Pour unstrained into a suitable glass.
Build	Pour the necessary ingredients directly into a glass without any pre-mixing, add ice only if required by the recipe. Mixed drinks made in this way are usually served with a swizzle stick.
Mix	Put the ingredients into the cone of the electric drink mixer and add crushed ice, if specified. Mix until the drink reaches the required consistency, then pour or strain into a glass.
Muddle	To extract oils or juice from an ingredient by pressing with a bar spoon or muddler.
Shake	Put ice into the cocktail shaker and pour in the necessary ingredients. Shake shortly and sharply unless otherwise instructed, and strain into the required glass.
Stir in	When topping with the final ingredient, use the bar spoon to stir as it is added.
Free pour	The method that a trained bartender uses to measure spirits into cocktails.
Strain	Either using the strainer at the top of the shaker or a fine strainer. This will remove pieces of fruit or ice from the drink prior to it being served.
Float/layer	Pour over a spoon in order for spirits of different volumes to be served in layers in one glass.

Highball glasses

CLASSIC COCKTAILS

Following is a list of classic cocktails. A classic cocktail is one which has been produced over many years. Like any chefs' recipes there are variations of ingredients and methods of production but customers will be able to easily request and identify the drink that they order.

Many of these drinks were produced to celebrate or commemorate specific occasions, and there are histories and stories attached to the drinks which customers often may not know and may like to hear.

This is by no means an exhaustive list but a sample of the many drinks and methods that can be used by a cocktail bartender.

TIP

Have a look at the UK Bartenders Guild website for more information on cocktails. www.ukbg.co.uk

Cocktail glasses

CLASSIC ALCOHOLIC COCKTAILS

COCKTAIL NAME	INGREDIENTS	SUGGESTED GLASS	SUGGESTED GARNISH	METHOD
Americano	Campari, sweet vermouth, soda water	Highball	Orange slice	Build
Bellini	Prosecco, peach puree	Champagne glass	None	Build
Between The Sheets	Triple sec, brandy, white rum, lime juice	Martini glass	Lemon peel	Shake and strain
Black Russian	Vodka, kahlua	Rocks glass		
Black Velvet	Champagne, guinness	Wine glass	None	Stir gently
Bloody Mary	Vodka, tomato juice, lemon juice, tabasco, Worcestershire sauce, salt and pepper	Highball glass	Lime segment, celery stick	Shaken. Customers may indicate how spicy they require it
Bloody Bull	Vodka, tomato juice, beef consommé	Highball glass	Lime segment	Shaken
Brandy Alexander	Brandy, crème de cacao, double cream	Martini glass or rocks	Nutmeg	Stir and strain
Buck's Fizz	Champagne, orange juice	Champagne glass	None	Stir gently
Bullshot	Vodka, beef consommé, tabasco, salt and pepper, lemon juice	Wine glass	Lime wedge	Shaken
Champagne Asta	Pernod, champagne	Champagne glass	None	Stir gently
Champagne Cocktail	Cube of white sugar, angostura bitters, peach brandy, champagne	Champagne glass	None	Build
Caiprinha	Cachaca, gomme syrup, fresh lime	Rocks glass	Lime wedge	Muddle

COCKTAIL NAME	INGREDIENTS	SUGGESTED GLASS	SUGGESTED GARNISH	METHOD
Cosmopolitan	Vodka, lime juice, cointreau, cranberry juice	Martini glass	Orange twist	Shaken
Tom Collins	London dry gin, gomme syrup, lemon syrup, soda	Wine glass	Lemon slice	Build
Daquiri	White rum, lemon juice, gomme syrup	Rocks glass	Lime wedge	Shaken
Gimlet	Gin, lime cordial *Variations*: Vodka Gimlet substitute vodka for gin	Rocks glass		Stir
Gin Fizz	Gin, lemon, gomme syrup, soda	Wine glass	Slice of orange and cherry	Build
Godfather	Whisky, amaretto	Rocks glass	None	Build
Grasshopper	Crème de menthe, white cacao	Rocks glass	None	Build
Harvey Wallbanger	Vodka, galliano, orange juice	Wine glass	Orange slice	Pour vodka and orange into the glass and pour the galliano over a spoon to float on top
Mai-Tai	White rum, myers rum, orange juice, orgeat, grenadine	Rocks glass	Orange slice	Shaken
Margarita	Tequila, triple sec, lemon juice	Rocks glass	None, check if the rim of the glass is to be salted	Classically a shaken drink but can be served 'frozen' which is produced in a blender
Manhattan Dry/Sweet/ Perfect Dry: Sweet: Perfect:	Canadian club, angostura bitters Dry vermouth, garnished with a twist Sweet vermouth, garnished with a cherry Sweet vermouth, garnished with a twist and cherry	Rocks glass		Mix and strain
Martini	Gin or vodka, dry vermouth	Rocks glass or Martini glass	Lemon twist, olive, ice	Shake or stir
Mojito	White rum, fresh lime, fresh mint, gomme syrup, soda	Rocks glass	Lime	Muddle lime and mint
Moscow Mule	Russian premium vodka, ginger beer	Rocks glass	Lime wedge	Build
Negroni	Gin, campari, sweet vermouth (soda) *Variations*: Negroski, substitute gin for vodka	Highball glass	Orange slice/ twist	Build

COCKTAIL NAME	INGREDIENTS	SUGGESTED GLASS	SUGGESTED GARNISH	METHOD
Old Fashioned	Bourbon, angostura bitters, sugar	Rocks glass	Orange slice	Soak sugar cube in bitters, crush and add bourbon
Pina Colada	White rum, pineapple juice, coconut cream	Hurricane glass	Pineapple wedge and cherry	Blend
Rusty Nail	Scotch, drambuie	Rocks glass	None	Build
Screwdriver	Vodka, orange juice	Highball	Orange	Build
Sea Breeze	Vodka, grapefruit juice, cranberry juice	Highball	Lime wedge	Build
Singapore Sling	Gin, cherry brandy, lemon juice, soda, gomme syrup	Highball	None	Shake
Stinger	Cognac, white crème de menthe	Rocks/cocktail	None	Build
Side Car	Cognac, triple sec, lemon juice	Rocks/cocktail	None	Shake
Tequila Sunrise	Tequila, orange juice, grenadine	White wine	Orange slice	Build, pour grenadine slowly
Whisky Sour	Whisky, gomme syrup, lemon juice *Variations*: Amaretto Sour, Apricot Sour, Vodka Sour, Gin Sour	Rocks	Orange slice, cherry	Shake and strain

 ## ACTIVITY

Choose three cocktails that are made using different methods. Practise making these with the correct garnish until each time you produce them they are of a consistent quality.

NON-ALCOHOLIC COCKTAILS

COCKTAIL NAME	INGREDIENTS	SUGGESTED GLASS	SUGGESTED GARNISH	METHOD
Virgin Mary	Tomato juice, lemon juice, tabasco, Worcestershire sauce, salt and pepper	Highball glass	Celery stick	Shake
St Clements	Orange juice, bitter lemon	Rocks glass	Orange slice	Build
Shirley Temple	Ginger ale, grenadine	Wine glass	Cherry	Build
Gentle Sea Breeze	Cranberry juice, pineapple juice	Highball glass	Pineapple wedge	Shake and strain
Egg Nog	Eggs, sugar, vanilla extract, cinnamon, mixed spice, milk	Highball glass	Cinnamon powder	Whisk all ingredients until fluffy
Virgin Colada	Fresh pineapple, coconut	Hurricane glass	Pineapple wedge and cherry	Place all ingredients in blender with ice.

ACTIVITY

Using a selection of soft drinks and cocktail-making skills devise and make a non-alcoholic cocktail suitable for an 11-year-old's birthday party.

STEP-BY-STEP: MAKING A SHAKEN COCKTAIL

1 *Use a Boston shaker, a Hawthorn strainer, a clean polished glass, ice and cocktail ingredients*

2 *Fill the shaker with ice cubes*

3 *Pour the ingredients of the cocktail into the shaker*

4 *Place lid or glass securely on to the top of the shaker*

5 *Move the shaker up and down across your body for approximately 15 seconds*

6 *Using a Hawthorn strainer pour the drink into the desired glass*

STEP-BY-STEP: MUDDLING A COCKTAIL

1 *Using brown demerara sugar and mint, a cocktail spoon and a muddler*

2 *First put sugar into a glass*

3 *Then add the mint*

4 *Pour in the base spirit*

5 *To muddle, grind the ingredients together to release the oils in the leaves of the herbs used*

Once muddled, top up the drink with ice and whatever other liquids should be used

STEP-BY-STEP: BLENDING A COCKTAIL

1 *Use a blender, ice, a clean glass and the cocktail ingredients*

2 *Fill the blender with ice*

3 *Pour in cocktail ingredients*

4 *Once blended pour all ingredients into a glass*

> **!** **REMEMBER**

Ensure that the blender is cleaned thoroughly between making each cocktail.

STEP-BY-STEP: RIMMING A GLASS WITH SALT OR SUGAR

1 *Use a clean polished glass, lemon juice, caster sugar, and two saucers*

2 *Pour lemon juice into the saucer*

3 *On a separate saucer pour caster sugar*

4 *Dip the top of the glass into the lemon juice*

5 *Then dip the glass into the sugar*

6 *Carefully ensuring that the whole rim is covered*

7 *When pouring the drink into the glass ensure that it does not wash the salt or sugar into the glass*

Assessment of knowledge and understanding

You have now learned about the responsibilities you have for preparing and serving cocktails. This will enable you to ensure your own positive actions contribute effectively towards the whole team.

To test your level of knowledge and understanding, answer the following short questions. These will help to prepare you for your summative (final) assessment.

Make sure that you keep this for easier referencing and along with your work for future inclusion in your portfolio.

Project 1

A guest has asked you to suggest a short cocktail list for a private function of 30 guests. The guest would like three alcoholic and two non-alcoholic cocktails, using a wide range of ingredients, equipment, accompaniments and techniques.

1 Prepare a plan of work for each cocktail in your chosen list, for you and your colleagues to work from. This should include the ingredients, accompaniments and equipment that should be used and how the cocktail should be served. Use diagrams or photographs to illustrate your answer.

Project 2

1 Write a checklist for a cocktail bartender to use at the beginning and end of a shift. Include which ingredients and accompaniments need to be prepared and which equipment should be used.

_____

_____

2 What is the size of a single measure of a spirit in England?

_____

3 Describe what a strainer is used for in cocktail making.

_____

4 Name three different types of cocktail glass.

i) _____ ii) _____

iii) _____

5 Name two different types of garnish and describe how they are prepared.

i) _____

ii) _____

6 Describe the method for making a shaken cocktail.

_____

_____

INDUSTRY PROFILE

Name: **BRIAN SILVA**

Position: BAR MANAGER

Establishment: RULES RESTAURANT

Current job role and main responsibilities:

I set the standards for the bar and create the cocktail list and choose what spirits are listed. I am also behind the bar during service and run the room from the bar.
I am responsible for all aspects of the bar from staff training to ordering and the profitability of the bar.
I also hand picked the staff and trained them in the areas needed.

How do you keep up-to-date with current beverage trends? Do you have a particular favourite, and why?
I am kept aware by my suppliers and being that we specialize in cocktails and whiskies, I am kept in the loop. I usually have people bring me in unusual spirits or mixers as these are a favourite of mine, especially aperitifs.

When did you realize that you wanted to pursue a career in the food service industry?
In my early 20s. I had worked in kitchens in my teens but the place to be seemed to be the bar.

Training:
I apprenticed at the Colonnade Hotel in Boston.
I worked my way up.

Experience:
I started as a bar back and was promoted to barman 6 months later. I was head barman after a year.
I opened the bar for a trendy French/Italian restaurant in Boston, Massachusetts and moved to the UK in 1989.
I worked for the IOD in Pall Mall for 5 years.
I moved to Home House in 1999 and opened the bar for them as bar manager.
I also oversaw the bar at Scott's in Mayfair in a dual role.
I was with the company for 5 years.
I then moved to the Connaught Hotel and worked with Angela Hartnett of Gordon Ramsay Group as her bar manager.
I was responsible for the beverage offering for the Connaught Bar and the American Bar. I had a team of 15.
I took time off when the hotel closed for a refit and then went to work as area group bar manager for Diageo PLC. I was responsible for three sites including the site at Terminal 5.
I left Diageo and am now the bar manager at Rules (and very happy to be).

What do you find rewarding about your job?
The customer contact.

What do you find the most challenging about the job?
Keeping up the enthusiasm and motivating the staff to do the same.

What advice would you give to students just beginning their career?
Take it slow and listen. You never stop learning. Treat people as you would want to be treated.

What traits do you consider essential for anyone entering a career in the food and drink sector?
Thick skin and a good sense of humour.

18

Prepare and serve wines

Unit 614 Prepare and serve wines
2DS4.1 Prepare service areas, equipment and stock for wine service
2DS4.2 Determine customer requirements for wine
2DS4.3 Present and serve wine

What do I need to do?
- Prepare for wine service.
- Correctly serve white wine, red wine, dessert wine and champagne to customers.
- Help customers with their wine choices.

What do I need to know?
- How wine is made.
- Where wine is made.
- How to describe the different grape varieties.
- How wine should be stored.
- What information should be written on a wine list.

Information covered in this chapter
- How wine is made.
- Grape varieties.
- Classification of wines.
- Opening and serving wine.

KEY WORDS

Old World
Wine made in Europe.

New World
Wine produced outside Europe.

Vintage
The year that grapes are picked and wine is produced.

Fermentation
The process of how alcohol is made.

Oenologist
The term for a wine maker.

Vineyard
A place where grapes are grown and wine is made.

INTRODUCTION

Wine bottles

Wine service is an important part of the customer's overall dining experience. Often a great deal of mystery surrounds wine but, in present times, there is no considered correct or incorrect way to drink wine. Instead customers should be able to feel relaxed and comfortable with what they order.

To enhance the customer's experience of ordering and drinking wine it is essential and good practice for the waiters and service staff of a restaurant to have a good working knowledge of their wine list.

HOW WINE IS MADE

Black ripened grapes

Wine is made from grapes. The grapes ripen during the summer months and are picked during the autumn, September–December in the northern hemisphere or Old World, March–May in the southern hemisphere or New World. Each year or 'vintage' that a wine is produced can differ in taste and quality from that of the previous year.

There are two different colours of grape: white grapes from which white wine is produced and red grapes from which both red and white wines are produced. Rosé wine is also produced from red grapes. The groups are further divided into different varieties or grape types.

Once the grapes are picked, they are crushed to extract the juice. The juice is then fermented to produce alcohol. In order to produce red wine, the skins of the red grapes are mixed with the grape juice, prior to fermentation. White wine is not fermented with the skins. Rosé wine is fermented with the red grape skins for only a short time.

White ripened grapes

Fermentation occurs when sugar and yeast react in a liquid, with a little warmth, to produce alcohol and carbon dioxide, which is released. In order to control this process extra yeast can be added to create a stronger wine. By law, wine is only allowed to be between 8 per cent and 15 per cent alcohol by volume.

After fermentation, some wines are matured. This maturation will change the flavour of the finished wine. Some wine is matured in stainless steel bins, which will result in a clean, crisp flavour. Other wines are matured in oak barrels that will give a woody, oaky, flavour to the wine.

Vineyard

GROWING GRAPES

Grapes are grown and wine is produced in vineyards or wineries.

Grapes are grown in regions worldwide where there is warmth in the summer and coolness in the winter. The weather is one factor that can affect the quality of the vintage and plays an important part in wine growing. If a summer is too hot the grapes could be too small and only a small amount of juice can be extracted, too wet and the grapes will contain too much water. If the late summer is not warm and sunny the grapes may not ripen sufficiently to produce enough sugar to react in the fermentation process. Ideally a wine producer (or oenologist) needs all the grapes in the vineyard to ripen equally at the same time

The soil and terrain can affect the grapes, thus impacting on the wine that is produced. Vines need to grow in sunny, well-drained soil. Different regions and indeed different vineyards will have different soil types, which will influence the flavours of the wine. If vines are grown in chalky soil then they will have resonance of that chalky flavour.

 ACTIVITY

Visit a supermarket or off-licence and have a look at the different wines that are available.

- What other countries are producing wine that are not mentioned in the following table?
- Can you identify which wines are produced in the Old World and which are New World?

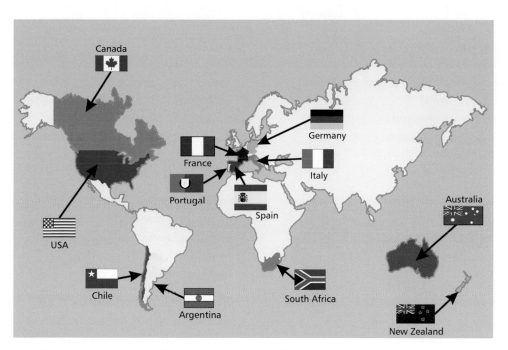

Map featuring wine-producing regions of the world

WINE-PRODUCING COUNTRIES AND SOME OF THEIR REGIONS

	COUNTRY	REGIONS
Old World countries	France	Bordeaux, Burgundy, Champagne, The Loire Valley
	Spain	Rioja
	Italy	Chianti, Montepulciano, Soave, Frascati
	Germany	
	Hungary	Tokai
New World wines	Australia	Hunter Valley, Mclaren Vale
	New Zealand	Marlborough, Hawkes Bay
	South Africa	Stellenbosch
	USA	Napa Valley
	Chile	Maipo Valley

GRAPE VARIETIES

Different grape varieties produce different types of wine. Most grape varieties are grown all over the world. Some grape varieties are known by different names in different areas of the world: Pinot Gris is recognized in France but in Italy the same grape is called Pinot Grigio.

WHITE WINE		RED WINE	
GRAPE VARIETY	DESCRIPTION	GRAPE VARIETY	DESCRIPTION
Chardonnay	Grape grown in both the Old and New World. New World Chardonnays are often aged in oak giving a rich woody wine. Old World Chardonnays can be sharper.	Cabernet Sauvignon	This grape is principally associated with Bordeaux but is grown all over the world. Has the aroma of blackcurrants and when blended with other grape varieties can form heavy, full-bodied wines.
Sauvignon Blanc	A sharp flavoured grape now prolifically grown in New Zealand. When it is fermented in oak it can become softer and more rounded.	Merlot	Originally grown in France but now grown worldwide. The wine produced gives aromas of stone fruits and can be smooth and well-rounded.
Viognier	A perfumed varietal which produces a dry crisp wine	Gamey	This grape is grown mostly in the Beaujolais region of France. It makes a light wine which can be served chilled.
Pinot Grigio/ Pinot Gris	A spicy flavoured grape grown predominantly in Italy, but also in France and the New World.	Pinot Noir	This grape is grown across the world and produces a wine that has the aroma of stone fruits. It is one of the grapes that is used in champagne production.
Gewurtztraminer	An interesting-flavoured grape with a honeyed aroma but a spicy flavour. Grown in Germany, France and the New World.	Sangiovese	Chianti is produced from this grape which is grown primarily in Italy. It produces intense cherry-flavoured wines.
Riesling	With light fragrant aroma the flavour of this grape can be deceptive, by being sharp and light. Germany grows the most Reisling but New Zealand is also producing a good range.	Tempranillo	The grape which is used only to produce Rioja in Spain. The wines are light with a slight spiciness.
Chenin Blanc/ Steen	Grapes producing wine with aroma of apples. Grown worldwide and the wine is normally blended with other grape varieties.	Zinfandel	Associated with Californian wine production, smells of autumn fruits, used to make rosé or blush wines.
Semillon	Grown in France and Australia, wine is yellow in colour and when grapes are left on the vine can be used to produce dessert wines.	Shiraz/Syrah	Grown across the wine-producing world to make a spicy, berry-flavoured wine. Can be blended with other grape varieties.

CLASSIFICATION OF WINES

In some wine-producing countries wines have been classified to aid their identification and preserve their integrity. The countries that have laid down these classifications are mainly in the Old World although they are beginning to spread to the New World.

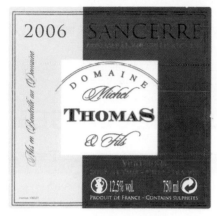

Example of a French wine label

Wine classifications exist to ensure the quality of the wine produced in a particular region. For example if a wine has champagne written on the label, by law it has to have been made from a blend of Chardonnay, Pinot Noir and Pinot Menieur grapes. The grapes must have been grown within a specific geographical area of the Champagne region and it must have been made to the correct alcoholic strength in the exact way specified. If any of these criteria have not been fulfilled then it cannot be described as champagne, but just a sparkling wine.

The best-known example of wine classifications exists in France. The main French wine classifications are as follows:

Vin de table: Table wine.

Vin de pays: Wine of a medium-quality grown within a specific geographic area from specified grapes.

Vin delimité de qualité supérieure (VDQS): A better-quality of wine than those previous, grown within a specific area from prescribed grape varieties, and made by an agreed method to an explicit alcohol content.

Appellation d'origine contrôllée: The best-quality wine made within a specific region, using exacting methods and grape varieties, to produce what is considered a fine wine.

 ACTIVITY

Have a look at the wine list within your establishment.

- Write down what country and region each wine comes from.
- Which grape variety or varieties is each wine made from?
- What is the vintage of each wine?

You will need to know all this information before you can serve wine confidently to your customers.

HOW CHAMPAGNE AND SPARKLING WINES ARE MADE

Champagne comes from the Champagne region of France but sparkling wine is produced all over the world. There are several different methods of producing sparkling wine once the initial wine production is complete. The principal method is to initiate a second fermentation and maturation process during which the carbon dioxide that is produced as a by-product is not released but forced back into the wine under pressure.

WINE EQUIPMENT AND WINE GLASSES

WINE EQUIPMENT

✓ Waiters' friend: The bottle opener specifically used to open wine at customers' tables.

✓ Ice bucket: Used to keep wine and sparkling wines cool, once opened.

✓ Decanter: Used to serve fine red wines that may have a sediment.

✓ Service cloths: Used to dry wine from an ice bucket and to catch drips.

Wine glasses are a definitive shape to ensure that they enhance the way the wine is drunk.

Champagne glass

Wine glass

Wine can be affected in three main areas:

- Ordering
- Presenting and opening
- Pouring

CHECKLIST FOR TAKING A WINE ORDER

✓ Before taking a wine order be aware of any vintage changes and availability of wines.

✓ Approach the host and make eye contact. Ask in a clear and audible manner if they would like to order any wine with their meal.

✓ As the customer orders, listen carefully and if necessary repeat back to customer. Send order to bar.

✓ Remove wine list after the wine order is taken, unless otherwise requested by customer.

✓ If white and red wine, or champagne is ordered ensure that sufficient glasses are available and placed on the table.

STEP-BY-STEP: POURING WINE

2 Ensure the flow is smooth and that the bottle at no point touches the edge of the glass

1 Hold the bottle of wine with the label facing upwards towards the customer at all times

3 The glass should be filled to no more than two-thirds

 REMEMBER

Wine should only be opened using a waiter's friend. When pouring wine always carry a wine cloth in your other hand, just in case of spills.

STEP-BY-STEP: HOLDING A CHAMPAGNE BOTTLE CORRECTLY

3 *Keeping the label facing upwards, use your fingers to hold the bottle steady as you pour*

1 *Example of champagne glasses*

2 *Tuck your thumb into the dimple at the bottom of the bottle*

! **REMEMBER**

Champagne is held in a pressurized bottle and if not handled correctly can have a dramatic effect!

Assessment of knowledge and understanding

You have now learned about the responsibilities you have for the service of wine. This will enable you to ensure your own positive actions contribute effectively towards the whole team.

To test your level of knowledge and understanding, answer the following short questions. These will help to prepare you for your summative (final) assessment.

Make sure that you keep this for easier referencing and along with your work for future inclusion in your portfolio.

Preparing for assessment checklist

- ■ List different grape varieties.
- ■ Demonstrate how to open and serve wine.

Project 1

1 Name two Old World wine producing countries and two New World wine producing countries.

_____

_____

2 What is a Waiter's friend?

_____

_____

3 What does the Vintage denote on a wine bottle?

_____

_____

4 When growing grapes what things can later affect the taste of the wine?

_____

_____

5 Name three white grape varieties and describe them.
  i) _____ ii) _____
  iii) _____

Project 2

1 List the equipment that is needed to open and serve a bottle of wine and a bottle of champagne.

_____

_____

2 Draw the outline of a champagne glass and a wine glass.

INDUSTRY PROFILE

Name: **MATTHEW MAWTUS**

Position: HEAD SOMMELIER

Establishment: L'ETRANGER RESTAURANT

Current job role and main responsibilities:
I am currently charged with the daily running of a 1000-bin wine list including the selection of wines, the purchasing of wines, building a balanced and broad wine list, ensuring the efficient and smooth running of 13 services per week in the restaurant including advising guests on their choice of wine for the meal, taking into consideration their budget, the food they are eating and the type and style of wine that I feel would be most beneficial to the guest in order to ensure that they leave the restaurant with great memories about the wine as well as the food.

What do you think gave you the edge to become Young Waiter of the Year 2007?
I feel that I allowed my personality to show during the competition, particularly during the service element. I also feel that I have gained a wealth of knowledge within the industry due to the fact that I have filled a number of positions within restaurants and hotels, thus giving me a broad experience base to draw from.

When did you realize that you wanted to pursue a career in the food and beverage service industry?
I took a job as a waiter at the age of 16 then when considering my choice of degree at university I realised that the food and beverage industry was something that I am particularly passionate about.

Training:
I have a BA in Hotel and Hospitality Management from the Scottish Hotel School, Strathclyde University, Glasgow. I also have an Advanced Level 3 with Merit in Wines and Spirits. The first restaurant I ever worked in is called the Milton of Crathes. However I attribute my first contact with fine dining as being in Camerons Restaurant, Glasgow Hilton. I feel that my time in Gordon Ramsay at Claridges was invaluable in terms of experience and contact with some of the leading figures in the Industry.

Experience:
The Milton of Crathes, waiter; *Albyn Hospital*, room service; *The Milton of Crathes*, commis chef; *Glasgow Hilton*, commis waiter, barman, room service, food and beverage supervisor; *Gordon Ramsay at Claridges*, commis sommelier; *L'Etranger Restaurant*, assistant sommelier, head sommelier.

What do you find rewarding about your job?
The constant challenge of learning more about my chosen field is exceptionally motivating. I also take a huge satisfaction from taking care of my guests and selecting the perfect wine to accompany their meal.

What do you find the most challenging about the job?
Difficult and ignorant guests can provide a challenge. I also find the hours are often very long and thankless.

What advice would you give to students just beginning their career?
Work as hard as you can, as the more you put in the more you get out. Allow your talent to shine, be yourself and most importantly believe in your ability.

Who is your mentor or main inspiration?
Hugues Lepin, ex-head sommelier of Gordon Ramsay at Claridges has been a huge influence to me. I also find the achievements of Marco Pierre White in the '80s and '90s, particularly at Harveys and The Oak Room to be very inspiring. I have also learned a huge amount from my parents.

What traits do you consider essential for anyone entering a career in the food and drink sector?
To be involved with the front-of-house you must be outgoing, personable, flexible, enthusiastic, quick thinking, quick witted, resourceful, understanding, caring and driven,

A brief personal profile
I am very interested in wine and other beverages, continually searching for new wines from obscure regions and talented, dynamic wine makers. I also take a great interest in cooking, particularly French and Italian cuisine.

Can you give one essential management tip or piece of industry advice?
Always be one step ahead of the competition and the guest as only then will you be able to provide something that little more special and memorable for your guest.

19

Maintain cellars and kegs

What do I need to do?

■ Know how to keep cellars clean and tidy.

■ Know how to keep equipment in good working order.

■ Know how to keep the cellar secure.

What do I need to know?

■ How to maintain safe and hygienic practices for cellars.

■ How to set up appropriate security measures.

■ How to keep the cellar clean and tidy.

■ How to correctly handle kegs and gas cylinders.

Information covered in this chapter

■ Cellar maintenance.

■ Cellar conditions.

■ Stock rotation.

■ Security of cellars.

■ Prepare kegs and gas for use.

KEY WORDS

Air line jumper
The piece of tubing that runs between the regulator and the keg coupler.

Bleed
To drain off liquid or gas, generally slowly, through a valve called a bleeder. To bleed down, or bleed off, means to release pressure slowly from a well or from pressurized equipment.

Cellar
A cellar is a room or rooms under a building, and usually below the surface of the ground, where provisions and other stores are kept.

CCTV
Closed Circuit Television is a video monitoring and security system using cameras that transmit visual information over a closed circuit through transmitters and receivers.

Dray
A drayman was historically the driver of a dray, a low, flat-bed wagon without sides, pulled generally by horses or mules that was used for transport of all kinds of goods. Now the term is really only used for brewery delivery men, even though routine horse-drawn deliveries are almost entirely extinct. Some breweries do still maintain teams of horses and a dray, but these are used only for special occasions such as festivals or opening new premises.

Keg
A keg is a stainless steel vessel that is used for the distribution of bulk beer. They come in various sizes, usually 50 and 100 litres.

Regulator
The regulator connects to the CO_2 tank. It steps the gas pressure down to a level that is correct for dispensing beer. Most kits come with a double gauge regulator. One gauge tells you the pressure going into the keg, the other gauge tells you how much air you have left in your air tank.

Wholesaler
A person, other than the brewer, manufacturer or rectifier, who sells alcohol beverages to a licensed retailer or to another person who holds a permit to sell alcohol beverages at wholesale.

INTRODUCTION

Cellar and keg maintenance are key to the smooth and efficient running of a bar. Cellars need to be clean and tidy, and drinks must be easy to find. They need to be well categorized and well stocked. Without these key aspects to cellar maintenance customers' needs may not be able to be met. Likewise in the maintenance of kegs there are key aspects with regard to the safety of changing between kegs, the use of gas and stock rotation that need to be carefully understood and procedures monitored in order to ensure the quality of the product for the customer.

This chapter will consider both these aspects – first the maintenance of cellars, second the maintenance of kegs.

CELLAR MAINTENANCE

Cellars are a store for all drink-related products that you sell in a hospitality outlet. They are subject to a lot of human traffic from staff and suppliers, meaning that they easily get dusty, dirty, messy and unhygienic. In addition to this they are usually behind the scenes and/or underground a hospitality outlet, and frequently out of sight of day-to-day traffic. This means that security is important too as these are the products that are most susceptible to theft and lack of accountability.

WHY ARE DRINKS PRODUCTS MORE SUSCEPTABLE TO THEFT?

- More accessible
- More immediate for consumption
- Increased behavioural effects on the person

Cellar area

HOW DO YOU KEEP A CELLAR CLEAN AND TIDY?

✓ Regularly clean the cellar.

✓ Ensure all drinks stored in the cellar have a specific place in the cellar.

✓ Do not keep drinks in any part of the cellar other than their allocated space.

✓ Regularly stock-take the cellar.

✓ Control the flow of human traffic – limit the people allowed access to the cellar.

✓ Ensure security procedures are maintained (see page 273).

✓ Store drinks appropriately and as per guidelines from wholesalers.

Making orders and receiving deliveries

One of the most important parts of cellar maintenance is having the correct stock levels available in your cellar. This also means correctly making orders and receiving deliveries:

1 Par levels – you must ensure that every product (beer, wine, soft drinks, etc.) has a minimum and maximum par level. This is the correct level of stock required to ensure that you don't overstock during quiet periods of business or understock during busy periods.

2 Once par levels are set, these need to be maintained. Depending on how busy your outlet is drinks orders will be made between once a week and daily. Within the cellar, when orders are made the following must be taken into consideration:

   a. Level of business – busy or quiet.

   b. Par levels.

   c. Orders from the individual outlets your cellar may supply (i.e. in a hotel).

3 Place the order with the appropriate wholesalers.

4 Receive delivery – when receiving the delivery of drinks, it is important that you check the following:

   a. The quantity on the delivery note is the quantity that you receive.

   b. Write down any anomalies between the delivery note and the actual delivery.

   c. Ensure the delivery person and the person receiving the order both sign the delivery note to confirm what was actually delivered. See example delivery note

 TIP

TIPS TO RECEIVING A DELIVERY

1 Check crates randomly to ensure that the delivery people have filled the whole crate and not left gaps in the middle of the crate.

2 Make sure you get a signature for what was delivered and any missing items.

3 Chase up the credit note from the company.

MATTHEW CLARK

Ship-to No.		Account No.	1049362
Order No.	3089	Document No.	2008659
Order Date	10/04/09	Document Date	20/04/09
Customer Reference No.		Load No.	
		Shipment	

INVOICE TO:

The Ship
Burnham Market
Norfolk

DELIVERED TO:

Number	Product Description	Quantity	Unit Price	Per	Goods	VAT Code
3	Tonic Water	36's	4.11	36		
2	Gin	1	9.86	Litre		
4	Vodka	1	9.86	Litre		
2	John Smiths	1	42.35	50L Keg		

Chargeable Containers Returned		Quantity	Value £	p	VAT	%	Goods & Containers	VAT	TOTAL
N 01	2 Doz Bottles & Case								
N 02	3 Doz Bottles & Case				15	%			
N 03	4 Doz Bottles & Case								
N 04	6 Syphons & Case								
N 06	1 Doz Pints & Case				Loss Returns				
N 08	1 Doz Litres & Case								
N 14	12 × 75 Bott & Case								
N 15	Empty Cases								
N 18	Empty 5 Star Case				TOTALS				
N 20	Grolsch Bottles & Case								
					For Customer Sg. G J Allen		For Company Sg.		Time Arrived
	TOTAL RETURNS £				Print Name		Print Name		

Company Copy   Ply 2 Customer Copy   All transactions are subject to our general terms and conditions overleaf   E & O. E.

Delivery note

ACTIVITY

Name five pieces of information that are missing from this delivery note

Storage conditions and recommendations for wine

■ Moderate *humidity* is important to keep the corks in good resilient condition and prevent them from shrinking. A relative humidity of 50–80 per cent is the acceptable range, but about 70 per cent is recommended. Excessive humidity will not harm the wine but will cause the labels and any other paper products, like cardboard boxes, you have in the cellar to rot. Insufficient humidity may cause the corks to dry out, lose their elasticity and thereby allow air to get into the bottle.

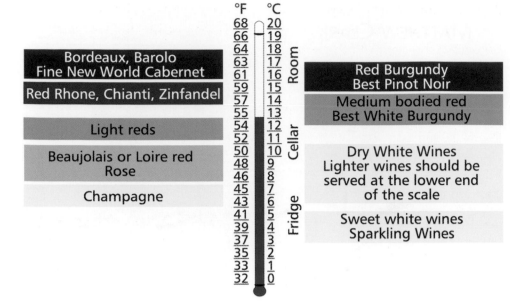

Wine storage temperature gauge

■ *Light* will prematurely age a bottle of wine. Clear bottles are most susceptible to this problem, but ultra-violet light will penetrate even dark coloured glass. Ultra-violet light may give a wine unpleasant aromas and ruin it. Extra care should be given to sparkling wines as they are more sensitive to light than other wines. It should be noted too, that incandescent or sodium vapour lights are better for a cellar than fluorescent lighting.

■ *Constant vibration* from machinery or a nearby road disturbs a red wine's sediment and can be harmful to all wine. This is not commonly a problem in the average home as dangerous extremes are rare and obvious. It should be remembered that excessive sound creates vibrations that may be harmful as well. Wines should be stored in such a way that you don't have to move them around to get at a particular bottle. Once a wine is laid down, it should stay there until it is opened.

■ The space should be *free from smells and debris*. Extraneous smells can enter through the cork and contaminate the wine. Proper ventilation will help with this problem and keep the cellar from giving the wine a musty taste. Debris that could be a home to insects that might infect the corks – untreated wood, food – should be removed. Never store fruits, vegetables, cheeses or any other food that is capable of fermenting.

■ *Table wine is stored horizontally* so that the wine stays in contact with the cork. This keeps the cork moist thereby preventing air from entering the wine. If bottles are stored with the labels uppermost, it will be easier to see the deposit of sediment that forms on the opposite side of the bottle when it comes time to open it. Fortified wines other than port, are stored standing upright.

A bin is a storage area in a wine cellar. With each successive harvest, wines are allocated the same bin year after year. Over time these bin numbers have become associated with the wine – Shiraz was stored in bin 50, Chardonnay in bin 65. Subsequently, it has become the case that bin numbers are sometimes brand names depicting a style of wine, and frequently have nothing to do with the origin of the grapes or where the wine has been stored.

Wine bottles

ACTIVITY

These aspects of storage can be applied to all forms of drink stored in cellars. Below are some more specific conditions for beer. Can you spot the similarities?

Storage conditions and recommendations for beer

Keep beer in a cold store or cellar and maintain the temperature at 11–13°C (52–56°F). Beer must be given time to condition before serving. Monitor stock rotation and selling dates. Clean the beer lines (pipes) thoroughly at least every 7 days. The same goes for the cellar – it should be kept spotlessly clean.

Stillage casks should be stored horizontally for a minimum of 48 hours prior to sale. Vent them on the day of delivery, peg them about 2 hours after delivery and tap them 24 to 48 hours before sale. Most beers should be sold within 3 days to avoid having too many on the bar at once. At closing time always insert a hard peg into the cask to preserve quality.

Train your staff to serve the perfect pint: always use a cool, clean and dry glass – preferably correctly branded; aim for a 10 mm deep head; remember, good presentation is vital and can encourage customers to return for more.

Tools required to maintain the cleanliness of cellars

In order to maintain a high level of cleanliness and ensure the quality of wines, beers and soft drinks, a series of tools are required. These include:

- Shelving, racks and cradles. Below are some pictures that illustrate the type of racks and cradles that can be used to store wines and spirits.

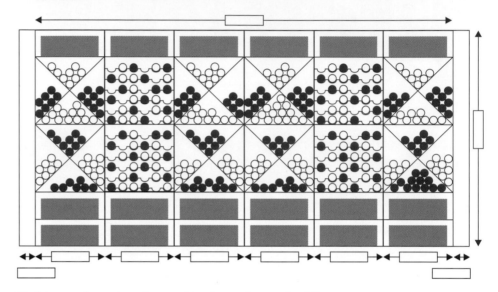

Shelving, racks and cradles used to store wines and spirits

Wine rack

A different type of wine rack

■ Wine cellar cooling units assist in regulating the temperature and humidity of wine rooms which experience very high or low temperatures. Wine cellar cooling units are generally straightforward to install, and in situ, are quiet and efficient.

Wine cellar cooling unit

■ Cleaning systems: Cellars need to be swept and floors cleaned with disinfectant frequently (at least twice a month). A busy cellar should be cleaned once a week.

CASE STUDY – STOCK ROTATION OF BEER

How old is my beer?

■ All beers have a best-before (BB) date label stuck to the top of the keg. When taking delivery of any beer it is of great importance first, that a best-before label is attached and second, that the date indicated will give you at least several weeks in which to sell it.

■ As in all food industries brewers are required by law to indicate the best-before date of their products. The label on the keg should indicate the product name and also the BB date. You will also see lots of other codes and numbers. Secret brewery stuff. The BB date is the important one.

■ Keg beers have quite a long shelf life, or cellar life in this case. This can in some cases be 8 weeks for keg beers and 4 weeks for cask ales.

■ So when the dray comes to the cellar door make sure of the following:

  – Keg beers: Make sure that the BB date gives you at least a month before it expires.

  – Cask ale beers: Make sure the BB date gives you at least 2 weeks before it expires.

  – Make sure that all kegs and casks are sealed properly.

  – No label, no delivery.

  – As a good customer of the brewery you are within your rights not to accept beer that you think does not give you a sufficient shelf-life.

  – Most brewers go out of their way to make sure you have good fresh beer, but it is up to you to check.

Why check?

■ If you have beer in your cellar that has passed it's best-before date, even if the keg or cask is unopened, most breweries or wholesalers will not give you any credit for your loss. So be warned.

And finally

■ To keep your beer fresh do not over-stock. You should plan on selling a full keg of any product, beer or lager, within at least a week. After that you could experience problems.

■ Cask beers should be sold within 3 days. It is better to have no beer to sell than sell beer that has gone off. Your customers will remember.

■ Best advice, make your local technician a nice cup of tea and he will give you the best advice for your particular business.

 ACTIVITY

Now apply this to wine:

■ How do you keep wine fresh and appropriately rotated?

■ How do you ensure you don't over order wine?

■ How long does wine last?

Ask at your workplace if you can help with taking the next wine order…

Security of cellars

Cellars must be kept secure at all times. Aspects of security include:

- *Locks*: Cellars must be kept locked at all times when the cellar/store person is not nearby.
- *Paperwork*: Logs must be kept to track goods in and out of the cellar. This may include delivery notes from suppliers, as well as requisitions from outlets (bars) that the cellar supplies. In a hotel a cellar may supply drink to many outlets including room service, restaurants, bars, cocktail bars and the kitchen.
- *Par levels*: Maximum and minimum levels of stock should be logged and maintained at all times in order to avoid running out of stock during busy periods and stock going out-of-date in quieter periods.
- *Authorized personnel*: Only allocated and authorized personnel should be allowed into the cellar at any time.
- *CCTV*: To monitor the comings and goings from the cellar to ensure that stock in and out of the cellar is appropriately logged.

RESEARCH ACTIVITY – WINE CELLAR FORMS

1 What forms are required to help maintain the par levels, ordering of stock and security in a wine cellar?

2 Ask your workplace or a work environment you are familiar with for copies of the different forms.

3 Write half-a-page about how they are used.

4 Show this to your teacher for feedback.

PREPARE KEGS AND GAS FOR USE

Kegs

Kegs can be used for the storage of beer, ales and ciders. In recent years some wines are also stored and served using a keg system. Kegs used in bars are generally delivered and collected by the supplier (wholesaler). Empty kegs are collected from the establishments and returned to the brewery where they are handled by a fully automatic cleaning and filling process. Breweries use their own facilities and systems to fill kegs to ensure the quality of the product. Usually no air or other liquid is able to enter the sterilized keg and therefore the beer is protected from contamination. When beer is delivered to an establishment, it is the responsibility of that establishment to ensure that kegs are stored and then dispensed properly so that the customer gets the freshest best-quality product possible.

Beer kegs

Gas cylinders

Two different types of gas are used in the dispensing of beer. They are:

- CO_2 (carbon dioxide) and
- CO_2/Nitrogen mix.

The sides of the gas cylinders are clearly labelled so that the type of gas can be easily identified and used according to organizational requirements.

The purpose of the gas is:

- To provide sufficient pressure to push the contents of the keg to the point of dispense.
- To fill the air space left in the keg above the beer when it is pushed from the keg.
- To keep the beer in good condition in the keg.
- To prevent the CO_2 which is already in the beer and which gives beer its 'fizz', from escaping.

Cylinders, as well as kegs, must be handled with great care as both are stored and used under constant pressure. They must be:

- Stored away from heat and direct sunlight.
- Always kept in an upright position.
- Securely clamped or chained to a wall.

Develop efficient and organized work habits

Kegs and gas cylinders are usually found in the cellar or in a specifically allocated room.

Storage is generally limited and therefore it is imperative to be organized to avoid constant unnecessary physical work in moving kegs and gas cylinders. Remember that kegs and gas cylinders are very heavy. It is also worth bearing in mind that kegs and gas cylinders are susceptible to movement and changes of atmosphere that can adversely affect the quality of the product.

■ Always keep kegs and gas cylinders in specified areas.

■ Plan your movements when handling kegs and gas cylinders to avoid any unnecessary lifting.

■ Ensure you are fully aware of the correct procedures when handling kegs and gas cylinders to avoid injury and accident.

■ If spillage occurs, make sure it is cleaned up immediately.

■ Always follow connecting and disconnecting procedures to ensure safety and security.

■ Always follow specific cleaning instructions to ensure freshness and quality of the beer and customer satisfaction.

Beer kegs

Fob detectors

Modern bars usually include fob detectors in the dispense system to eliminate beer wastage, caused by excess gas, which otherwise occurs;

■ when a keg becomes empty

■ when a new keg is tapped

■ when first drinks are pulled in the morning from a part-used keg.

The fob detector is normally attached to the wall over the keg and is linked up with the beer lines. It acts as a control mechanism, the float inside it allowing the dispense system to operate only while there is a continuous flow of beer from the keg. If gas or foam accumulate in the beer lines, the detector cuts off the system. If this happens because the keg is empty, the system will only work again when a new keg is connected.

Fob detectors must be cleaned every week, with the beer lines, to prevent dispensing problems. Before starting to clean make sure the vent valve lever is in the upright vertical position and the float lift lever is in the 'lift' position.

■ When chamber fills, return vent valve lever to the horizontal position.

■ When the lines have been rinsed with water, move float lever to 'beer flow' position before re-tapping the keg.

■ Do not use sponge pellets when cleaning the fob detector.

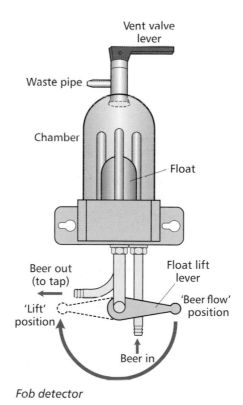

Fob detector

ACTIVITY

Can you follow these steps yourself in your work environment?

How to use the fob detector:

■ When beer stops coming through the tap, this means the keg is empty.

■ In the cellar disconnect empty keg and connect a full keg.

■ Bleed the fob detector through the small valve at the top.

■ Make sure the fob glass is full to the top. Close valve after use.

■ Then and only then press the release button upwards.

■ Check that the ball rises to the top of the fob glass.

■ When fob detector glass is full and the ball is at the top, pull the release button back down into the down position.

■ Do not leave ball release button in the up position.

Fob detectors

ACTIVITY

Get your supervisor to watch you:

■ Check a keg is empty.

■ Check a gas cylinder is empty.

■ Change a keg (disconnect, remove, replace and reconnect).

■ Change a gas cylinder (disconnect, remove, replace and reconnect).

CHANGING KEGS AND GAS CYLINDERS

Kegs and gas cylinders are changed when they are empty. They will generally not be empty at the same time, but when one is empty it must be changed immediately.

Kegs will be empty when:

■ There is no beer coming out of the tap.

■ The beer is very 'heady'.

■ The keg is very light.

Gas cylinders will be empty when:

■ The beer is flat.

■ There is no pressure.

■ The cylinder is very light.

■ The pressure gauge is reading empty.

Disconnecting and removing kegs

Always follow manufacturer's instructions when disconnecting kegs:

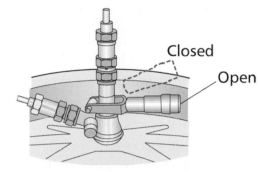

- Ensure gas is turned off and leads are removed and stored until needed for the next keg.

- Pull the lever on the coupling head upwards and turn the coupling head anti-clockwise until it is released from the keg.

Keg coupling head

- Empty kegs should be stored in a separate part of the cellar from full and used kegs. They should not be stacked more than two high.

- When lifting kegs, follow moving procedures to avoid injury.

- Never try to remove any parts of the keg, especially the extractor tube, as this action could cause great injury.

Disconnecting gas cylinders

Always follow manufacturer's instructions when disconnecting gas cylinders:

- Turn off the valve on the gas cylinder before disconnecting, unscrew connector.

- Check the gauge to make sure the cylinder is empty.

- Remove the gas leads carefully, this will have to be done with a spanner.

- The gas cylinders will be held securely to a wall by a chain or clamp. This stops the cylinder from falling. If a cylinder falls over, the valve may be damaged causing gas to escape. As the gas is escaping, the cylinder may actually be propelled around the cellar where it is stored, due to the pressure in the cylinder. This can cause not only a great deal of damage to the cellar, but also injure someone who may enter the cellar at that time. Undo the chain before moving the gas cylinder.

- Move gas cylinders carefully, usually by rolling to the storage area.

Disconnecting a gas cylinder

CONNECTING NEW KEGS AND GAS CYLINDERS CORRECTLY

Connecting kegs

Always follow manufacturer's instructions:

- Make sure you are using the appropriate beer.

■ Always use the FIFO (first in first out) system to ensure the freshest product possible.

■ Kegs should be handled carefully to avoid unnecessary agitation, especially just before tapping.

■ There will be a protective cover over the valve, which must be removed. The type of beer in the keg will also be printed on this cover, as well as on the side of the keg.

■ Remove the protective cover.

■ When tapping a keg, do not lean over the keg. This will ensure your safety as well as avoiding you getting wet with beer, should the valve be faulty.

■ Use a clean coupling head and insert into the keg. Turn clockwise, but do not over-tighten.

■ Make sure the beer and gas lines are correctly connected.

■ Pull the lever on the coupling head down until it clicks. This allows it to flow.

■ If you are connecting more than one keg creating a 'bank', do not connect more kegs on to one another than specified by the manufacturer.

Tapping the keg

■ Ensure handle is in 'closed' position.

■ Position keg coupler above valve so that locating lugs align with slots in neck.

■ Fit coupler in keg neck and turn clockwise a quarter turn or 90°.

Important: do not tighten beyond limit

■ Connect gas line to side of the coupler.

■ Pull out handle and depress until it locks into position.

■ Connect beer line to top of the coupler.

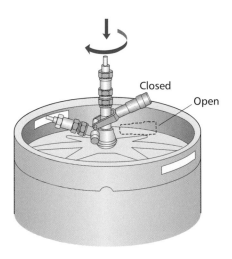

Closed

Open

Tapping a keg

Connecting gas cylinders

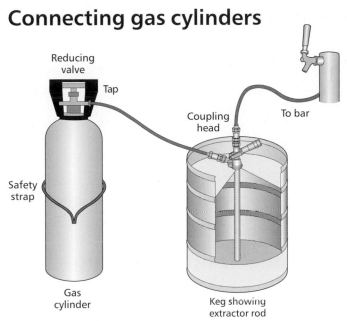

Connecting a gas cylinder and keg

It is important to be aware of the properties of CO_2. It is odourless, colourless, it sinks to the ground and you cannot see it.

Always follow manufacturer's instructions:

- Remember that gas cylinders are under a great deal of pressure so they must be handled carefully.
- Make sure that the cylinder is securely attached to the wall to prevent it from falling over.
- Do not use gas cylinders that have passed their expiry date.
- Remove the protective tape from the outlet valve.
- Very quickly turn the valve on and then off again. This blows away any dust or moisture that may be on the valve, and will allow you to check that you are not accidentally connecting an empty cylinder.
- Connect the reducing valve to the cylinder. You should use a new washer – these are small plastic rings. Tighten the nut with a spanner.
- When the gas is connected, do not forget to turn it on!
- Check the meter to ensure that the pressure is as required.
- If you hear hissing, therefore a leak, inform your supervisor.
- If you suspect a leak, but cannot hear a noise, squeeze some liquid soap or soapy water over the joint. If bubbles form, then there is a leak.

Changing a gas cylinder

Checking a pressurized keg

Gas cylinder control panel

Changing a gas cylinder

1 Shut off to the right completely (clockwise).

2 Disconnect slowly, allowing gas to escape. Leave used cylinder secured to wall until all the fittings have been disconnected and all gas noises stop.

3 Remove old cylinder and secure new cylinder to wall bracket.

4 Connect to new CO_2 cylinder using good or new washer.

5 Open to the left (counter-clockwise) very slowly until gas noise stops, then open all the way till knob stops.

The figure on the previous page shows how the gas cylinder and the keg are connected to one another.

New kegs or gas cylinder is not operating correctly

If you discover that there is something not quite right with the keg or gas cylinder, for example, you detect a leak, this must be reported to your supervisor immediately. A new keg or gas cylinder must be used in place of the damaged one, which must be labelled with its fault, so it can be returned to the brewery or gas supplier.

Note

■ Ale does not use gas and therefore does not have connectors to a gas cylinder.

■ They are also stored on their sides instead of upright.

■ The picture shows the connector for a keg of ale.

STORING USED KEGS AND GAS CYLINDERS

All used kegs and gas cylinders must be stored according to organizational requirements:

■ There must be an allocated storage area from where the brewery and the gas supplier will collect their respective kegs or cylinders.

- All kegs must be stored carefully to ensure the safety of staff.
- Do not stack the kegs on top of one another unless an interleaving sheet of plywood or similar material separates them to avoid toppling of kegs.
- Gas cylinders must be stored upright fixed to a wall or lying down.
- All kegs and cylinders must be stored in a dry area where they are not exposed to extreme temperatures.
- Kegs and cylinders must also be in a secure place where they will not be stolen.

MOVING A KEG

Always follow these techniques to avoid injury or accidents:

- Wear sturdy shoes and gloves to protect against metal splinters.
- Stand in front of the upright keg, feet apart to give you balance. Place hands at 'ten to two' position on top rim of keg.
- Use your body weight to tilt the keg slightly towards you so that it is balanced on the rim. Move smoothly, do not jerk!
- Use your hands to turn the keg so that it moves on its rim to the required position. Move your feet as you go to avoid twisting your body. Allow returning to the upright position.
- Gas cylinders can also be rolled in a similar manner, being very careful not to tip the cylinder on to yourself.

Assessment of knowledge and understanding

You have now learned about cellar maintenance and how to safely use kegs and gas cylinders including: cleanliness and security of cellars; storage of bar-related products in the cellar; how to safely replace, store and swap between empty and full kegs and gas cylinders, in order to ensure the quality of drinks sold in a hospitality outlet.

To test your level of knowledge and understanding, answer the following short questions. These will help to prepare you for your summative (final) assessment.

Consider your responses to the following questions:

Cellar maintenance

1 Why do you think drinks products are more susceptible to theft?

_____

2 Why should you monitor and control the personnel allowed in and out of the cellar?

_____

3 What should you do in the case of breakages in the cellar?

_____

4 How often should the cellar be cleaned?

_____

5 How often should cellar equipment be checked to ensure that it is clean and in good working order?

_____

6 What might happen if cellar equipment is not kept in good working order?

_____

7 What could happen if the cellar environmental conditions are not adhered to appropriately?

_____

Kegs and gas cylinders

1 List the safety points to remember when tapping a keg and changing a gas cylinder.

_____

2 Why should gas cylinders be securely fixed to the wall?

_____

3 Why should you always inform someone that you are going to the cellar?

_____

4 Explain FIFO in the context of kegs and cylinders.

_____

5 Why is there a protective cover over the keg valve?

_____

6 Why should you **not** use gas cylinders that have passed their expiry date?

_____

7 How can you check that beer is not old?

_____

Practical exercises

Ask your supervisor to observe you:

■ Changing a keg.

■ Changing a gas cylinder.

Ask your supervisor how to:

■ 'Bleed' excess air from the system.

Show your supervisor:

■ The different connections for each type of beer served in your organization.

■ A safe method of moving and storing used kegs and gas cylinders.

INDUSTRY PROFILE

Name: **MARK STROOBANDT**

Position: MASTER BEER SOMMELIER AND DIRECTOR THE F&B PARTNERSHIP

Establishment: LONDON, DUBLIN, BIRMINGHAM, WORKING GLOBALLY

Current job role and main responsibilities:
Director The F&B Partnership and master beer sommelier. Responsible for developing and creating drinks and food training programmes and events. Delivering content through face to face and on the job training, presentations, tastings and master class. I do media work including press launches, TV and radio plus training other trainers within our team.

How do you stay in touch and keep up-to-date with the latest trends in speciality beers?
Mainly through personal relationships with brewers, brand owners and operators within the On and Off trade, but also trade magazines, press, internet and consumer feed-back.

When did you realize that you wanted to pursue a career in the food and beverage service industry?
During my first year at law school in Ghent, Belgium I worked in a speciality beer bar to fund my studies and it is there I realized that I liked it more than studying law. The bar owner introduced me to many brewers and opened a new world of speciality beers to me and instilled a passion and desire for more knowledge which led me to take various courses and a stint at a catering college in Brussels.

Training:
Draught master training course with InBev Belgium; brewery courses with Belgian brewers; catering college CERIA in Brussels; Train 2 Train course with Belgo restaurants, London; BRI beer appreciation course; BIIAB ABCQ course; beer academy foundation course.

Experience:
Hopduvel, speciality beer bar in Ghent, Belgium: bartender, beer sommelier; Waterhuis a/d Bierkant, speciality beer bar in Ghent, Belgium: general manager; Belgo restaurant group: head bartender, executive bar and drinks development manager; self employed: consultant to various breweries and On and Off trade companies; The F&B Partnership: director and master beer sommelier.

What do you find rewarding about your job?
Working with a great business partner and support team and the ability to pass on my knowledge and instil passion. I love changing hearts and minds on people's perception about beer, and beer and food.

What do you find the most challenging about the job?
Overcoming old-fashioned thinking, preconceived ideas and inefficient work practices with people who are reluctant to change their thinking.

What advice would you give to students just beginning their career?
Whatever happens in the world people still will love to eat and drink and you can play a pivotal role in that. You need to reach a point where you have to be honest with yourself and admit you actually like doing this line of work and that you can be great at it and that catering is a rewarding, challenging, but above all, fun career.

Who is your mentor or main inspiration?
Many people along my career path have inspired me and I draw from people with passion and belief in what they do. These have been people I work with or people who aspire to achieve great things within our industry.

What traits do you consider essential for anyone entering a career in the food and drink sector?
See it as career where the sky is the limit; have a passion for food and drink; love what you do and be proud of what you do as not many can do it well; never stop learning and always find out the why to better understand; be a team player but don't be afraid to lead; you need people skills and the ability to cope with stress; know how to smile and how to deliver great service; don't let work overtake your life.

A brief personal profile
Marc is a regular commentator for beer in the trade and consumer press. He was awarded an honorary knighthood by the Chevalerie du Fourquest des Brasseurs of the Confederation of Belgian Brewers and he is also Commander in the Order of De Roze Olifant. Marc has just completed and is about to embark on another media tour in the US encompassing press, TV and radio communicating his passion and love of beer to the trade and consumer. Marc has worked with clients such as Inbev UK, Anheuser-Busch, Carlsberg UK, The Belgian Embassy, The Belgian Tourist Board, Majestic Wine, Harvey Nichols, Leith School of Food and Wine, Fortis Bank and Coca-Cola.

Can you give one essential management tip or piece of industry advice?
Only great service will do, retail is detail and the customer is king as they spend the money.

20

Clean drink dispense lines

Unit 616 (2DS6) Clean drink dispense lines

2DS6.1 Clean drink dispense lines

What do I need to do?

- Prepare the drink dispense line system ready for cleaning.
- Clean the drink dispense line.
- Know how to check that pipes are clean and free from debris, detergent and water.
- Know how to check the drink is of the correct quality for service.

What do I need to know?

- How to clean drink dispense lines.
- How to dilute cleaning materials appropriately.
- How to get the appropriate equipment together to clean dispense lines.

Information covered in this chapter

- Policies and legislations on beer line cleaning.
- Line cleaning chemicals and equipment.
- Line cleaning procedures.
- Cleaning the drinks dispense lines.

KEY WORDS

Bacteria

Bacteria found in beer is not significantly hazardous to human health; however, its effect is noticeable in the appearance, aroma and taste of beer. The presence of bacteria results in an 'off taste' and cloudy appearance that makes beer unappetizing. A beer that tastes sour, vinegar-like, or smells like rotten eggs may indicate a beer system is contaminated with beer-spoiling bacteria.

Beer stones

The raw materials, grains and water, that are used in the brewing process contain calcium. Oxalic acids or salts are present in hops and may be created during the process of changing barley into malt. The combination of these ingredients and the fact that beer is dispensed at cold temperatures may result in calcium oxalate deposits known as beer stone.

Faucet handles

Sometimes called a faucet knob or tap handle. This is the lever that you pull on the faucet to make the beer come out.

Faucets

This is where the beer comes out. There are lots of parts inside the faucet, so it should be cleaned regularly.

Keg couplers

This piece attaches to the keg and actually taps it. There are six different types of keg couplers used throughout the world. Which ones you will need will depend upon which brand of beer you dispense.

Litmus paper

Paper with powder extracted from certain plants that tests the pH of a substance. Acid turns red while base turns blue; neutral remains white. The stronger the acid or base, the more intense red or blue the colour of the litmus paper.

Yeast

May result from an extremely small amount left from the brewing process, or it may be wild yeast which floats in the air. It is usually found as a surface growth on components of a beer system that are exposed to the air such as faucets, keg couplers, and drains and can be recognized by its white or grey colour.

INTRODUCTION

It is essential to clean drink dispense lines on a regular basis in order to prevent the build up of bacteria, yeast, mould, and even beer stones. Dirty lines lower the quality and taste of drinks dispensed through those lines. It is important to regularly clean drinks lines, faucets and keg couplers to ensure the dispense of high quality drinks, including beer.

CASE STUDY – *THE PUBLICAN*

Dirty beer lines could break the law

15 November, 2006
By Phil Mellows

Licensees warned at Beer Forum

Publicans could be contravening food safety laws by not cleaning their beer lines properly.

The warning came at a Beer Forum organized by *The Publican* in which industry opinion-formers debated the issues facing the pub beer market and discussed the results of *The Publican*'s 2006 Beer Report survey – including the fact that 11 per cent of licensees admit to not cleaning their lines weekly, as recommended by brewers.

Recent estimates have been much higher, with the suggestion from some quarters that up to eight in 10 pubs are not cleaning their lines at least once a week. Forum attendees were shocked, if less than surprised, that so many admit their poor practice, and that as many as 23 per cent say they have not had any cellar management training.

Courtesy of The Publican, *www.thepublican.com*

BREWERY POLICIES ON LINE CLEANING

Suppliers of beer and post-mix drinks know the importance of proper line cleaning and the impact it will have on their products, reputation and sales. Most suppliers publish line cleaning procedures and schedules within their quality assurance policies. These policies are monitored and enforced by contracted distributors where legal, depending on state statutes.

A review of the individual brewery policies reveals that there is a consensus that it is important to clean a draft system at a *minimum of once every two weeks*. But *once a week is the recommended frequency* for cleaning lines where used in high volume.

The cleaning process and chemicals used to clean and sanitize the system will also vary with the type and length of the drink dispensing system.

Legislation

Legislation regarding the cleaning of drink dispense lines includes:

■ In most EU countries it is a mandatory obligation as part of food and hygiene legislation that beer lines are sanitized regularly and to a set standard.

■ It is part of an employer's 'duty of care' to ensure the workplace is a safe environment to work (Health and Safety at Work Act, 1974), in addition the workplace has a 'duty of care' to the customer to ensure that they are frequenting an environment that is also safe.

■ Control of Substances Hazardous to Health – COSHH.

Using chemicals or other hazardous substances at work can put people's health at risk. So the law requires employers to control exposure to hazardous substances to prevent ill-health. For further information, please go to the following website: http://www.hse.gov.uk/coshh/

In relation to the cleaning of drink dispense lines, please note the following:

1 Always have available COSHH information sheets for all chemicals used (contact your supplier for further information).

2 Always store cleaning chemicals out of childrens' reach.

3 Always keep chemicals in the supplier's container until needed for use.

4 Always rinse clean measuring vessel immediately after use.

5 Always use manufacturer's measuring vessel where supplied.

6 Always wear protective goggles, gloves and apron when handling chemicals.

7 Never put cleaning chemicals into containers intended for other products including aluminium containers.

8 Never put cleaning chemicals into cups or glasses; they may be drunk in error.

9 Never use cleaning chemicals for any purpose other than that for which they are supplied.

10 Never mix chemicals with one another.

Line-cleaning chemicals

An effective line-cleaning chemical must be used to attack the enemies of beer previously mentioned. Line cleaners will be either caustic with a high pH, or acidic with a low pH depending on the line conditions and the type of system being cleaned.

Alkaline (caustic) cleaners attack and dissolve proteins, carbohydrates, hop resins and bio-films. They also are very effective in killing mould, bacteria and yeast.

 **ACTIVITY**

Can you remember what the enemies of beer are?

Acid line cleaners dissolve minerals that are commonly referred to as beer stone.

Both caustic and acid line cleaners can be very dangerous if not handled and used properly. You should always follow the directions printed on the package and strictly adhere to the manufacturer's recommended concentration levels. Using the proper concentration level is the safest and most cost-effective method for beer line cleaning.

You should always wear personal safety equipment including eye protection and rubber gloves when handling line-cleaning chemicals. It is also important to never mix an alkaline solution with an acid solution.

ACTIVITY

What will happen if you mix an alkaline solution with an acid solution?

CLEANING THE DRINKS DISPENSE LINES

Line-cleaning procedure

There are two unique methods employed to clean draught beer dispensing systems:

- *Pressurized cleaning*: This method is usually done by putting the cleaning agent into a plastic or metal container and forcing it through the drinks lines via the use of a hand pump or gas pressure (CO_2 or compressed air).

The containers have a means of connecting the drinks system either through a faucet adaptor or a coupler for the beer valve (tap). Pressurized cleaning containers make it quick and easy to clean picnic pumps, direct draw and short-draw systems of less than 20 feet in length.

- *Re-circulating cleaning*: Uses a motorized electric pump that is especially built for beer line cleaning. These pumps are equipped with connectors to enable cleaning the system from the tap or faucet end.

Re-circulating cleaning is always the best choice for long draw systems that are over 20 feet (i.e. the drink is being pulled from its original container to the glass over a length of 20 feet of pipes). The turbulent flow of the cleaning solution is up to 80 times more effective than simply allowing the cleaning solution to soak inside the beer lines as is the case through pressurized cleaning.

No matter what type of cleaning system you are using, it is recommended that a proven three-step cleaning procedure is used to ensure that the lines are thoroughly cleaned and sanitized in order to maintain the integrity of the drink.

1 Begin by flushing the beer from the lines with water. This eliminates beer from the lines so as not to dilute the cleaning properties of the chemical.

2 Next, clean the lines with the appropriate solution. Allow chemicals to circulate or soak in the lines for at least 10 minutes.

3 The final step is to thoroughly flush the chemical from the lines with water. After the water rinse cycle is completed, it is recommended to check the pH level with a pH tester or litmus paper to ensure that no cleaning solution remains in the lines. Then reconnect the kegs and allow some beer to run through the faucet and discard to make sure all the lines are completely refilled with beer.

Line-cleaning equipment

1 Two buckets (receptacles) – one for clean water and one for cleaning detergent.

2 One smaller bucket to place sparklers and other loose pieces of equipment from dispense end of pumps and lines.

3 Correct cleaning chemicals.

4 Litmus paper (if supplied by cleaning chemical company).

5 COSHH hand-outs to go with the cleaning chemicals used.

6 Damp cloth.

Swan neck beer dispenser

With and without sparkler beer taps

A STEP-BY-STEP METHOD FOR CLEANING DRINKS DISPENSE LINES

1 Preparing the drinks dispense line ready for cleaning (if using a gas pump cleaning system)

■ Fill water cleaning container with water.

■ Turn off gas supply to keg couplers.

■ Check that float ball is at top of fob detector to indicate the gas pressure.

■ Connect keg couplers to cleaning main and press to open position.

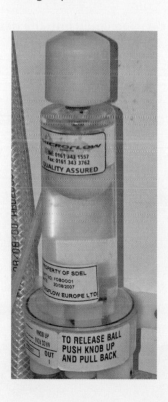

■ Turn on cleaning main gas pump.

■ Unscrew sparklers from dispense taps and immerse in a receptacle containing diluted detergent.

■ Place a receptacle under each dispense tap and flush through system until all traces of drink are removed.

2 Clean the drinks dispense line using correctly diluted cleaning agents and recommended equipment

■ Measure the correct quantity of pipe cleaning liquid into the detergent cleaning container. If separate detergent container is available, fill with cold water and mix thoroughly. If only one container is available re-use water container.

■ If using a cleaning main with two containers, turn the selector cock from water to detergent container.

■ Fill the system with detergent solution.

■ If a fob detector or beer monitor is fitted, the manual vent valve must be opened for a few seconds to allow detergent solution to flow down the vent pipe.

■ Allow dispense equipment to soak for 15 minutes.

■ After 15 minutes pull fresh cleaning fluid through system again – the water will either feel slimey or if a dye has been used in the cleaning fluid, you will notice a different colour to the liquid.

■ Rinse out cleaning fluid container thoroughly with fresh water and refill with fresh water or use separate fresh water container if available.

3 Make sure cleaned pipes and taps are free from debris, detergent and water

■ If using a cleaning main with two containers, turn the selector cock from detergent to water container.

■ Flush out the system with at least two gallons of water per dispenser.

■ Flush through system until all traces of detergent are removed.

■ Check with litmus paper supplied with cleaning fluid if available.

■ If a fob detector or beer monitor is fitted, open the manual vent valve to rinse detergent from the vent pipe.

■ Turn off gas supply to cleaning pump.

■ Reconnect keg couplers to drinks containers in use.

■ Turn on gas supply to drinks containers.

■ Switch on inline flash coolers.

■ Flush through system until all traces of water are removed.

■ Rinse sparklers in running water and refit to dispense taps.

- Drain and rinse cleaning containers, and replace caps.
- Pull through to drink (beer or soft drink) and test for clarity and taste.
- The outside of the pipes may be cleaned with a warm damp cloth.

4 Ensure that the drink is of the correct quality for service

- By following the above steps you can be sure that the drinks served are of the correct quality.
- In addition, you should taste test each drink that has had its lines cleaned.

CASE STUDY – JUST ICE!

A recent UK government SMART award has helped fund a ground-breaking project at 42 Technology Limited – work which could soon see landlords, hoteliers and club managers enjoying significant time and cost savings associated with the tedious task of cleaning beer dispense lines. More importantly to the brewer and drinker, the innovative method aspires to guarantee a sparkling delivery from barrel to glass.

The process is based upon ice technology originally pioneered at Bristol University. Working in close association with Brewing Research International, 42 Technology developed a prototype process which will enable beer dispense systems to be cleaned every time a barrel or keg is changed; using nothing more than a fine slurry of ice which scours the components as it is pumped through. No cleaning fluids, no special solutions, just ice!

It is widely known that the nature of many draught beers causes microbiological action in the beer dispense lines – cask beer, for example, is after all a 'living' product.

Although modern kegs ensure their contents remain in a high quality, sterile condition, the final journey to the glass can be a very unhygienic path through couplers, joints, lines, fob detectors and eventually taps. All of which provide a perfect environment for the cultivation of yeast and bacterial colonies, with the unmistakable result of foul-tasting, contaminated beer with a tainted aroma and poor appearance.

To make matters even worse, deposits known as 'beer stone', a calcium deposit that builds up over many months, also act as a haven for the biological constituents. After just one treatment with the ice slurry, a substantial amount of beer stone is removed, giving a clear indication that the ice slurry can be effective at both removing and preventing build-up of beer stone in dispense line systems.

Lengthy trials of 42 Technology's new ice process have shown that slugs of ice pumped through entire beer dispense systems will remove build-ups of microbiological organisms that are unaffected by existing cleaning methods.

Traditional cleaning, involving regular use of powerful chemicals is known to kill most of the contamination, but does not typically remove the denatured organisms from the line, leaving behind a foothold for the next generation of biofilm. Such chemical systems have a number of disadvantages which in practice means that beer lines are cleaned poorly or far too infrequently. In addition to being extremely unfriendly to the environment, the hazards of using these chemicals are often under-estimated. Many end-users are failing to observe or are simply unaware of the strict safety guidelines. Unfortunately, it is very rare to find them using protective gloves, goggles or face masks that are deemed vital, by Health and Safety regulations, when dealing with these extremely corrosive chemicals.

The application of ice technology, in its ideal embodiment, could be an integrated cleaning system which runs automatically, with little intervention from the landlord. The ice slurry itself has to be produced from a liquid with a freezing point suppressant. This enables the suspension of ice crystals giving the required flow characteristics. Fortunately, alcohol is an ideal freezing point suppressant, making it highly suitable for use as the working fluid to make the ice slurry. This opens the possibility that it might not be necessary to flush the system at all! Such an approach may have the potential to almost completely eliminate beer loss and the labour required to clean lines.

Courtesy of 42 Technology, September 2003

Assessment of knowledge and understanding

You have now learned about the procedures involved in cleaning drinks dispense lines and the best practice required for this task.

To test your level of knowledge and understanding, answer the following short questions. These will help to prepare you for your summative (final) assessment.

1 Why is it important to clean drink dispense lines?

2 Why is it important to make sure cleaning agents are correctly diluted?

3 What equipment do you need to clean drink dispense lines?

4 Why should online beverages be tested after cleaning the pipes and lines?

5 Why should the lines be thoroughly rinsed with clean water after cleaning and before use?

6 Identify the type of unexpected situations that might occur and discuss how to deal with these situations.

Project 1

Go to a bar/pub near you and ask if you can watch them cleaning the drink dispense lines.

Research task

Research and investigate how and why the following form in drinks dispense lines:

■ bacteria

■ yeast

■ mould

■ beer stones

Ask your assessor to evaluate you based on completing the following tasks:

1 disconnecting a fob detector

2 disconnecting a keg

3 disconnecting a gas cylinder

4 connecting a fob detector

5 connecting a keg

6 connecting a gas cylinder

21

Receive, handle and store drinks stock

Unit 619 Receive, store and issue drinks stock

2DS2.1 Receive drinks deliveries

2DS2.2 Store and issue drinks stock

What do I need to do?
■ Know how bar items are ordered.
■ Know how and where bar items are stored.

What do I need to know?
■ How drinks and bar stock are delivered.
■ How bar stock is stored.
■ How bar stock is issued from stores to a bar.
■ How stock-takes are carried out.

Information covered in this chapter
■ The goods receiving and storage cycle.
■ Drinks deliveries.
■ Storing drinks and bar products.
■ Issuing drinks and bar products.
■ Stock-takes and inventories.
■ Ordering stock.

KEY WORDS

Stock
Produce or beverages in the store room.

Deliveries
When ordered goods arrive.

Inventory
Another term for a stock list.

INTRODUCTION

Receiving, storing and issuing drinks stock is an important part of the operation of a bar or restaurant. It is a function that not only occurs in the bar but in kitchens and retail outlets as well.

The entire function occurs in a cycle of which each part is dependent on the other areas. In large operations this process is very formal and includes a clear recording process for all the transactions, in smaller operations this process would be less formal and would depend more on the employees' integrity. The important factor is that bar and drinks stock is expensive and needs to be bought, stored and sold in the correct manner.

TIP

This is a very formal approach to stock control. It will occur in all premises but in a more informal approach.

GOODS RECEIVING AND STORAGE CYCLE

Within the subject of stock all the areas are related and have an impact on one another. Stock cannot be issued without the establishment knowing how much they have already. Drinks cannot be issued if they are not being held within the establishment.

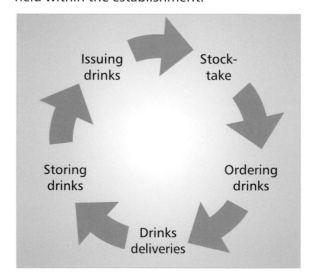

The storage cycle

DRINKS DELIVERIES

Deliveries of beverage stock should be organized at a time convenient to the establishment. For example, if the establishment is busy from lunch-time through the afternoon then arrangements should be made for the deliveries to be done first thing in the morning.

Stock being delivered

When the delivery arrives a member of staff should check the delivery and sign the delivery note given to the company to acknowledge receipt of the goods.

CHECKLIST FOR DELIVERIES

✓ Have the correct items been delivered?

✓ Is there the correct amount of items?

✓ Are any of the items broken or damaged?

✓ Have any items been substituted?

✓ Are the items within their 'use-by' dates?

If there are any discrepancies or items missing from the delivery then this should be noted on the delivery note. Once the delivery note has been returned to the company they will issue an invoice for the establishment to pay.

STORING DRINKS AND BAR PRODUCTS

Alcohol store

Alcohol is an expensive commodity, therefore it needs to be stored in a secure area. Depending on the size of the establishment this can range from a large cellar where thousands of pounds of stock is held, to a cupboard behind the bar where a few bottles of spirits are kept.

There are a few things that should be in place in cellars or alcohol stores, these include:

- The area should be able to be locked or secured to prevent unauthorized access.
- The area should be free from pests or infestation.
- The area should be cool, well-ventilated and dry, not exposed to excessive heat or damp.
- The area should have suitable shelving.
- The area should be able to be kept clean and tidy.
- The area should be well lit and employees should be able to locate items easily.
- A clear system of organization should be used. Items could be placed in alphabetical order, to ensure that they can be easily located.

When putting stock into the store a 'first in first out' policy should be used. All the existing stock should be taken off the shelves in the stores and the newest stock is placed at the back of the shelf with the most recent dates at the front. By using this system the establishment can ensure that it is selling only items that are legally deemed fit for human consumption.

The stores should contain enough stock to supply a few services but large amounts of stock should not be held within an establishment as it can have financial implications for the premises.

> **TIP**
>
> First in First out ensures that the stock with the nearest 'use-by' date is at the front of the shelves and can be utilized first.

ACTIVITY

Imagine that you are organizing your drinks stores at work and you notice that you have four cases of cider that need to be sold or used by the end of the following month.

■ What action could you suggest to your supervisor to enhance the selling of these products?

■ Design some marketing material for the items.

THE STORAGE OF DIFFERENT BAR ITEMS

TYPE OF DELIVERY	WHERE IT SHOULD BE STORED	PROBLEMS
Crated bottled drinks	The bottles can be stored within the crates and the crates can be stacked safely. Often the empty bottles need to be returned in the crates.	The empty crates can use a great deal of space.
Boxed bottled drinks	The bottles can be delivered in boxes, frequently cardboard. The bottles need to be removed from the boxes and placed on shelves.	If a bottle is damaged or a cardboard box gets damp the box can become damaged.
Beer kegs	These are bulky to store, and need to be kept clearly in 'use-by' date order.	Real ale casks need to be stored on their sides for 48 hours prior to being poured.
Gas cylinders	Gas cylinders need to be stored upright in an area where they cannot be knocked over or damaged.	A cage is needed.
Bar equipment	On shelving at an appropriate height to be easily accessed.	Electrical equipment could become damaged if not stored correctly.
Glasses	Glasses can be stored in specially designed crates or boxes for glass storage.	Ensure boxes are carefully placed on shelves, if over-stacked they may damage the glassware.

TIP

When ordering drinks from the stores it is important to ensure that you state the correct name of the item as well as the size of the item and the quantity needed.

ISSUING DRINKS AND BAR PRODUCTS

In larger establishments alcoholic beverages need to be issued from the stores to the bar. At the end of each service or shift the bartender on duty will identify which stock needs to be replenished in preparation for the next shift. There will be a 'par level', an amount of stock that will be required to service the bar during a shift. The bartender will order any items that are not up to the par level. He will order these from the stores which will generate the order to be delivered to the bar.

This is now increasingly done electronically where a tally of the items sold is communicated with the stores who can automatically produce a bar order from that. This is very dependent on not just the stock that is sold being registered in the point of sale system, but any drinks that may be given as complementary and breakages being recorded in the system as well.

STOCK-TAKES AND INVENTORIES

A stock-take, or inventory, is carried out to get a snapshot of the amount in size and value of all beverages within the establishment. It is vital for the financial records of the business and it is important for the managers and owners to have clear and accurate information.

Stock-takes can be carried out on either a weekly, monthly or annual basis. Each item that is in stock, both in the bar and in the stores, will be counted and recorded. The amount of the items that have been bought during the period needs to be recorded within the stock-take, as do the amounts that have been sold, damaged or given away. This will be matched against how much of each item has been sold to ensure that none is being stolen or lost without being recorded.

It is vital that all members of staff record any movements of stock correctly, then the stock-takes will be as accurate as possible.

Stored kegs

 TIP

Do not discuss the cost price of stock with your customers, remember the profit is what will pay your wages!

ORDERING DRINKS AND BAR PRODUCTS

The stock-take can generate a drinks order to the supplier. The order can be placed daily, weekly, or even monthly, depending on the size of the order needed or the space for storage available within an establishment. It is generally good practice not to hold too much stock within an establishment but to have a regular supplier who can deliver frequently.

The prices that are agreed with the supplier will be negotiated prior to the order being placed.

The order can be placed on the telephone, by fax or by email and the delivery date and time should be indicated on the order. Some suppliers will let the establishment know if they have a shortage of a product prior to the delivery. This can give the establishment an opportunity to get the product from another source.

Assessment of knowledge and understanding

You have now learned about how to receive, handle and store drinks stock.

To test your level of knowledge and understanding, answer the following short questions. These will help to prepare you for your summative (final) assessment.

Make sure that you keep this for easier referencing and along with your work for future inclusion in your portfolio.

Preparing for assessment checklist

■ Have a look at the stores in an establishment where you work or study. Why are they organized in the way that they are?

Project 1

1 Draw up a stock-take form for a small bar.

2 What would your par level be for the products in that bar?

3 How often would you carry out a stock-take and why?

4 How would stock be issued for the bar?

Project 2

1 Design a store for the drinks stock in a small bar.

2 What methods of securing the stock would be used?

3 How often would you order stock from the suppliers?

4 Where would you store glasses in the store?

22

Maintain a vending machine

Unit 1GEN6 Maintain a vending machine

1GEN6.1 Clean a merchandising vending machine

1GEN6.2 Clean a drinks vending machine

1GEN6.3 Fill a vending machine

1GEN6.4 Display vending goods

What do I need to do?

- Isolate the electricity supply.
- Wear protective clothing.
- Clean the vending machine.
- Test the vending machine.
- Restock the vending machine.
- Display items correctly.
- Complete documentation.
- Tidy up.

What do I need to know?

- How to clean and maintain a merchandising vending machine.
- How to present vending goods.

Information covered in this chapter

This unit is about cleaning the inside and outside of a merchandising vending machine, testing the machine, and completing any relevant documentation. The unit also covers comparable activities for drinks machines, procedures for filling chilled food, drinks and ambient vending machines. This chapter will also describe the methods for presenting vending goods.

KEY WORDS

Vending

A vending machine is a machine that provides various snacks, beverages and other products to consumers. The idea is to vend products without the use of a cashier. Items sold via vending machines vary by country and region.

24-hour service

Round-the-clock continual service for consumers.

Food hazards

A hazard is anything that could cause harm to the consumer. There are three main hazards that may arise with food or drink from vending machines. These are contamination by:

■ Bacteria or other micro-organisms that cause food poisoning.

■ Chemicals, for example, cleaning materials or pest baits.

■ Foreign materials such as glass, metal or plastic.

Merchandising

The methods, practices and operations carried out to promote and sell certain products.

Maintenance

Regular servicing and up-keep of the vending machine.

INTRODUCTION

The type of organization will determine to a large extent the delivery and service system requirements. Those where large numbers of people must be served quickly such as educational establishments, industrial plants and hospitals will usually provide a cafeteria-style service. However automatic vending will be used as a supplement service for irregular hours catering.

An example of some of the types of food and drink in a vending machine

The history of vending dates back as far as 215 BC and was devised by a Greek mathematician. Initially in Europe and North America, the use of automatic vending was in the form of candies and sweets. Other items such as cold drinks and hot drinks soon followed. Today, many complex menus which can include complete meals are available through vending machines. Some contain heated elements to cook or reheat foods before dispensing them. Others are refrigerated to hold cold salads, sandwiches, snacks, drinks and even iced desserts.

Food for vending machines can be prepared by the establishment using them or by an outside vending company that delivers fresh foods at frequent intervals. These companies will maintain the machines and ensure that they are fully stocked.

The fast turnover of the food and a good supply service are essential for the safety and success of vending machines. The display of the food and drink is also an important issue as they must be presented attractively to enhance the sales potential.

Food hygiene should be practised, with all precautions and legal responsibilities involved in the following:

1 Protecting the vending food from risk of contamination.

2 Preventing organisms from multiplying whilst in the vending machine to an extent which would pose a health risk to customers and employees.

3 Destroying any harmful bacteria in food by thorough heat treatment when serving hot food and drink.

The essentials of food and personal hygiene for vending are:

- Keep yourself clean and wear clean protective clothing.
- Always wash your hands thoroughly after using the toilet, after every break, and before starting work.
- Do not smoke or eat when handling food or cleaning machines.
- Keep chilled foods at the required temperature.
- Ensure cuts and sores are covered with a waterproof and high-visibility dressing.
- Tell your supervisor before starting work if you are suffering from sickness or diarrhoea, fever or an infected wound.

! REMEMBER

There are a number of advantages to the use of vending machines:

- *Convenience*: Vended goods are available 24 hours a day and machines can be sited anywhere.

- *Increased staff productivity*: Research conducted by NOP showed that an average size business with 50 staff could be spending more than £85,000 of its annual wages bill in time spent by employees making their own tea and coffee.

- *Reduced wastage*: Providing customer demand has been gauged correctly, wastage is reduced significantly and also better portion control can be maintained.

- *Ease of maintenance*: A permanent member of the team can be trained to supply and clean the vending machines on a regular basis.

- *Variety*: Vending machines offer a complete range of assorted products. Vending machines that serve drinks can now offer different drinks with various tasting options depending on whether a person prefers their tea or coffee strong or weak.

TYPES OF VENDING MACHINE

There are basically four types of vending machine:

■ Beverage vending: Can either mix ingredients to produce a specific beverage or will already have a pre-mixed beverage inside each cup to be selected.

■ Chilled food vending: Can be for the selling of sandwiches and snack foods that require refrigeration.

■ Merchandise vending: These are usually glass-fronted vending machines so that the customer can view the products for sale. A example of this type is a vending machine selling confectionery.

■ Micro-vending system: This system provides a range of hot or cold foods from which the customer can make a selection and heat in an accompanying microwave oven.

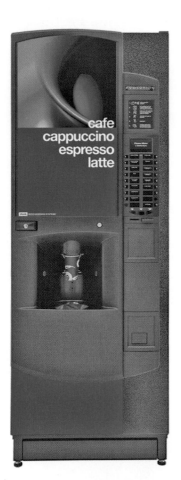

Coffee vending machine

IMAGE COURTESY OF CRANE MERCHANDISING SYSTEMS (CMS)

Soft drinks vending machine

Burger vending machine

CLEANING A VENDING MACHINE

Good hygiene practice must be followed by all food handlers and servers. Chapter 1 (Maintain a safe, hygienic and secure working environment) covers this feature in some depth.

Regular cleaning and supply of stock is always required through demand and this might necessitate numerous daily visits to the vending machine to clean and restock the items that have been used. Staff should be trained in the techniques of cleaning and restocking all types of vending machines.

The following list of key features needs to be considered when undertaking this task:

Key features for cleaning a vending machine

1 Always try to clean and restock the vending machine when the demand is at its lowest which will help to minimize potential loss of sales.

2 Always wear the correct protective clothing to minimize potential accidents and help to safeguard against spillages.

3 Where possible before cleaning, the vending machine should be isolated from the mains supply to avoid any electrical accidents.

4 The vending machine's supplier will always have a set of written recommendations and instructions for use, cleaning and maintenance. These should always be followed especially with reference to nominated cleaning agents.

5 Select the nominated cleaning agents and prepare them for use. Always ensure that the sanitizers and sterilizers are used correctly.

6 Temperatures must be monitored during this process to ensure that the limit has not been exceeded with reference to refrigeration temperatures and the temperatures for hot beverages and foods. The monitoring of temperatures should always be undertaken to reassure that the temperature limit is not surpassed. Food that has been exposed to unsafe temperatures should be discarded immediately.

7 Clean the vending machine according to the manufacturer's recommendations.

8 Dismantle any internal working parts for cleaning according to the health and hygiene standards.

9 Always wipe down the internal and external surfaces of the vending machine to maintain the clean outlook of the service. Ensure that the external surfaces are clean, dry and smear free.

10 Test the vending machine to ensure that it works correctly.

11 Complete any records especially those that the Environmental Health Officer may want to inspect.

12 Always leave the area around the vending machine clear of any rubbish and in a clean condition.

> **! REMEMBER**
>
> It is important that the food safety management system is reviewed when new types of products are introduced to a vending system, different vending machines are used, or new types of clients acquired.

FILLING A VENDING MACHINE

It is important to always supply enough stock to meet the demand of your customers. You should always carefully check the condition of all stock in the vending machine to ensure it is in the optimum condition.

Key features for stocking a vending machine

1 Isolate the electricity supply for safety.

2 Remove and dispose of any stock in the vending machine that has passed its expiry date or is not in optimum condition.

! REMEMBER

The up-to-date results of the procedure must be available for inspection by an Environmental Health Officer as required.

Charts which detail times and regularity of checks and cleaning will suffice when accompanied by supporting documents such as details of HACCP.

3 Check the dates on all the stock and always place the older items at the front of the vending machine so that these are used first, following the principle of stock rotation.

4 Always supply enough stock to meet the demand and ensure that all labelling and packaging is correct.

5 Check the slow-selling items very carefully for the correct expiry dates on the packaging and for signs of deterioration in the commodity.

6 Refill all appropriate containers with the relevant powders and products and ensure that all correct cups, plates and napkins are available in or near the vending machines.

7 Check that the vending machine is in full working order.

8 Complete any records especially those that the Environmental Health Officer may want to inspect.

A clean and fully-stocked vending machine

TRY THIS!

Using the control chart try and create your own version for foods that must be kept chilled or frozen.

Hazard analysis chart

A hazard analysis chart should be used to help with the maintenance, cleaning and supply of vending machines. An example of the type of documentation to use for ambient temperature ingredients used in vending machines is shown in the table on the following page.

Temperature control of ingredients for vending machines

The control of temperature is essential in restricting the growth of bacteria and minimizing the risk of food poisoning and deterioration and spoilage of food. For high risk foods in particular, keeping them chilled or hot is the single most important control in ensuring their safety.

Bacteria need warmth to live and multiply. Generally, at temperatures of 8°C or less their growth is inhibited and at 63°C or above most are killed. The range between these two temperatures is known as the danger-zone where bacteria will grow rapidly and therefore it is necessary to avoid keeping foods at these temperatures.

The temperatures required in the Food Hygiene (England) Regulations 2006 Schedule 4 refer to the temperature of the food itself. In vending it is often more practical for routine checks to measure air temperature and the relationship between the two needs to be understood and periodically checked.

HAZARD ANALYSIS CONTROL CHART

PROCESS STEP	HAZARDS	CONTROLS	MONITORING	CORRECTIVE ACTION
Purchase of products	Presence of micro-organisms, toxins or foreign matter.	Buy from reputable supplier.	Check supplier has accreditation from reputable audit organization.	Warn or change supplier.
Delivery to warehouse	Presence of foreign materials.	Visual check of delivery vehicle.	Delivery record check.	Reject delivery.
Storage in a warehouse	Pest infestation.	Pest control in place. FIFO in the warehouse.	Pest control contract. Warehouse check.	Reject product.
Transport to a vending machine	Presence of foreign materials.	Vans cleaned to schedule.	Cleaning record.	Reject product. Review with driver.
Filling and cleaning vending machine	Microbiological growth in machine.	Operator trained to clean properly and with sufficient frequency.	Operators audited.	Retrain operator. Clean machine.
Storage and dispensing	Microbiological contamination of water.	Connect to a source of drinking water.	Site survey form ensures water source is drinking water.	Disconnect machine.

THE DISPLAY OF VENDING GOODS

During the restocking of the vending machine it is important that you consider how the vending goods should be displayed in a merchandise vending machine. With the correct and vibrant display of the goods contained in the vending machine it is probable that this form of marketing will help to increase sales.

If certain products have sold out and suitable replacement products are used, it is important to provide correct information on the vending machine to inform the customer of the change of product. The label must be visible at all times so that an informed selection can be made.

The use of menus can be employed to help give information to customers and these have become a successful way of selling products in sophisticated vending machines which sell hot and cold meals. An example of a vending machine menu is shown on page 310.

Some vending machines have computerized displays which will give price information. The operator should always check that these prices are correct alongside any pricing information that may also be displayed.

A vending machine menu

Assessment of knowledge and understanding

You have now learned about maintaining the service of a vending machine. This will enable you to ensure your own positive knowledge and skills will contribute effectively towards the food and drink service operation.

To test your level of knowledge and understanding, answer the following short questions. These will help to prepare you for your summative (final) assessment.

Cleaning the vending machine

1 State why it is important to check the electricity supply is safely isolated.

_____

2 State why it is important that the interior and exterior of the machine is left clean, dry and free from smears.

_____

3 Why is it important to keep the area immediately around the vending machine clean and tidy?

_____

4 Why is it important to conduct a test of the vending machine after cleaning?

_____

Filling a vending machine

1 What procedures need to be followed if faults or problems are identified?

2 Why is it important that the interior of the machine is clean prior to re-stocking of goods?

3 Why is it necessary to carry out temperature tests in vending machines?

4 Why should stock rotation procedures be followed?

5 What type of documentation needs to be accurately completed?

Display vending goods

1 State two ways that items should be presented to help maximize sales.

2 Why should information changes be clear, up-to-date and accurate?

23

Prepare and serve dispensed and instant hot drinks

Unit 2DS7 Prepare and serve dispensed and instant hot drinks

2DS7.1 Prepare work area and equipment for service

2DS7.2 Prepare and serve hot drinks

What do I need to do?

- Prepare equipment and work areas for service.
- Make sure you have sufficient supplies of drink ingredients and accompaniments.
- Give customers information about drinks.
- Make and serve drinks.
- Clean and tidy the service area.

What do I need to know?

- What equipment is needed for serving instant hot drinks.
- Information about the drinks, ingredients, services and accompaniments.

Information covered in this chapter

This unit is about preparing basic equipment such as small dispensing machines, kettles, urns, coffee and tea pots.

The unit also covers the preparation and service of hot drinks such as coffee, tea and hot chocolate.

KEY WORDS

Instant hot drink
Through various manufacturing processes the drink such as tea or coffee is dehydrated into the form of powder or granules. These can be re-hydrated with hot water to provide a drink similar to conventional coffee or tea.

Dispensing machine
A machine that provides various snacks, beverages and other products to consumers.

Food hazards
A term used by food safety organizations to classify foods that require time and temperature control to keep them safe for human consumption.

Sufficient supplies
Ensuring that the ingredients required to produce beverages are in constant supply for the needs of service.

Accompaniments
Ingredients such as sugar, milk and cream to go with a specific beverage.

INTRODUCTION

Usually the term beverage refers to a selection of hot drinks on a menu. This will include coffee, tea, tisanes, chocolate, milk-based drinks and other proprietary drinks such as Horlicks. The service of these particular beverages has expanded over the years from being served in a traditional format and now the service has developed to meet the modern customer's needs. An implication of this is the traditional service of morning coffee, which described coffee to be served in a tea cup, with a saucer and accompanied with hot milk and white sugar. Today the service of morning coffee will depend on the services on offer in a particular establishment and the customer expectation or demands may differ. The service of a morning coffee may now be in a mug or a cup of variable sizes, served with milk or cream and the option of a saccharine-based sweetener or unrefined sugar.

The use of instant and dispensed beverages has increased due to the growing quality of the product, the variety available and the ease of use and service. These types of beverages can be purchased in the form of powders, individual bags, granules, syrups and pre-ground beans.

There are some key requirements that beverage service staff should have:

- Good product knowledge.

- Competent technical skills.

- Progressive social skills.

- A good team work ethic.

- The ability to communicate.

- The ability to solve problems efficiently.

CLASSIFICATION OF A BEVERAGE SERVICE

For the service of beverages to operate effectively it should be viewed as a sequence of events that is primarily concerned with the effective delivery of hot drinks to the customer and to enhance the customer experience at the same time. For this to happen a standard production system is often developed for different areas of the hospitality industry, which consists of eight set stages:

A traditional service of coffee

1 Preparation and cleaning for the service to include preparation and service equipment.

2 Ensuring sufficient beverage ingredients are stored ready for use.

3 Taking the beverage order clearly.

4 Effective service of the beverage.

5 Presentation of the bill.

6 Clearing and cleaning down.

7 Washing the service equipment thoroughly.

8 Clearing down following the period of service.

THE PREPARATION FOR SERVICE

There are certain set tasks and duties which need to be carried out to help guarantee that sufficient preparation has been made for the expected volume of business for each service. There are three categories to follow in this initial set up stage:

- Preparation of equipment that is used to prepare or make the beverage.

- Preparation of service equipment.

- Preparation of other equipment.

> **! REMEMBER**
>
> A potential contamination hazard is anything that could cause harm to the customer. There are three main hazards that may arise with beverages. These are contamination by:
>
> - Bacteria or other micro-organisms that cause food poisoning.
>
> - Chemicals for cleaning.
>
> - Foreign materials such as glass, metal or plastic.

A coffee shop prepared ready for service

Preparation equipment

Kettles, urns, small vending machines and coffee and tea pots will need to be prepared before service. Good hygiene practice is required to be followed by all staff and servers. Regular cleaning and routine checking of the condition of the equipment is important to help maintain a consistent service. Staff should be trained in the techniques of cleaning and checking of all types of equipment. However the following list of key features needs to be considered when undertaking this task:

KEY FEATURES FOR EQUIPMENT PREPARATION

1 Always try to thoroughly clean and check the working functions of all equipment prior to service.

2 Always wear the correct protective clothing to minimize potential accidents and help to safeguard against spillages. Wearing a protective coat over your service uniform whilst you undertake these preparation duties will help safeguard against potential spillages.

3 Where possible before cleaning any small vending machines, they should always be isolated from the mains supply to avoid any electrical accidents.

4 Certain equipment will always have a set of written recommendations and instructions for use, cleaning and maintenance. These should always be followed especially with reference to nominated cleaning agents.

5 Select the nominated cleaning agents and prepare them for use. Always ensure that the sanitizers and sterilizers are used correctly.

6 Dismantle any internal working parts for cleaning according to the health and hygiene standards.

7 Test the equipment to ensure that it works correctly.

8 Complete any records especially those that the Environmental Health Officer may want to inspect.

Service equipment

Cups, mugs, saucers, cutlery, glassware and trays should also be checked for cleanliness and inspections must be made to ensure that no chips, cracks or broken elements are apparent.

Great care must be exercised when handling glassware. Any broken glass should be cleared up at once. The use of a small piece of plasticine or blu-tack is useful for collecting slivers. Be particularly careful to remove any broken glass from sinks. All glassware should be thoroughly inspected for flaws before use and any that are faulty should be rejected. Ensure that the type of glass being used is appropriate to the work at hand especially if hot liquids are to be placed inside glassware.

Crockery must always be checked to make sure they are dishwasher proof as certain crockery items that have been decorated with metallic edges may not be suitable for dishwashers. When using dishwashers you should only use

Care should be taken to ensure that all glassware is clean and free from chips and cracks

the recommended detergent and no more than the suggested amount. Other procedures that should be followed in the cleaning of crockery are as follows:

- Avoid stacking dirty crockery.
- Do not mix cutlery and crockery together when cleaning to avoid possible breakages.
- Remove left-over drinks from the bottom of cups immediately after use.
- Rinse items as soon as possible after use to prevent possible staining.
- Do not use scouring pads to remove stains as these might prematurely scratch the surface of crockery and increase the likelihood of further staining.
- When loading the dishwasher space crockery properly and do not over-fill.

Other equipment

Dishwashers, refrigeration units and thermometers will also be used from time to time in the preparation and service of instant beverages.

The capacity of the dishwasher should preferably be larger than the operational limit necessary. Invariably slow dishwashing increases the amount of equipment required to be in use during service and will expand the storage space required in the preparation area. Dishwashing can be undertaken manually, washing by hand with brushes, cloths and detergents. If the operation has the capacity to support this system, it can work very well and will help to make certain that crockery and glassware are cleaned correctly.

Washing dishes

Using the semi-automatic system of loading soiled crockery and glassware into dishwashing machines will help to save labour and can be just as thorough in the cleaning of these items. Most machines will operate at up to 60°C for general cleaning, although low-temperature cleaning is now widely used to maintain electricity efficiency. However, dishwashers are costly to purchase so care should be taken to maintain them, ensuring the dishwasher is cleaned regularly to prevent a build up of limescale, particularly in hard water zones. You can contact your local water supplier to find out how hard your water supply is and adjust your dishwasher accordingly.

As well as taking care of the food that you store in your refrigerator to make sure that it lasts for as long as possible, you should also look after the refrigeration and freezer units. You should regularly clean your refrigerator. Clean on a regular basis, preferably at a time of day when it is at it's most empty, so that you do not have to remove many different items and try to store them all safely during cleaning.

Place perishable goods in the freezer to keep them cold but fruit and vegetables may be left out at room temperature. Whilst you have everything out of the refrigerator, take advantage of this time to throw away any products that are out-of-date.

A walk-in refrigeration unit

Fill a large sink with warm water and detergent, remove all the refrigeration trays, drawers and racks from the inside and wash thoroughly. Also clean the inside of the refrigerator along the sides and base, with fresh warm water and a soft detergent. Once the drawers and trays have been dried, they can be repositioned along with the contents of the fridge.

It is very important to clean up any spillages or food that has dropped on to the shelves, as they could come into contact with other foods and spoil or cross-contaminate them. Looking after your fresh food and your refrigerator will bring about many benefits.

By ensuring that your refrigeration and freezer system is well maintained, reliability is improved and also the chance of these complex systems breaking down is reduced. Changes and repairs to a refrigeration system require the assistance of a suitably qualified refrigeration maintenance contractor. By identifying possible problems early and maintaining a hygienic routine, appropriate help can be requested quickly.

Have a maintenance schedule

This will ensure the system is checked frequently. The employer should ensure that they have the correct type of maintenance contract. Keep condensers clean and free from blockages so that there is enough space for good airflow away from the unit. Also check ventilation, because a compressor in a poorly-ventilated area will run hotter than necessary.

De-ice evaporators

Ice will build up over time, but excessive ice might indicate that a drain is blocked or that the unit is too close to the thermostat. Ask your line manager to investigate this.

Check noisy compressors

This could indicate that the bearings are becoming worn. Compressor reliability may be reduced if the oil level is too low or too high.

Check the oil level regularly and if a change is noticed, have a qualified service technician investigate.

Monitor pipework

Vibrating pipework is more likely to fracture, resulting in a major refrigerant leak. Consult your refrigeration maintenance contractor to ensure that pipes are properly secured. Insulation on pipework should also be in good condition to prevent unnecessary heat gains.

A small refrigeration unit

THE STORAGE OF INGREDIENTS

All ingredients required for service should be stored in optimum condition ready for use.

Tea

- Tea is purchased in tea bags, loose leaf, instant granules or pods designed for tea-makers.
- Should be kept in a dry container with a sealed lid.
- Should be kept in a clean and well-ventilated area.
- Should be stored away from excess moisture.
- Should be stored away from strong smelling ingredients because tea can absorb strong odours.

Tea

Coffee

- Coffee is purchased as instant granules, ground beans, pods for coffee-makers and as the bean itself.
- Should be stored in a clean and well-ventilated area.
- An air-tight container should be used for ground and instant coffee to help ensure that the oils do not evaporate, causing a loss of flavour and aroma.
- Should be stored away from excess moisture.
- Should be stored away from strong smelling ingredients because coffee can absorb strong odours.

Coffee

Chocolate

Chocolate

- Chocolate is purchased as a powder, in block form or as a chocolate bar.
- Should be stored in a clean and well-ventilated area.
- An air-tight container should be used for all chocolate to help ensure that the oils do not evaporate, causing a loss of flavour and aroma.
- Should be stored away from excess moisture.
- Should be stored away from strong smelling ingredients because chocolate can absorb strong odours.

Syrups

- Syrups are purchased in bottles or re-sealable air-tight containers.
- The flavours can be vanilla, hazelnut, almond, chocolate and cinnamon and are used predominantly to flavour coffee.
- Should be stored in a clean and well-ventilated area.
- Should be stored away from excess moisture.
- Should be stored away from strong smelling ingredients because syrups can absorb strong odours.

Syrup

Sugar

- Sugar is purchased in cubes, sticks, granulated, unrefined or partially refined state.
- Should be stored in a clean and well-ventilated area.
- Should be stored away from excess moisture.
- Should be stored away from strong smelling ingredients to prevent absorption of strong odours.

Sugar

Milk

- Milk is purchased in fresh (skimmed, semi-skimmed or full-fat versions), powdered or ultra high temperature treated (UHT) portions.
- Should be refrigerated if fresh or in an opened UHT tetrapack.
- Powdered milk or UHT portions should be stored in a clean and well-ventilated area.
- Should be stored away from strong smelling ingredients to prevent absorption of strong odours.
- Always check the 'use-by' date on the label.

Milk

Cream

- Cream is purchased fresh (single, whipping or double) or in UHT format.
- Should be refrigerated.
- UHT cream portions should be stored in a clean and well-ventilated area.
- Should be stored away from strong smelling ingredients to prevent absorption of strong odours.
- Always check the 'use-by' date on the label.

Cream

IDENTIFYING THE CUSTOMER REQUIREMENTS

Taking the orders from customers can be a long but important process. It is essential that the information received and recorded is accurate because this will be the detail the production areas require and will also provide essential information for the billing process. There are four basic order-taking methods to consider:

1 *Duplicate*: The order is taken and copied to the production area and the second copy is retained by the server for reference to service and billing.

2 *Triplicate*: The order is taken and copied to the production area and the cashier for billing. The third copy is retained by the server for service references.

3 *Service with the order*: Taking the order and immediately serving the required product. This system is used in a bar or counter methods of service.

4 *Pre-ordered*: This may be part of a function service or room service in a hotel. However, the triplicate system may also be used as part of this process.

There will be opportunities to up-sell and promote drinks or accompaniments to customers. This personal selling will contribute to the promotion of sales where there are specific sales promotions being undertaken by the employer. Service staff should be informed of the products that they are selling so that a well informed choice can be made by the customer.

Service staff must have a full knowledge of the products that they sell and serve

THE MAKING AND SERVICE OF INSTANT BEVERAGES

! REMEMBER

The provision of good service is dependent on teamwork among service staff and staff from other departments.

Tea

The type of tea that has been ordered will depend on how much tea should be used per cup or per pot. It is advisable to use a measure for loose tea products as this will ensure that a standard product is maintained. Alternative portioning methods are of course the use of tea bags or granulated tea.

However, because tea is predominantly an infusion, to achieve a good end result the following rules should apply:

1 Heat the tea pot before putting in the tea.
2 Measure the tea quantity exactly.
3 Always use freshly boiled water, ensuring that the water is at boiling point when pouring into the pot.
4 Allow the tea to brew for between 3 and 6 minutes depending on the type of tea used.
5 Remove the tea from the pot unless the customer specifically asks for it to remain. If loose tea is used a tea strainer should be provided for the customer.
6 Serve milk separately with sugar or a saccharine-based sweetener.

Fruit-flavoured teas and herbal infusions are commonly described as tisanes. They have gained popularity because of their purported medicinal uses and often they do not contain caffeine.

Examples of some of these are:

- Fruit teas: lemon, blackcurrant, orange, strawberry and cherry.
- Herbal teas: mint, peppermint, chamomile and rosehip.

These teas should generally be served in china pots or made by the cup and infused in a similar way to tea.

Mint tea

Coffee

The methods of brewing coffee can vary dependent on the type of coffee to be served. Coffee beans can be purchased and ground to order to ensure the maximum flavour and strength of the coffee. Ready-ground coffee will be purchased in vacuum packs that are sealed in order to maintain the freshness of the coffee inside. These packets will contain set quantities to make 4.5 litres of coffee using a coffee machine – usually 350 g is sufficient to make this amount of coffee.

The rules to observe when producing ground coffee to be brewed in a machine are as follows:

1 Purchase the correct type and grind of coffee for the type of machine in use.

2 Ensure all the equipment is clean before use.

3 Use a set measure for the coffee.

4 Add boiling water if using a cafetière or cold fresh water if using a coffee machine.

5 The infusion time must be controlled according to the type of coffee being used.

6 Do not boil the coffee whilst it is being infused as this will create a bitter flavour.

7 Strain or push the plunger down in the cafetière and serve.

8 Offer with hot or cold milk or cream separately and sugar or a saccharine-based sweetener.

9 The best serving temperature is 82°C for the coffee and 68°C for the milk or cream.

A cafetière of coffee (can be served with portions of UHT milk and sugar sachets)

A guideline for the quantity of coffee to use for a cafetière can be:

■ Two level dessert spoons for a three-cup size cafetière.

■ Six level dessert spoons for an eight-cup size cafetière.

■ Nine level dessert spoons for a twelve-cup size cafetière.

To make an instant coffee it will require approximately 75 grams of instant coffee for 4.5 litres of boiled water. If producing a single portion of coffee to be served in a cup or mug the coffee should be measured into the cup and fresh boiled water that has been allowed to cool for a few seconds will then be poured into the cup. Stir well until all of the instant coffee has been saturated and mixed in.

Espresso and Cappuccino

Machines that are used in making this form of Italian coffee can provide cups of coffee in a few seconds. The method involves passing steam through the finely ground coffee and infusing under pressure. The advantage of this method is that each cup of coffee is freshly made to order.

Served black this type of coffee is known as an Espresso and is served in a small cup. A double Espresso is served in a slightly larger cup. If a Cappuccino is required fresh milk is heated for each cup using a pressurized steam injector which froths the milk at the same time as heating it. Syrups can be added to create flavour variations if requested. These beverages have become very popular in cafes.

Hot chocolate

As with coffee, there are a variety of ways of making drinking or hot chocolate. The different methods will derive different results such as the thickness, flavour and colour of the finished drink. Many vendors will use powdered drinking chocolate as a quick and efficient way of producing a standard hot chocolate drink. The manufacturer's instructions and recipe should be followed to produce a consistent drink, but there are some fundamental rules to follow:

1 Ensure that the chocolate powder has been correctly stored.

2 Make sure all the equipment is clean before use.

3 Use a set measure for the chocolate powder unless using individual sachets for a one-cup product.

4 Add boiling water or boiled milk if preferred to create a creamier drink.

5 Stir well until all of the chocolate powder has dissolved into the liquid and there are no lumps apparent in the drink.

6 Offer sugar or a saccharine-based sweetener separately.

7 The best serving temperature is 82°C for the chocolate drink.

8 Syrups can be added to create flavour variations if requested.

9 The drink can be finished with a little whipped cream floated on top and decorated with dusted cocoa or fine chocolate shavings.

A hot chocolate drink finished with whipped cream and chocolate shavings

An alternative recipe is to make the chocolate drink using a good quality chocolate bar. Dark chocolate is usually the best to use because it has a higher cocoa content and therefore it will produce a stronger flavour and colour. This will create a thicker consistency to a normal powdered version. To make four cups the following recipe can be used:

175 g   dark chocolate, chopped into small pieces

175 ml water

450 ml fresh milk

Using a saucepan, melt the chocolate with the water, whisking until the mixture thickens. Heat the milk in a separate saucepan and add the chocolate mixture. Stir well until the chocolate is completely amalgamated. Divide between four cups or mugs and serve as for hot chocolate.

PRESENTING THE BILL

In cafes and smaller tea shops the duplicate billing method is generally used. This is where the customer will make the payment directly with the cashier, server or waiter according to the guidelines of the business. As further checks are received the items are entered onto the overall bill for a particular table or customer.

When the customer requests the bill, the server or waiter must collect it from the cashier who must first check that all items are entered and priced correctly and then total it up. The top copy of the bill is presented to the customer, usually on a side plate and folded in half or placed in a bill wallet. In some smaller operations the server or waiter will undertake the task of the cashier too.

On receiving the necessary payment from the customer, the server or waiter returns the bill and payment to the cashier who will receipt both copies of the bill and return the receipted top copy plus any change that is due to the customer. This is returned to the customer promptly.

The principle of providing a bill with the order immediately is used where the customer's order is set on an electronic billing system, such as a cash register. When the order has been completed, the visual display unit (VDU) will show the customer the required total sum owed. The VDU may also show the amount of change that needs to be returned to the customer and will also print a receipt or an itemized bill for the customer if required. This system will speed up the process of billing the customer and is used in many coffee shops, airport lounges, cafeterias and tea shops.

CLEARING AND CLEANING DOWN

After the service of the beverage and when the customer has finished and vacated their seat or table, this section will need to be cleared and cleaned as quickly and efficiently as possible to 'turn-over' the area for further custom during the service period.

A waitress clears a table using a tray to collect the glassware and crockery

The collection of all sullied crockery, glassware and cutlery should be undertaken by the service team and transported to the production area for washing. If linen tablecloths or napkins have been used these should be exchanged for fresh clean and pressed replacements. All of the soiled linen should be placed in the designated area (usually a laundry basket) and returned to the linen room.

Check the accompaniments that are requested by customers to ensure that they are replenished and ready for use. All tables that have not used linen should be wiped clean using a clean cloth and a sanitizer. Tables and chairs should be re-aligned and any required menus, merchandising or table decoration placed on the table ready for the next customer. The washing and cleaning of equipment is covered under the heading 'preparation for service', page 315.

CLEARING DOWN FOLLOWING THE PERIOD OF SERVICE

After the service period, there will be a variety of tasks and duties to be carried out in order to clear down from the previous service and to begin preparations for the next service. During this sequence it is an important requirement that all cleaning programmes and management systems are followed. Detailed cleaning schedules need to be completed and these will be undertaken on a daily, weekly and sometimes monthly basis. Maintenance checks should also be undertaken alongside this process of clearing and cleaning down.

Other set tasks will help to clean and prepare for the next service session:

■ Switch off any hotplates, small vending or coffee machines. Clear away any crockery or glassware from the hotplate area and restock as required with a fresh set.

A waiter cleaning down the bar area

- Return all cleaned and polished cutlery to their correct storage place.
- Collect all cruets, accompaniments such as sugar bowls and cocoa dusters and refill. Return to their correct storage place.
- Clear down the bar area and put all equipment away. Wash and polish all used glassware. Remove all empty bottles and empty all bins, clean and dry them.
- All beverage service equipment should be cleaned and put away in storage.
- All perishable materials should be returned to their correct storage point.
- Kettles and urns should all be cleaned and left standing with cold water in them – to be emptied and refilled for the next service.
- All tea pots and coffee pots should be cleaned and relocated to their storage area.
- Ensure all trays are wiped down and stacked correctly.
- Sweep and mop all flooring.
- Remove plugs having switched off all electrical sockets.

Assessment of knowledge and understanding

You have now learned about preparing and serving dispensed and instant hot beverages. This will ensure your own knowledge and skills will contribute effectively towards the food and drink service operation of your establishment.

To test your level of knowledge and understanding, answer the following short questions. These will help to prepare you for your summative (final) assessment.

Prepare the work area and equipment for service

1 Describe two reasons why safe and hygienic working practices should be observed when preparing and serving hot drinks.

i) _____ ii) _____

2 Why should all drinks, ingredients and accompaniments be available and ready for immediate use?

_____

3 Why is it important to check for damage in all work areas and service equipment before taking orders?

_____

4 Explain what should happen if a fault is found on an electric kettle before service.

_____

Prepare and serve hot drinks

1 Explain two hygienic working practices you should use when preparing and serving a pot of tea for two customers.

i) _____ ii) _____

2 Describe why information about products given to customers should be accurate.

_____

3 Why and to whom should all customer incidents be reported?

_____

4 Explain why customer and service areas should be kept clean, tidy and free from rubbish and used equipment.

_____

24

Prepare and serve hot drinks

Unit 618 Prepare and serve hot drinks using specialist equipment

What do I need to do?

■ Prepare a wide range of hot drinks.

■ Prepare the work area for hot drinks service.

What do I need to know?

■ How hot drinks are produced.

■ Which hot drinks are served.

■ How to take hot drinks orders.

Information covered in this chapter

■ Coffee growing and production.

■ Different methods of making coffee.

■ Types of tea and different blends available.

KEY WORDS

Fair Trade
Movement that supports fair payment of produce to growers.

Tisanes
Herbal infusions for drinking.

INTRODUCTION

The sales of hot drinks in the UK have grown vastly in the last few years. Chains of coffee shops dominate nearly every high street. Coffee and tea service is also an important part of restaurant and food service as it is the last impression that a customer will take with them of the premises.

To be able to consistently make and serve a high standard of a range of coffee and tea is a skill that needs to be learnt and practised. It is important to understand where and how both coffee and tea are made. There are many different varieties of each and these will be identified. The different methods of making tea and, especially, coffee will be looked at then finally, step-by-step guides to making a range of coffees will be given.

Coffee

HOW COFFEE IS PRODUCED

The coffee bean is the seed of the coffee plant, the bean is found at the centre of the berry of the plant. Coffee beans are grown in equatorial regions of the world. These include central and South America, central Africa, India and Indonesia. The berries are picked and are then dried, either in the sun or by machine to remove the outer pulp of the berry. At this stage the beans are known as green coffee, and are sold and exported overseas. It is at this point that the coffee beans are decaffeinated by soaking them in hot water to remove the caffeine.

Roasting coffee transforms the chemical and physical properties of green coffee beans into roasted coffee products. The roasters operate at about 200°C and the length of time that beans are roasted will affect the flavour of the finished coffee. When roasted, the green coffee bean expands to nearly double its original size, changing in colour and density. As the bean absorbs heat, the colour shifts to yellow and then to a light 'cinnamon' brown, then to a dark and oily colour. During roasting oils appear on the surface of the bean. The roast will continue to darken until it is removed from the heat source.

Once roasted the beans will either be vacuum-packed to preserve their flavour and texture, or alternatively they will be ground in preparation for use and vacuum-packed.

COFFEE BEAN VARIETIES

The majority of coffee comes from either the Arabica coffee bean or the Robusta coffee bean. The Arabica bean has many different varietals which will be recognized.

ARABICA VARIETIES OF COFFEE

VARIETY	CHARACTERISTICS
Colombian	Coffee was first introduced to the country of Colombia in the early 1800s. When Colombian coffee is freshly roasted it has a bright acidity, is heavy in body and is intensely aromatic. Columbia is the second-largest coffee growing country in the world after Brazil.
Costa Rican Tarrazu	Dark, strong beans from Costa Rica in the Caribbean.
Ethiopian Harrar	From the region of Harrar, Ethiopia. Known for its complex, fruity flavour that resembles a dry red wine.
Colombian Milds	Includes coffees from Colombia, Kenya and Tanzania, all of which are washed Arabicas.

VARIETY	CHARACTERISTICS
Jamaican Blue Mountain	From the Blue Mountain region of Jamaica. Due to its popularity, it fetches a high price in the market.
Java	From the island of Java in Indonesia. This coffee was once so widely traded that 'java' became a slang term for coffee.
Kenyan	Known among coffee enthusiasts to have a bright, acidic flavour
Santos	Named after Brazil's famous port which the coffee passes through. A low-acidic light-bodied brew.

FAIRTRADE

Fairtrade is a movement which promotes the payment of a fair price in relation to the production of both coffee and tea. Fairtrade's intention is to deliberately work with impoverished producers and workers in order to help them move from a position of vulnerability to security. It also aims to help them actively become more involved in their own organizations.

Fairtrade and ethically-sold coffee has been available in the UK for many years and they tend to be slightly more expensive than other brands, but their popularity has increased and many customers actively seek these products.

✓ TIP

Does your establishment offer Fairtrade products? If so are your customers aware of them?

 ACTIVITY

Have a look in your local high street at the different coffee and tea shops that there are. Write down the different types of coffee and tea that they serve.

- Note the different methods by which they serve the teas and coffees, look at the cups that they use, and how they dispense milk and sugar.
- Name some of the different beans that coffee is made from.
- What blends and types of tea are on offer?

DIFFERENT METHODS OF MAKING COFFEE

Coffee-making is called brewing and the beverage coffee is formed by introducing water to ground coffee beans. There are four main methods: boiling, pressure, gravity and steeping.

METHODS OF BREWING COFFEE

METHOD	TYPE	DESCRIPTION
Boiling 	Turkish coffee	A very early method of making coffee and is still used in the Middle East, North Africa, East Africa, Turkey, Greece, and the Balkans. Water is placed together with very finely ground coffee in a narrow-topped pot, called an *ibrik* and is allowed to briefly come to the boil. It is usually drunk sweet, in which case sugar is added to the pot and boiled with the coffee; it is also often flavoured with cardamom in Arab countries and served in small cups. The result is very strong coffee with foam on the top and a thick layer of sludgy grounds at the bottom.
Pressure 	Espresso	Espresso is made with hot water at between 91°C and 96°C forced under high pressure through tightly-packed, finely-ground coffee. It can be served alone and is the basis for many coffee drinks. It is one of the strongest-tasting forms of coffee regularly consumed, with a distinctive flavour and crema, a layer of emulsified oils in the form of a colloidal foam standing over the liquid.
	Aeropress coffee and espresso maker	The Aeropress is a recently popularized device similar to the French Press. Hot water is poured into a ground coffee mixture, but the coffee is pressed out under moderate pressure a relatively short time later through a paper microfilter, without accumulating the considerable amounts of bitter sediment associated with a French Press.
	Single-serving coffee machine	Various types of machines force hot water under pressure through a coffee pod composed of finely ground coffee sandwiched between two layers of filter paper or a proprietary capsule containing ground coffee. These are normally used in the home but some are available in cafes.
	Moka pot	Also known as 'Italian coffeepot' this is a three-chamber design which boils water in the lower section and forces the boiling water through the separated coffee grounds in the middle section. The resultant coffee is collected in the upper section. It usually sits directly on a heater or stove. Generally used domestically.
Gravity 	Filter coffee	Also known as American coffee this is made by letting hot water drip on to coffee grounds held in a coffee filter (paper or perforated metal). Strength varies according to the ratio of water to coffee and the fineness of the grind, but is typically weaker than Espresso, though the final product contains more caffeine.

DIFFERENT METHODS OF MAKING COFFEE

METHOD	TYPE	DESCRIPTION
	Electric percolator	Common in some households today but differs from the pressure percolator described previously. It uses the pressure of the boiling water to force it to a chamber above the grounds, but relies on gravity to pass the water down through the grounds, where it then repeats the process until shut off by an internal timer.
	Cold press	Cold water is poured over coffee grounds and allowed to steep for 8 to 24 hours. The coffee is then filtered, usually through a very thick filter, removing all particles. This process produces a very strong concentrate which can be stored in a refrigerated, airtight container for up to 8 weeks. The coffee can then be prepared for drinking by adding hot water to the concentrate at an approximately 3:1 ratio (water to concentrate), but can be adjusted to the drinker's preference. The coffee prepared by this method is very low-acid with a smooth taste, and is often preferred by those with sensitive stomachs. Others, however, feel this method strips coffee of its bold flavour and character. Because this method is not common, there are few appliances designed for it.
Steeping 	Cafetière or French Press	A tall, narrow glass cylinder with a plunger that includes a wire mesh filter composed of metal or nylon. The coffee and hot water are combined in the cylinder (normally for 4 to 7 minutes) before the plunger, in the form of a metal foil, is depressed, leaving the coffee at the top ready to be poured. It is important to pay attention to the grind of the coffee beans, a rather coarse grind must be used.
	Coffee bags	Much rarer than their tea equivalents and also much bulkier as more coffee is required in a coffee bag than tea in a tea bag.
	Malaysian coffee	Brewed using a 'sock', which is really just a muslin bag shaped like a filter into which coffee is loaded then steeped in hot water. This same method is used in Colombia to make *tinta*, black coffee that is often served with *panela*, a sugar concentrate in cake form.
	Vacuum brewer	This consists of two chambers: a pot below, atop of which is set a bowl or funnel with its siphon descending nearly to the bottom of the pot. The bottom of the bowl is blocked by a filter of glass, cloth or plastic, and the bowl and pot are joined by a gasket that forms a tight seal. Water is placed in the pot, the coffee grounds are placed in the bowl, and the whole apparatus is set over a burner. As the water heats, it is forced by the increasing vapour pressure up the siphon and into the bowl where it mixes with the grounds. When all the water possible has been forced into the bowl the brewer is removed from the heat. As the water vapour in the pot cools, it contracts, forming a partial vacuum and drawing the coffee down through the filter.

 **ACTIVITY**

- How is coffee made in the premises that you are working/training in?
- Have you been trained in all the different methods that are used?
- Draw a diagram of how you have been trained to serve coffee in your premises.

TYPES OF COFFEE THAT CAN BE OFFERED

Espresso

This is a small shot of black coffee, served in a small cup with a saucer. To prepare, place one pull of ground coffee from the grinder into the single cup handle, flatten, then wipe the excess grinds off the rim. Brew the coffee for 20 seconds only. The coffee should have a small white froth, called crema, on the top.

Double Espresso

This is a slightly larger shot of coffee and is prepared by using a double shot of ground coffee into the double handle. It is served in a large cup and saucer. The coffee is brewed for 20 seconds only and should have a small white froth on top of it.

Cappuccino

This is a shot of Espresso in a large cup and saucer topped up with steamed milk and froth and sprinkled with powdered chocolate.

Caffe Latte

This is a shot of Espresso with steamed milk with no froth served in a glass on a saucer.

Macchiato

This is a shot of Espresso with a spoonful of foam over the top, a small Macchiato is served in a small cup and saucer and a large Macchiato is served in a large cup and saucer.

Filter Coffee/American Coffee

This is made by the pot through the filter coffee machine. To prepare place a clean paper filter into the metal filter of the machine, empty one bag of ground filter coffee into the filter paper. Pour one jug of cold fresh water into the machine and place jug under the filter. The coffee will take about 7 minutes to brew. The coffee can be kept warm on the hot plate of the machine for about 15 minutes before it becomes stale. Filter coffee is served in a filter coffee pot with a jug of warm milk and an empty large cup and saucer.

Liqueur Coffees

A liqueur coffee is a coffee with a measure (25 ml shot) of a specific liqueur. This brew is usually served in a clear, clean, pre-heated, liqueur coffee glass with the coffee at the bottom and the cream floated on the surface.

TYPES OF LIQUEUR COFFEE

LIQUEUR COFFEE	LIQUEUR/SPIRIT
Highland Coffee	Scotch whisky
Irish Coffee	Irish whiskey
Brandy Coffee	Brandy
Cafe Royale	Brandy
Parisienne Coffee	Brandy
French Coffee	French brandy
Calypso Coffee	Rum
Baileys Coffee	Baileys Irish Cream
English Coffee	Gin
Jamaican Coffee	Tia Maria and Rum
Monk's Coffee	Benedictine
Seville Coffee	Cointreau
Witch's Coffee	Strega
Russian Coffee	Vodka

A coffee liqueur

TEAS

Tea is a beverage synonymous with Britain, millions of cups are drunk every day. Teas are made from the processed leaves of the tea bush, *Camellia sinensis*, a shrub first grown in south-western China. The raw leaves are affected by the soil in which they grow, the climate, the weather and the time of picking, much like grapes in winemaking. The leaves which make the best tea are newest on the bush and the plant is regularly pruned to encourage new growth. Tea buds are picked by hand.

IMAGE COURTESY OF ISTOCKPHOTO.COM/FLAVIA BOTTAZZINI

Tea bushes

CHECKLIST FOR TEA PROCESSING

✓ Once picked, tea buds are taken to a factory and air dried.

✓ The dried leaves are then rolled to crush the leaves further.

✓ The leaves are then placed in a humid atmosphere and left to ferment and oxidize.

✓ The tea is then sorted by the size of the leaves and packed to be shipped.

✓ Once the tea leaves reach the UK, the different growths are blended to form loose leaf tea or tea bags.

Where tea is grown

Although originating from China, tea is also grown in India and Indonesia. Importing tea to the UK played an important part in British history and many trade routes around the world existed to import tea into Britain (see map overleaf).

Varieties of tea

There are countless varieties of tea which fall into three broad categories:

Oolong tea: The raw leaves are sun-wilted and then bruised, which exposes their juices to the air, so the leaves oxidize and start to turn brown.

Black tea: Made from leaves that are allowed to oxidize for longer, giving the strong, dark tastes found in familiar Indian teas like Assam and Darjeeling.

Green tea: The most common in China, green teas are made from unoxidized leaves, which are simply heated, rolled and then dried. Dragon Well from Hangzhou is one of China's most famous green teas.

Map of tea growing areas

DIFFERENT TYPES OF TEA

TEA	COUNTRY	DESCRIPTION
Assam Tea	India	Assam is a major growing area covering the Brahmaputra valley, stretching from the Himalayas down to the Bay of Bengal. There are 655 estates covering some 168 000 hectares. Assam tea has distinctive flecked brown and gold leaves known as 'orange' when dried. Its flavour is robust and bright with a smooth malt pungency.
India Tea	India	A blend of teas from all parts of India, this is often served as afternoon tea or after a meal. It is full-bodied, refreshing and with delicate hints of its regional origins.
Darjeeling	India	Regarded as the 'champagne of teas', Darjeeling is grown on 100 estates on the foothills of the Himalayas, on over 18 000 hectares at about 7000 ft. Light and delicate in flavour and aroma, and with undertones of muscatel, Darjeeling is an ideal complement to dinner or afternoon tea. The first 'flushes' (pluckings) are thought to produce the best Darjeeling vintage but all crops are of very high quality.
Lapsang Souchong	China	Perhaps the most famous black tea, the best coming from the hills in north Fujian. Its unique smokey and tarry taste is acquired through drying over pine wood fires.
Green Teas	China	These are unfermented teas, highly favoured by the Chinese themselves, the most well-known being: Longjing (Dragonwell) from Zheijiang; Gunpowder (its name deriving from a similarity in appearance to early powder and shot); Taiping Hon Kui (Monkey King) from Anhui; and Youngxi Huo Qing (Firegreen).
Dimbula	Ceylon/Sri Lanka	Probably the most famous of Ceylon teas, Dimbula is cultivated on estates first planted with tea when their coffee crops failed in 1870. Grown 5000 ft above sea level, all Dimbula teas are light and bright in colour with a crisp strong flavour which leaves the mouth feeling fresh and clean.

TEA	COUNTRY	DESCRIPTION
Uva	Ceylon/Sri Lanka	Uva is a fine flavoured tea from the eastern slopes of the central mountains in Sri Lanka. It is bright in colour and has a dry, crisp taste. Uva teas make an ideal morning drink or an after-lunch tea.
Nuwara Eliya	Ceylon/Sri Lanka	Nuwara teas are light and delicate in character, bright in colour and with a fragrant flavour. Their excellence is particularly heightened when taken with lemon rather than milk.

BLENDED TEAS

VARIETY	CHARACTERISTICS
Jasmine Tea	China tea is mixed with jasmine flowers while oxidizing, and occasionally some are left in the tea as a decoration.
Earl Grey Tea	Said to have been blended for the second Earl Grey by a mandarin after a successful diplomatic mission with China, the blend was originally made from black China tea and treated with the natural oil of the citrus bergamot fruit. Earl Grey is renowned for its perfumed aroma and flavour. Nowadays the teas used in Earl Grey vary, and there are as many perceptions of Earl Grey as there are Earl Grey drinkers on account of the interaction between bergamot oil and different teas
English Breakfast	This is traditionally a pungent blend of Assam and Ceylon teas that help to digest a full English breakfast and get the day off to a good brisk start. The essence of early morning tea, or as the Indians call it 'bed' tea, is its strength and ability to wake and stimulate the metabolism. Many English Breakfast blends also include tea from Africa to give a coppery brightness to the colour.
Afternoon Tea	A blend of delicate Darjeeling tea and high-grown Ceylon tea to produce a refreshing and light tea, Afternoon Tea also makes an ideal companion to cucumber sandwiches, cream pastries and fruit cake. The essence of Afternoon Tea blends is not their strength but their flavour.

HERBAL TEAS OR TISANES

A herbal tea or tisane is any herbal infusion other than from the leaves of the tea bush. Herbal teas can be made with fresh or dried flowers, leaves, seeds or roots, generally by pouring boiling water over the plant parts and letting them steep for a few minutes. Seeds and roots can also be boiled on a stove. The tisane is then strained, sweetened if so desired, and served. Many companies produce herbal tea bags for such infusions. There are many different fruit and herbal teas available including chamomile tea, mint tea, lemon verbena tea and nettle tea.

 TIP

The list of herbal teas is vast, almost any herb can be made into a tea or infusion.

HOT DRINKS EQUIPMENT

An espresso machine

Filter coffee machine

HOT DRINKS SERVICE

Prior to the customer's order being taken it is important that the waiter is aware of all the different hot beverages that are available.

When taking the customer's order the waiter must ensure that they have all the relevant information about the customers' drinks.

CHECKLIST

- ✓ Do the customers want milk or lemon with their tea?
- ✓ Do they want a decaffeinated coffee?
- ✓ Do they require semi-skimmed or skimmed milk with their beverage?
- ✓ Would they like milk or cream with their coffee?

Cups and saucers must be carried on a tray at all times. The tray should be loaded so that the saucers are piled up and the cups are arranged around the tray. The tray should also have teaspoons, and milk jugs if necessary.

When serving the customers their drinks place the cups in front of each customer first. When putting the tea or coffee pots on the table, ensure that the spout is not facing a customer as they could get scalded or burnt by the steam.

When placing a coffee or tea cup and saucer in front of a customer the handle of the cup should be on the right-hand side, with the teaspoon placed diagonally from the top of the cup to the handle.

 TIP

Customers should never be asked if they want 'white or black coffee' but if they want their coffee 'with or without milk'.

 REMEMBER

Caffe Latte is a long milky drink.

STEP-BY-STEP: MAKING A CAFFE LATTE

1 *Make a double espresso in a glass (see 'making an espresso' on page 348)*

2 *Pour milk but not froth into the glass*

3 *When placing the glass in front of the customer, place the handle facing to the right-hand side and the teaspoon from top to right*

STEP-BY-STEP: MAKING FILTER COFFEE

1 *To make filter coffee the following are needed: a working filter coffee machine, a clean filter, ground coffee and fresh cold water*

2 *Remove filter holder and place filter into it*

3 *Put entire bag of coffee into the filter*

4 *Slide filter back into the machine*

5 *Pour the cold water into the machine. The machine will slowly drip the filter coffee through*

 REMEMBER

If the coffee does not filter, do not add a second jug of water, get your supervisor.

STEP-BY-STEP: MAKING A CAPPUCINO

1 *Froth and polish a jug of milk*

2 *Make a double espresso (see 'making an espresso' on page 348)*

3 *Pour milk and froth into the cup by nudging the jug gently, a spoon should not need to be used if the milk is of the correct consistency*

4 *Ensure that there is an equal amount of both warm milk and froth in the cup*

5 *When placing the cup and saucer in front of the customer, place the hand of the cup facing to the right hand side and the teaspoon from top to right*

6 *Chocolate powder or flavoured syrups can be added to the drink prior to service if the customer desires*

 REMEMBER

Do not boil the milk or it will affect the taste of the drink and could burn the mouth of the customer.

STEP-BY-STEP: MAKING AN ESPRESSO/DOUBLE ESPRESSO

1 *Fill the metal filter with freshly ground coffee*

2 *Temper or compress the coffee*

3 *Attach the coffee filter to the machine. Place warmed demi-tasse under the spout of the filter*

4 *Turn machine on for 20 to 25 seconds*

5 *When placing the tea cup and saucer in front of the customer, place the hand of the cup facing to the right-hand side and the teaspoon from top to right*

A double espresso is made using exactly the same method but with twice the amount of coffee and is served in a large cup

---

!   **REMEMBER**

Espresso is a short beverage and should only fill half the cup.

STEP-BY-STEP: MAKING A MACCHIATO

1 *Make a double espresso (see 'making an espresso' on page 348)*

2 *Spoon some of the froth only on to the espresso*

3 *When placing the cup and saucer in front of the customer, place the hand of the cup facing to the right- hand side and the teaspoon from top to right*

 REMEMBER

Macchiato can be served as both a double and a single drink.

STEP-BY-STEP: MAKING A HOT CHOCOLATE

1 *Place two dessert spoons of chocolate chips into a glass*

2 *Pour a small amount of hot milk into the glass and stir until the chocolate has completely melted*

3 *Top up the glass with hot milk*

 REMEMBER

Place a metal spoon into the glass before adding hot liquid, to prevent accidents.

STEP-BY-STEP: MAKING A COFFEE LIQUEUR

1 *Put three brown sugar cubes and a metal teaspoon into a liqueur coffee glass*

2 *Make a double espresso (see 'making an espresso' on page 348), and pour into the glass. Stir until all the sugar is dissolved. Add the liqueur of choice*

3 *Place the tip of a warm dessert spoon on the surface of the coffee. Pour the cold cream at a slow steady pace from a jug*

4 *The layer of cream should be about 2 cm on the surface of the drink. The liqueur coffee needs to be served to the customer rapidly as the cream can sink*

> **! REMEMBER**
>
> Always place a metal spoon into the glass before adding the hot liquid to conduct the heat away from the glass and prevent it from cracking.

STEP-BY-STEP: MAKING ICED TEA

1 *Fill the cocktail shaker with ice*

2 *Pour hot tea into a shaker*

3 *Add lemon slices and juice to taste*

4 *Add sugar syrup to taste*

5 *Shake and pour into chilled glass*

Assessment of knowledge and understanding

You have now learned about the responsibilities you have to prepare and serve hot drinks. This will enable you to ensure your own positive actions contribute effectively towards the whole team.

To test your level of knowledge and understanding, answer the following short questions. These will help to prepare you for your summative (final) assessment.

Make sure that you keep this for easier referencing and along with your work for future inclusion in your portfolio.

Preparing for assessment checklist

■ Ensure that you can prepare a wide selection of the hot drinks available.

■ Ensure that you know the correct service and accompaniments for each beverage.

Project 1

1 Prepare the following beverages for one order:
One Espresso.
One Cappuccino.
One pot of English Breakfast Tea.

2 Explain what sequence you have prepared the beverages in and why.
_____

3 Take a photograph or draw a diagram of the order that you have prepared.
_____

Project 2

1 Design a hot drinks list for a high street coffee shop or cafe.
_____

2 Why have you included or excluded certain drinks?
_____

3 What drinks could you offer to children?
_____

4 Are you offering decaffeinated drinks?
_____

5 Are any of your drinks Fairtrade?
_____

Glossary of terms

24-hour service Round-the-clock continual service for consumers.

Accompaniments Items of food that are served to complement the main dish such as a sauce, relish or seasoning. Also includes ingredients such as sugar, milk and cream to go with a specific beverage.

Air line jumper The piece of tubing that runs between the regulator and the key coupler.

Alcohol A beverage that is intoxicating.

Bacteria (in beer) Bacteria found in beer is not significantly hazardous to human health; however, its effect is noticeable in the appearance, aroma and taste of beer. The presence of bacteria results in an 'off taste' and cloudy appearance that makes beer unappetizing. A beer that tastes sour, vinegar-like, or smells like rotten eggs may indicate a beer system is contaminated with beer-spoiling bacteria.

Bain-marie A water bath that is used to keep food hot during service.

Bar A place where alcoholic and non-alcoholic beverages are sold and served.

Beer stones The raw materials, grains and water that are used in the brewing process contain calcium. Oxalic acids or salts are present in hops and may be created during the process of changing barley into malt. The combination of these ingredients and the fact that beer is dispensed at cold temperatures may result in calcium oxalate deposits known as beer stone.

Bleed To drain off liquid or gas, generally slowly, through a valve called a bleeder. To bleed down, or bleed off, means to release pressure slowly from a well or from pressurized equipment.

Body language How a person's physical appearance and actions can indicate what they are thinking and feeling.

Buffet Type of service where the customers can help themselves to the dishes they require, with little or no assistance.

Canteen A type of foodservice outlet in which customers can help themselves, assisted in their choice by the employees.

Carvery A specialised type of buffet where a roast meat is served to the customer.

Carving trolley A classical service where the roast meat dish is brought to the customers' table and carved to their specifications in front of them.

Cashier A cashier is a person responsible for totalling the amount due for a purchase, charging the consumer for that amount, and then collecting payment for the goods or services exchanged.

CCTV Closed Circuit Television is a video monitoring and security system using cameras that transmit visual information over a closed circuit through transmitters and receivers.

Cellar A cellar is a room or rooms under a building, and usually below the surface of the ground, where provisions and other stores are kept.

Cocktail A term used for a drink mixed from two or more alcoholic beverages.

Colleagues People who work at the same level as yourself in your own organization or other organizations, and staff whose work you are responsible for.

Communication Giving and receiving information, listening and understanding.

Condiment Salt and/or pepper.

Confidential information Information that you should only share with certain people, for example your manager or personnel officer.

Conveyor belt This consists of two or more pulleys, with a continuous belt that rotates around them. One or both of the pulleys are powered, moving the belt and the material on the belt forward. The powered pulley is called the drive pulley while the unpowered pulley is called the idler.

Covers A word used to describe the quantity of customers at a table.

Credit Money available for a customer to borrow during the duration of their stay/visit. Arrangement for deferred payment for goods and services.

Crockery Crockery is the general term for the dishes used in serving and eating food, including the plates, bowls and cups. Generally made from porcelain or china.

Cross-contamination If a chopping board is not cleaned properly before another food is cut on the same board a transference of contamination can happen.

Crumbing down The action of removing crumbs and debris from a table either using a crumber or a napkin.

Customers These include individual clients, plus other departments within your organization and external organizations to whom you may provide a service (internal and external users of your service).

Cutlery This refers to any hand implement used in preparing, serving and eating food. It is more usually known as silverware, whereas cutlery can have the more specific meaning of knives and other cutting instruments.

Deliveries When ordered goods arrive.

Discrimination The unfair treatment of a person or group of people

Dispensing machine A machine that provides various snacks, beverages and other products to consumers.

Disposable crockery Plates, cups etc. that can be used only once.

Draught A drink that is dispensed directly from a tap.

Dray A drayman was historically the driver of a dray, a low, flat-bed wagon without sides, pulled generally by horses or mules that was used for transport of all kinds of goods. Now the term is really only used for brewery delivery men, even though routine horse-drawn deliveries are almost entirely extinct. Some breweries do still maintain teams of horses and a dray, but these are used only for special occasions such as festivals or opening new premises.

EPOS Electronic Point of Sale. Data recorded at checkout and used for forecasting and stock control.

Equal opportunities The term applied to the laws that prevent discrimination.

Eye contact Look directly at the face of a person.

Fair Trade Movement that supports fair payment of produce to growers.

Faucet handles Sometimes called a faucet knob or tap handle. This is the lever that you pull on the faucet to make the beer come out.

Faucets This is where the beer comes out. There are a lot of parts inside the faucet, so it would be cleaned regularly.

Feedback Giving colleagues and team members your assessment of the positive and negative aspects of the way they work and potential outcomes from set objectives.

Fermentation The process of how alcohol is made.

Flair The art of entertaining customers while making cocktails, by juggling and throwing cocktail equipment, glasses and bottles.

Float An amount of money placed in a till/EPOS at the start of the shift and used to provide change for cash transactions. The float is always kept at the same value and is the first thing to be placed in the till at the start of the shift and the first amount of money to be removed from the till at the end of shift, prior to reconciliation taking place. It may be removed in change for reuse during the next shift.

Food bacteria Bacteria were first observed by Antoine van Leeuwenhoek in 1676, using a single-lens microscope of his own design. Food bacteria are a group of single cell micro-organisms, and although the vast majority of bacteria are harmless or beneficial, a few bacteria are pathogenic and these are food bacteria that will cause illness.

Food hazards Is a term used by food safety organizations to classify foods that require time and temperature control to keep them safe for human consumption. Foods that contain moisture, protein and are neutral to slightly acidic are typically labelled as a potential food hazard and strict storage conditions are imposed.

Hazard A hazard is something with the potential to cause harm.

Health Achieving health and remaining healthy is an active process. Maintaining effective strategies for staying healthy and improving one's health is of utmost importance.

Heat lamp A light used to keep food hot during service.

Hygiene Hygiene is the practice of keeping the body clean to prevent infection and illness, and the avoidance of contact with infectious agents.

In writing For example, short memorandums and messages.

Instant hot drink Through various manufacturing processes the drink such as tea or coffee is dehydrated into the form of powder or granules. These can be re-hydrated with hot water to provide a drink similar to conventional coffee or tea.

Inventory Another term for a stock list.

Keg A keg is a stainless steel vessel that is used for the distribution of bulk beer. They come in various sizes, usually 50 and 100 litres.

Keg couplers This piece attaches to the keg and actually taps it. There are six different types of keg couplers used throughout the world. Which ones you will need will depend upon which brand of beer you dispense.

Legislation Legislation is a law which has been circulated by the government. The term may refer to a single law, or the collective body of enacted law, while 'statute' is also used to refer to a single law. Before an item of legislation becomes law it may be known as a bill, which is typically also known as 'legislation' while it remains under active consideration.

Limits of your job What you are and are not allowed to do in the workplace.

Liqueur Sweetened alcoholic beverage.

Litmus paper Paper with powder extracted from certain plants that tests the pH of a substance. Acid turns red while base turns blue; neutral remains white. The stronger the acid or base, the more intense the red or blue the colour of the litmus paper.

Maintenance Regular servicing and up-keep of equipment.

Merchandising The methods, practices and operations carried out to promote and sell certain products.

Mise-en-place French term for setting up the restaurant, literally means to put in place, or do the preparation for.

Mixology The art of cocktail making.

Napkins A napkin or serviette is a rectangle of cloth or paper used at the table for wiping the mouth while eating. It is usually small and folded.

New World Wine produced outside Europe.

Oenologist The term for a wine maker.

Old World Wine made in Europe.

Payment In return for goods or services, a customer/guest is required to provide monetary value through cash, cheques or credit cards.

PDQ 'Process Data Quickly'. Usually used in reference to PDQ terminals – these are the terminals used by businesses to manually swipe or input customer card details in order to take payments.

Personal hygiene Hygiene refers to practices associated with ensuring good health and cleanliness.

PIN 'Personal Identification Number'. A number you choose and use to gain access to various accounts or to provide authorization for charges to a credit/debit card. This information should be kept by the customer and is private.

Position number The number given to each seat at a table, in order to identify them.

Prioritizing Placing your aspects of your work in order of the most important.

Promotional offer A method of increasing sales or merchandise through advertising; any activity designed to enhance sales.

Redeem To pay off, buy back, or to clear a debt by payment.

Refrigerated trolleys Trolleys with a chiller unit to keep food items at a safe temperature.

Regulator The regular connects to the CO_2 tank. It steps the gas pressure down to a level that is correct for dispensing beer. Most kits come with a double gauge regulator. One gauge tells you the pressure going into the keg, the other gauge tells you how much air you have left in your air tank.

Risk A risk is the likelihood of the hazard's potential being realized.

Security Being protected against danger or loss. Security is a concept similar to safety. Individuals or actions that infringe upon the condition of protection are responsible for the breach of security.

Silver service The name applied to the service of food on to an individual's plate using cutlery.

Soup tureen A dish used for serving soup.

Spirits A generic term for alcohol that has been distilled, typically 37 to 50 per cent alcohol per volume.

Staphylococci *Staphylococcus* can cause a wide variety of diseases in humans and other animals through either toxin production or invasion. Staphylococcal toxins are a common cause of food poisoning, as they can grow in improperly stored food.

Still room Area in a restaurant, normally, but not always, in the kitchen. The area is used to prepare bread items and hot beverages.

Stock Produce or beverages in the store room.

Stock level Stock level is a term used to describe an amount of stock that is maintained below the cycle stock to buffer against running out of any particular ingredient. Safety stock levels exist to counter uncertainties in supply and demand. For example, if a restaurant were to continually run out of ingredients, they would need to keep some extra stock of ingredients on hand so they could attempt to meet demand.

Stock rotation system This is the practice used in restaurants and food production areas, of moving products with an earlier sell-by date to the front of a shelf, so they get picked up and sold first, and of moving products with a later sell-by date to the back.

Sufficient supplies Ensuring that the ingredients required to produce food and beverages are in constant supply for the needs of service.

Table seating The term used for an individual's cutlery and glasses on the table.

Tablecloths The cloths used to cover a table.

Take-away service Food produced in an outlet and sold for consumption elsewhere.

Tetrapaks The generic term for cartons that contain liquid.

Tisanes Herbal infusions for drinking.

Vending The idea is to vend products without the use of a cashier. Items sold via vending machines vary by country and region. A vending machine provides various snacks, beverages and other products to consumers.

Vending machine hazards Contamination by bacteria or other micro-organisms that cause food poisoning. Chemicals, for example, cleaning materials or pest baits, and foreign materials such as glass, metal or plastic.

Vineyard A place where grapes are grown and wine is made.

Vintage The year that grapes are picked and wine is produced.

Virgin Cocktail containing no alcohol.

Voucher A voucher is a bond which is worth a certain monetary value and which may only be spent for specific reasons or on specific goods.

Waiter's stations Sideboards within the restaurant that waiters use to prepare and store items for service.

Walkouts When a customer walks out of the establishment/organization without providing payment for goods and/or services received during their stay or visit.

Waste items Rubbish to be thrown away or recycled.

Weights and Measures Act The legislation concerning the size of drinks that can be poured and the alcoholic strength.

Wholesaler A person, other than the brewer, manufacturer or rectifier, who sells alcoholic beverages to a licensed retailer or to another person who holds a permit to sell alcohol beverages at wholesale.

Workplace The place where an employee will work.

Yeast May result from an extremely small amount left from the brewing process, or it may be wild yeast which floats in the air. It is usually found as a surface growth on components of a beer system that are exposed to the air such as faucets, keg couplers and drains and can be recognized by its white or grey colour.

Index